Stumbling Toward God
A Memoir

By
Lona Rae

A record of the experiences and epiphanies that have guided one woman's spiritual path.

Copyright December 26, 2023

Lona Rae Babbington

lonarae.books@yahoo.com

Dedicated to

My Children:
Rebecca Rae
John David
Mary Elizabeth

My Grandchildren:
Tracie Diane
Scott Spencer
Terri Lynn
Raymond Jay

My Greatgrandchildren:
Samantha
Tyler
Dillon Jay
Devon Michael
Alexis Paige
Angel Marie
Evelyn Elizabeth
William Steven
Jacob Edward
Scarlett Annalise

My Great-Greatgrandchild

Calliope Rose

And all those to come. . . . .

In the nearly 90 years I have lived, the world has changed with such incredible swiftness that my childhood seems like a fantasy. But my memories, and the memories of those who came before me, may be the only legacy I can leave to those who come after me.

With love to my ancestors, my descendants, my extended family, and my many friends. –

Lona Rae

"*You need to claim the events of your life to make yourself yours. When you truly possess all you have been and done, which may take some time, you are fierce with reality.*"

- Florida Scott Maxwell

"*There is no light without shadow and no psychic wholeness without imperfection.*"

- Carl Jung

Stumbling Toward God

A Meditation upon Persimmons

When I was seven or eight, I had a secret place in the woods behind our house, just close enough to home that I could hear if my mother called me – or, I suppose, if I called her, although I don't think it occurred to me that I might need to call anyone, ever. My private place was on a hillside overlooking a small creek that ran over smooth sandstone, pooled into shady homes for tadpoles or flattened out into skating rinks for water bugs, until it finally fell off down a steep bluff into what was surely a foreign land. My private hideaway was inside a triangle of three persimmon trees, their narrow trunks set close together, their branches low, with honeysuckle vines growing tightly all around except for one small place where I had pulled the vines away so I could crawl inside. I fit neatly and safely, like a young bird in its nest.

While I sat there in my hidey-hole, I may have pondered the secrets of the cosmos, or read a book, or practiced making a cat's cradle with a long circle of string, or watched tadpoles lose their tails in a fruit jar full of water, or sipped nectar from the nipped-off ends of honeysuckle blossoms or attempted with solitary difficulty the art of whistling. (There are a great many things that are difficult to learn all by yourself, but if you don't ask for help you avoid the embarrassment of clumsy efforts and miss that almost sensuous surge of triumph when you finally succeed all by yourself.) I may have done all those things, or none of them, although I have certainly done all of them at some time, somewhere – memory is a baffling trickster. But what I absolutely do remember very clearly is wondering, one whole summer, if it could possibly be true that inside a persimmon seed you might find – if you were very lucky – a tiny knife or fork or spoon. I hope I also wondered, although I'm not at all sure that I did, why God (whose existence I had not yet questioned) would conceal such an astonishing surprise in such an unlikely and inconvenient place. But I have never really believed the old folktale (among many others) that, depending on what dining artifacts persimmons were producing in a particular year, the winter weather was being foretold. Especially when, eventually, I realized that God was probably producing persimmon seeds long before human beings began producing, or even realizing they needed, either forks or spoons. Or, for that matter, weather forecasts.

3

Prologue

It was January of 2021 as I began, after spending the last 10 months of my life in survival mode, secluded from the Covid-19 pandemic of 2020-21 in one-half of a duplex in Murray, Kentucky, locked in almost as carefully and completely as a medieval anchorite, although certainly with more conveniences. Julian of Norwich comes to mind, born sometime in 1342 in England, boarded up in her anchorage against the wall of an old church in Conisford, waiting out the Black Death, the bubonic plague that killed nearly 50 percent of the world's population.

Julian was apparently supported by the church to which her anchorage was attached and dependent upon its parishioners. She had a window in her little home through which she held audiences with those who came to her for advice. I am supported by savings and Social Security and visited (carefully masked) by my three children who have already heard more advice from me, mostly unsolicited, than I was probably equipped to give, and probably learned far more from my many mistakes than from my loving (and occasionally insistent) suggestions.

Julian had what she called "showings" during those years and wrote about them–the first woman whose spiritual writings were published in English. She is now an acclaimed mystic. I am no mystic, and certainly no saint, as the events of my life have proved over and over again. But time has also shown me a great deal about both life and things of the spirit, and I have been reflecting on my own small awakenings and feeling the urge to put my thoughts into writing. It may well be a family trait, passed down through the maternal line. If so I am, as a Hank Williams Jr.'s song goes, just fulfilling "a family tradition." There it is again, like grace notes: all my life music has played through my mind as commentary, a lyrical score underwriting my thoughts, my dreams, my intuitions.

Reviewing the past can seem like looking into a kaleidoscope – one of those childhood toys I bought my children for Christmas when they were small, along with tin trucks and tinker toys, building blocks, and baby dolls that blinked their eyes and even wet tiny diapers. For it is in a kaleidoscope with its scattering of multi-colored rocks that, refracted through prisms somewhere inside the tube, form and re-form beautiful patterns with just a slight turn of the tube. It is an illusion but a fascinating one. Sometimes I think we may all live in an illusion. I am not alone in such thoughts. The Hindus even have a word for it: maya.

The kaleidoscope patterns seem an appropriate metaphor for the changing patterns of life-as-lived and life-as-remembered. My life-remembered is, of course, uniquely different than the life-remembered by my children, my siblings, and my friends. Perhaps I have different "rocks" in my mental kaleidoscope. I offer this as a kind of apology to anyone who is hurt, shocked, or angered by my vision/version of a past we shared. Life-lived and life-remembered are both, after all, always a matter of perspective. The writer Scott Peck, when attempting to write about himself, said, "It is not just that the autobiographer is too close to his subject, I suspect, but also that he is prone to suffer from the delusion that he understands the subject: himself."

About this writing business: my mother's mother was a poet. I still have the originals of most of her poems, stored in one of those letter-sized boxes that a single ream of typing paper used to come in before computers demanded several reams, now sold by the case. Her poems were written on whatever was close at hand: scraps of paper, used envelopes, pieces torn from brown paper shopping bags, versions inserted into letters she wrote on lined paper to me or my mother. I read one of them at her funeral: "When my apprenticeship is over . ." it began. Could she have been channeling Alfred Lord Tennyson? I've always believed she was a bit of a psychic. She once told me that in the distant past she had had frequent conversations with her deceased mother and experimented with seances where a group of friends gathered round a table and, their palms flat on the surface, tried to persuade it to move.

I've attended a lot of Zoom meetings recently, and someone has compared those to seances, with people appearing and disappearing like spirits of the past and present, occasionally speaking in spectral voices from above slates on which are written robotic names like "Z324." At one Zoom prayer meeting, we were "bombed" by a group of invaders who apparently had nothing better to do and thought it was great fun to interrupt our meeting with a cascade of pornographic videos. The minister, who happened to be a woman (ministers come in all sizes, shapes, and genders these days), told us to close our eyes while she got rid of the invaders, but I suspect at least one or two of the ladies might have stayed on to watch. I left when someone changed the name on one of the more erotic displays to mine.

I was a grown woman before I knew that women could be ministers. In my youth women were not often even invited to pray publicly. I distinctly recall one Sunday morning at New Hope Baptist Church (my religious alma mater) when one of my mother's older friends was offered the opportunity. and dropped dead before she could say "Amen." Now my oldest daughter is an Episcopal deacon and thus properly ordained. So far, she is still alive after praying publicly, even "officially" from the pulpit, and quite often.

My sister Kay wrote poetry too. She died in March of 2020, so suddenly, sitting in her favorite chair in their family room after breakfast, waiting for her husband of 60 years to return from a trip down the hall to bring her an anti-nausea pill she had requested. One of her children read one of her poems at her funeral. For the last 50 years or so I haven't been much of a churchgoer, although I'm not opposed to churches (or Zoom prayer meetings). Kay's funeral was the last religious service I personally attended before the coronavirus locked so many of our generation inside our homes or buried us in our final resting places. I hope she watched her memorial service from heaven's vestibule, or wherever souls are housed for safekeeping (and perhaps recycling) and knew finally and forever in how much esteem she was held by those she had worked so hard to love and protect.

And, of course, I also have poems. And stories, whole books of stories, some published and some unfinished and stored now in a black-lidded box in a corner of the guest room closet. And novels: one published, one lost forever in the slush pile of a publisher, two complete but always far from final, four half-finished, one in so many drafts I'll probably never sort it out.

My life has been filled with words: in three newspapers, the *Metropolis News,* where I began as an assistant to the editor, and two where I was editor: the *Downers Grove Graphic* and the *DuPage County Times*; in two magazines: *Office Appliances* and *Office Design*. There were ten years of words at the American Institute of Steel Construction where I started as a secretary and became Director of Public Relations and scribbled away at everything from publicity releases to convention and conference brochures and articles for industry magazines. And I should not forget the wills and deeds, divorce petitions and briefs when I worked as a legal secretary. This is, incidentally, an excellent interim occupation for wives who must leave careers behind to follow husbands and raise children and reinvent themselves when life throws them a curve--or simply thrusts them into a new consequence of their own indecision (or indiscretion!).

When I retired at 70 and realized I would probably die of boredom unless I found something constructive to do, I fell into genealogy like a pig into mud (sheer delight if you're a pig) and ended with five books of genealogies. Those have been shared with local libraries, families, and my own children, who need to know (I believe) who came before we got here. Several years ago, I gave each of my children a book containing photographs and memories of their own childhoods, so I must acknowledge that my reflections here may seem to contain too little of them and too much of me. That, too, is an assessment of my life: too little for them and too much for me.

For Christmas in 2021 I gave each of them a copy of an autobiography, *"Reflections on a Not-Quite-Ordinary Life,"* somewhat edited to at least partially obscure those few details that seemed blatantly inappropriate for future generations. (Or perhaps I simply left something to their imaginations.) The present book has also been modified for public consumption, should that ever occur. (Some names have been changed to protect the innocent, *and* the guilty.)

A few days ago, I was reading someone else's book, *Seeing through the Visible World*, by June Singer, a Jungian psychologist. As she described her own early life, her realization that "there might be more beyond the familiar world than [she] had thought, only that [she] could not see it," and her determination to "try to expand [her] ability to see," I was struck by how parallel our lives and goals had been, from early childhood doubts to revelatory discoveries in the bookcases of public libraries, seasons of marriage and parenting, then encounters with the ideas of Carl Jung, an introduction to gnostic and early Christian mystics, a brush with Eastern yogis, and eventual seduction into the mysteries of quantum physics. A sentence in her Preface stopped me in my tracks as she described her solitary adolescent Sunday treks to local churches seeking enlightenment, or at least *truth*, only to realize: "There was little room in those churches for me, *stumbling toward God*, to find my own way." That sentence, but especially the single phrase "*stumbling toward God*," seemed to describe the essence of my entire life.

As I have gone stumbling along, often tripping over my own ego and falling flat on my face more than occasionally, I have seemed to reinvent myself over and over again. Author John Rogers describes it well when he says, ". . . in life we are re-born many times." Another writer explains, "We die to old ways of being to be reborn in our need, dependency, and control to be reborn in reliance on Spirit." And perhaps, as Eastern religions claim and Western religions hint, we are reborn after physical death as well. Who knows? I certainly hope so. I yearn to read, perhaps even to live, more pages of the story of life on this beautiful earth.

About those ancestors of mine: My father's people were all from Germany, arriving in America in the 1840s and '50s. They settled in southern Illinois and farmed the land they found there, built and worshipped in Lutheran churches, and some of those kin led, I believe, "lives of quiet desperation." My mother's people were a motley crew. The Rectors were among two boatloads of immigrants brought from Germany to work in an Englishman's silver mines, only to discover that there was no silver, there would be no mines, and they found themselves housed instead in an abandoned Indian encampment. They flourished, and one of those ancestors founded the first Lutheran church in America. The English Quaker John Stokes' descendants left the Carolinas and, by way of Kentucky, founded with two other families the first settlement in what would become Union County, Illinois. The Chaudoins were French Huguenots who fled religious persecution; one served under General Washington in the Revolutionary War. If you detect a deliberate religious/spiritual connection underlying these selections, you are not mistaken.

It's hard to know where to begin. However, still, I have decided to begin before my own beginning, for I believe it is true that everything from before is buried deep in our unconscious, perhaps embedded in our DNA, perhaps alive in our brains as a kind of "race memory," perhaps stored in an even more pervasive (and persuasive) spiritual reality that some philosophers, psychologists, physicists, and even theologians, describe as "universal consciousness." I have always wondered if that might be the only way a mother robin could know how to build a nest or beavers to construct a dam. Such creative creatures we all are. And so, first of all:

Roots

The religious passion of English puritans
and the cold fury of German valkyries
war silently within my bones.
My father's Lutheran reserve
holds aloof, stoic and shuddering,
from my mother's missionary fervor.
My head does not always

overrule my heart.

I revel too often in solitude,
a sometimes unholy seclusion,
living somewhere inside my head.
My children must have been jealous
when I left them to roam
in that foreign land behind my eyes,
knocking on my knee, my heart:
"Mommy, come out and play."
But I did not know how to play.
Someone I loved once told me:
"You have never been a child."
Perhaps that's true.

- Lona Rae

"Until the missing story of ourselves is told, nothing besides told can suffice us: we shall go on quietly craving it."

- Laura Riding

"Tell me the tales that to me were so dear, Long, long ago; Long, long ago;

Ah, yes, you told me you ne'er would forget, Long, long ago, long ago."

-Thomas Haynes Bayly

Who I Came From

It may seem odd to begin what is intended to be a spiritual autobiography with events that happened and people who were born long years ago--even centuries--before I was born. But I came into a world that had already been created, a culture that had evolved, families that had existed long before I was brought into the world nearly 90 years ago in the front bedroom of the house my mother's father had built in a little community in Southern Illinois that the natives fondly called "Fudgetown." And no, it was not an ethnic enclave humorously named for a clan of dark-skinned folk--excepting perhaps those who had been temporarily tattooed darkly by the coaldust from the local mines. Fudgetown was the local pronunciation of "Fergestown," probably so named for (or by) an original settler who was no kin of mine. It was always just a "wide spot in the road," but it's still *on* the map.

Alex Haley looked for his own "*Roots*" in the histories of his own families, just as I have looked for mine, though perhaps not for the same reasons. In the places where I grew up, and even in the southern culture where I live today, the first question the locals still ask a stranger is, "Who are your folks?" For while it may no longer be taken for gospel truth that the "sins of the fathers are visited upon their children even unto the fourth and fifth generation," there is still a suspicion—often *taken* for truth—that some traits are "in the blood." Suppose your father, your grandfather, or even your uncle on your mother's side was a bad actor. In that case, folks want to know, alert to the possibility that bad blood can bubble up again into "toil and trouble," as Shakespeare's witches once prophesized. I've known a witch or two in my time. At least they said they were. I suspect they were more likely intrigued by the possibility of obtaining some mystical power by simply laying claim to it.

But there is surely always some "good blood" mixed in with all the rest. As I struggle to explain my fascination with my ancestors, I am reminded of a Christmas present from my granddaughter Terri: a simple strip of wood on which are the words, "Great women raise great women raise great women." It is perhaps a bow to ego (you are free to speculate on *whose* ego that might be), but it has still found a home atop the mirror on the chest of drawers in my bedroom. And only this morning one of my "spiritual gurus," the Franciscan Richard Rohr, wrote affirming his own curiosity and conviction of the importance of both *abuelitas* (grandmothers) and the faith of his own ancestors. He quotes Paul's letter to Timothy, "I thank God, whom I serve with a pure conscience, *as my forefathers did* …when I call to remembrance the genuine faith that is in you, *which dwelt first in your grandmother Lois and your mother Eunice*, and I am persuaded is in you also. Therefore I remind you to stir up the gift of God which is in you . . . For God has not given us a spirit of fear, but of power and of love and of a sound mind." *(My italics added.)*

And I breathe a sigh of "Ah yes, there it is. That is what I have always looked for: power, love, a pure conscience and a sound mind, free of fear." But, like my forefathers and fore*mothers*, I too have had to work for it, most often by "stirring up the gift of God."

In Rohr's view (and in mine, though he bears considerably more spiritual expertise): "Humans throughout history have often had a strong appreciation for and connection with their ancestors. I think the collective notion of oneness is what Christians were trying to verbalize when they made a late addition to the ancient Apostles' Creed: 'I believe in the communion of saints.' They were offering us the idea that *the dead are at one with the living*. . . The whole thing, all of life, is *one*, just at different stages, all of it loved corporately by God (and, one hopes, by us). Within this worldview, we are saved not by being privately perfect, but by being 'part of the body,' humble links in the great chain of history."

I like that: to think of those ancestors of mine as "a community of saints" and myself as a "humble link in the great chain of history." I shall ignore even the possibility that there could ever be such a thing as purgatory. My understanding of God refuses to allow it.

The Buddhist monk Thich Nhat Hanh, another spiritual teacher, would agree with Rohr. He tells of how, after his mother's death, he grieved terribly for more than a year until one night he dreamed of "sitting with her, and we were having a wonderful talk. She looked young and beautiful, her hair flowing down. . . as if she had never died." When he woke, "The impression that my mother was still with me was very clear. I understood then that the idea of having lost my mother was just an idea. It was obvious in that moment that *my mother is always alive in me*."

In my own life there have been such occasional vignettes, moments that have seemed to stand out from the rest, like separating "wheat from chaff" (the grain from the hulls). I'm sure there is far more "chaff" than wheat in the memories that follow, but there are indeed nuggets of truth here: *my* truth, some (but not all) found buried in the distant past and now exhumed, like the acorns squirrels bury in the warm summer ground to be dug up in the depth of winter. It is my winter season. But, as my father--a farmer all his life and so attuned to the seasons--always believed, I too believe in springtime.

For reasons that will become clear as my story unfolds, I was born in the front bedroom of my mother's parents' home in Fudgetown, and since my mother and I lived with them for the first three years of my life, I was always very close to them, perhaps too close. Having since spent twelve years helping my youngest daughter raise her three children, I understand far better how different family dynamics are when three generations, rather than the conventional two, are involved. When bonds are formed at a very early age, they never really dissolve, nor are bonds easy to create when they have not been allowed to form in those first years. I believe there's an old adage, perhaps of Catholic origin, "Bring up a child in the way it should go, and when it is old, it will not depart therefrom." But in my experience, the child may also struggle very hard to "depart," to get way. I've always been fond of Francis Thompson's poem that begins, "I fled Him down the nights and days, I fled Him down the turning of the years . . ." And Pogo's refrain (again, in my view, and edited for gender, of course): "I have met the enemy, and she is me."

My mother's parents were Miles Marion and LeMaude (Stokes) Jennings. Daddypa, or "Pa," as I later called him, was born in 1884 at a "wide spot in the road" called Rock in Pope County, Illinois (which partially adjoins northeast Massac County, where my father was born and raised). Pa was one of 15 children and had served three years (1906—1909) as a medic in Cuba with Teddy Roosevelt's Rough Riders during the Cuban Pacification. He enlisted at

Paducah, Kentucky, and was discharged at Ft. Bayard, New Mexico, went back to Rock and lived briefly with his father and younger siblings (his mother had died in 1904) before going north to work at the Kankakee Mental Hospital in northern Illinois. It was there he met my grandmother.

Maude (I've always called her "Danty," an infant attempt at "Granny," which I never outgrew) was already working there as a nurse. She was still unmarried at the age of 29. In her day, they would have called her a spinster, even an "old maid," but today she would be considered a "career woman," a rather unusual state for that day and time for, in 1910, she was a single woman working 250 miles from home and family. She had attended a nursing school at Creal Springs in Williamson County. A portion of the old brick building was still standing when my mother pointed it out to me 20 years ago on one of our frequent Sunday drives to visit the sites of her own lives-remembered.

A year later they both returned to Union County, Illinois, where Danty was born in 1881, and all her family had lived for a hundred years to work in the Anna State Hospital before being married in that county in October of 1910. On the day she and Pa were married, they simply went down to the county courthouse and had the ceremony performed, but they didn't live together for nearly a year. (Marriage between employees at the hospital was forbidden.) She always said that she did change her white nurse's cap for a clean one. One of my cousins, Aunt Mary's daughter Kathy, told me in confidence that her mother had told *her* in confidence that Danty had told *her* in confidence that the newlyweds hadn't slept together for the first year they were married. I'm sure that was true. And it has always amused me (perhaps a delight in saying something shocking?) to introduce their story by saying, "My grandparents met in an insane asylum." Well, they did!

When they finally set up housekeeping, Miles and Maude made their home at Mt. Pleasant, also known thereabouts as the Stokes Family Settlement and later as Lick Creek. Their two oldest children were born there. They eventually had three daughters: Mary Almeda Jennings, who married Lewis Turner; Maude Evelyn Jennings (my mother), who married Raymond Korte; and Maxine Lucille Jennings, who married Frank Mussa. All three of the women survived their husbands and never remarried. The women were all great talkers, but when the three couples were together the men seemed to have very little to talk about. Lewis was English and worked all his adult life in a stove factory; Frank was Italian and became a welder in a steel mill; my father was German, always a farmer who tilled the soil. Perhaps the only thing they had in common was that they had married sisters.

The Jennings Family

Pa's father, George Jennings, was a dirt-poor farmer and father of 15 children (at least 12 lived to maturity) who lived a hardscrabble life on a farm at Rock. But his ancestors included the Revolutionary War veteran John Chaudoin (later Shadowen), a descendant of a French Huguenot family from the German-speaking area of Alsace-Lorraine, a Province bordering on Germany and Switzerland. The Chaudoin family first settled in America at or near "Manikintown" in Goochland County, Virginia. The ancestors of George's wife, Mary Susan Rector, first arrived in America in the early 1700s, part of two boatloads of German folks who were the original settlers of the Germanna colonies in Virginia. One of those settlers, Henry Hager (my 9th great-grandparent) formed the first

Lutheran Church in America in about 1717. I managed to trace the Rector family far back into the 15th century in Germany.

I have been unable to trace the Jennings family back farther than my 3rd-great-grandfather, Joseph Jennings, who married Elizabeth Chaudoin, a daughter of John Chaudoin (the Revolutionary War veteran), in Green County, Kentucky, in July of 1814. The courthouse was still standing in 2006 when I went there to get a copy of their Marriage Bond, so I probably walked in Joseph's footsteps of nearly 200 years before, and I held in my own hand the paper he had signed with his "X."

Joseph and Elizabeth moved to Illinois with their large family (at least ten children) in 1836, coming by wagon and crossing the Ohio River at Golconda, Illinois, where a ferry was operated. Rock, their destination, was only about 10 miles west of the river. One of their children, Benjamin Franklin Jennings (b. 1829 in Kentucky), was my great-great-grandfather. Joseph favored naming his sons after famous men, mostly presidents. I will not bore anyone with reciting the results of his lack of ingenuity. But I will note that my first husband and I lived in Golconda when we first married. Our little house was high on a hill overlooking the Ohio, and from there we could probably see the places where that ferry left Kentucky and docked in Illinois.

The family settled on a plot of ground Joseph had purchased in Pope County in the community that is still known as "Rock," a barren piece of ground just barely able to support the family. But they survived. The only trace of Joseph in Kentucky that I have been able to discover, other than the 1830 census, is an old newspaper story indicating that a Joseph Jennings was imprisoned for "stealing chickens." (And in his defense, if it *was* him, he did have all those children to feed.) In Illinois, a story from another source indicates more certainly that he had found the body of a man who had drowned in the Ohio River and was paid $1.00 for his services in that connection. Joseph died in 1849, probably at home in Rock. His wife lived on for 20 years, residing with one or another of her children as the years passed and dying in 1870. I am sure they were both buried somewhere in Pope County, but no one remembers where. I believe it was most probably in Mt. Zion Cemetery, but there are no markers.

Their son Benjamin married Matilda Corder on 20 July 1851 in Pope County. She was born about 1832 at Crab Orchard, Illinois, in what is now Williamson County, and it is probable (though not absolutely certain) that her father was William Corder and that her mother was the former Frances "Fanny" Lawson (shown in the 1850 census as "insane"). Matilda was living with the Robertson family in 1850, next door to William and Fanny Corder. She was probably "working out" as a mother's helper to the Robertsons' large family. William Corder was a shoemaker, and so was Benjamin Franklin Jennings. I believe he learned his trade from William in about 1850 and brought William's daughter Matilda home to Pope County to marry her.

Benjamin died in 1903, but Matilda lived until 1924, taking turns residing with her children. In 1910, she was living with George (my great-grandfather) but died in 1924 at the home of her daughter, Mahala Jennings Day, in Creal Springs. According to Matilda's obituary in the book *Rock Community in Pope County, Illinois*," she was 93 when she died, and the mother of 12 children; 8 predeceased her. And of her marriage to Benjamin: "He was a shoemaker for many years. Aunt Tilda assisted him in his work, *doing most all of the sewing and a lot of other work*. She lost her eyesight about 30 years ago and was deprived the pleasure of viewing the faces of her loved ones and the beauties of nature..."

One of Pa's favorite stories was of the day the very large Jennings family accompanied their grandmother's coffin, borne on a wagon–the road was impassable by car–down a muddy unpaved track to the family plot in the graveyard and of the hilarity which accompanied their progress. Pa always remembered it as "the best time the family had had in years." The road to the grave site in Mt. Zion Cemetery (Pope County) is well-kept these days.

My mother, born in 1913, would have been 11 years old when her great-grandmother Matilda died. Her chief recollection was that, when visiting her Uncle Frank and Aunt Ethel, the children would be allowed to fill Grandma's pipe with tobacco because the old lady smoked a pipe as long as she lived, not an unusual or unladylike habit in that day and time. I smoked (NOT a clay pipe) from the time I was 16 until I stopped a few days after my youngest grandchild was born in 1983. That was 40 years ago. My great-great-grandmother apparently suffered no ill-effects from her habit; she died at 93. I'm 89 now; so far, so good.

Benjamin and Matilda's oldest child was my great-grandfather, George Jennings (1852-1930). He married Mary Susan Rector, the daughter of John Rector and Melvina Jane Barton Rector, on 4 Sep 1875 in Pope County, Illinois, at the home of her parents. She would bear him 15 children. Family tradition says that Mary was an immaculate housekeeper, even with her large family and frequent pregnancies, and her daughters were accomplished homemakers and seamstresses. So was my mother, one of her many granddaughters.

I would be remiss if I did not also note that my great-grandfather George was not held in quite such high esteem as the mother of his children. He lived in Johnson City as he grew older. Two of his daughters, Lillie and Amelia, had married and raised their families there. But his granddaughter Betty Jennings (my great-uncle Roy's youngest daughter) told me they were all ashamed of him. He had a pushcart that he trundled around Johnson City, selling vegetables or whatever salable object he might have discovered in his travels about town. And he was often unkempt. He died in 1930, four years before I was born. I do hope he didn't steal any chickens. One chicken thief in the family was quite enough.

The Chaudoins (aka "Shadowens")

The ancestors of Elizabeth Chaudoin Jennings (Joseph's wife), my 3rd great-grandmother, continue back to the Alsace-Lorraine valley in France.

Elizabeth was the daughter of John Chaudoin (1761-1848), a veteran of the Revolutionary War. He married Sarah Wilkinson (1766-1852) in Chesterfield County, Virginia, in February 1788, according to a "minister's return" verifying the ceremony. They were both born in Chesterfield County; he died in Williamson County, Illinois, and Sarah six years later in Hamilton County. Neither of them could either read or write. They had at least fourteen children; Elizabeth was the oldest.

When John applied for a Veteran's pension in 1832, he dictated (and signed with an "X") an account of his service, that while living in Buckingham County, Virginia, he served two three months tours of duty in the U.S. Army as a substitute for another. It was customary for those drafted to "hire" a substitute if, for some reason, they did not wish to or could not serve. He spent the first of those tours guarding the prisoners and was in no battles. But on the second tour, he "marched into North Carolina towards Hillsburg *under*

General Washington and . . . did nothing more than follow the enemy to and fro, having never overtaken them."

In August of 1771, he was drafted himself into service and placed under the command of Captain Cunnigan, with whom he marched to Little York, Virginia, where General Washington took command as general-in-chief. Here they remained, besieging Little York, which was in the possession of the British under Lord Cornwallis, until the 18th or 19th of October, when the enemy surrendered. He was injured just before Cornwallis' surrender but retained in service to guard prisoners at Little Fork, serving three weeks past his term sometime in December.

He was granted his pension, and after he died in 1848, his widow Sarah Wilkinson Chaudoin received a widow's pension. The last name Chaudoin was anglicized to "Shadowen" when members of the family began to leave Virginia and Tennessee, spreading out into the world.

John, who had a twin brother, was the son of Francois Chaudoin Sr., who was born sometime in May 1720 in the Normandy District of France and died about 1799 in Buckingham County, Virginia. John 's mother was Sarah Weaver, the daughter of the French Huguenot Samuel Weaver, also one of the original settlers of Manikantowne, who had married Francoise L'Orange.

Francoise L'Orange (wife of Samuel Weaver) was also the daughter of French Huguenots and was born either in France or, quite probably, at sea on the Nassau, the last of their four ships to arrive in America. Her father, Jean Velas L'Orange, with "wife and child," is shown on the list of 191 passengers. Francoise's mother is believed to be the former Francoise Rouvierre.

Manikantowne was one of the settlements in the 10,000 acres granted to the French Huguenot refugees by the Virginia House of Burgesses (on the instruction of King William of England) on the south side of the James River, about 15-25 miles west of present-day Richmond, Virginia. The Huguenots were fleeing religious persecution in France, where they had been subjected to midnight raids, robbery, beatings, extortion, dismemberment, drowning, and burning at the stake. Those who fled France in the early 1700s went first to England, and King William then transported them on four ships to the American colonies in Virginia. The English word "refugee" was first used in reference to the French word "refugie" for the Huguenots and is still considered a badge of honor to their descendants, conjuring up the history and memory of the tragic original families and their sufferings, and suggesting strength, stamina, and courage under persecution.

The Huguenots in Manikantowne (which included some of my ancestors) formed an Episcopal Church, which has continued in existence (though, of course, not in the same building!) until the present day.

The Chaudoin, Weaver, and l'Orange Families were all among the French Huguenots who left France in the early 1700s to escape religious persecution and were settled in Virginia in the early 1700s. In about the same time frame, the Rector and Fischback families were among the German families who came from Germany to Virginia in 1714 and 1717 to work in a mining enterprise that Virginia Governor Spotswood hoped to establish on his properties there.

The Rectors

The ancestors of my great-grandmother Mary Susan Rector Jennings, George's wife and Pa's mother, have been traced back to the 15th Century in Germany. She was one of eleven children born (as previously stated) to John H. Rector (1828-1881) and his wife, the former Melvina Jane Barton (1830-1864). Both were born in Rhea County, Tennessee, and died in Pope County, Illinois, and are buried there in Sulphur Springs Cemetery.

John H. Rector (my great-great-grandfather) was the direct descendant of one of the original Germanna colonists, two large groups of settlers who came to Virginia from Germany in the early 1700s. I have traced this branch of my family back to Heinrich "Henry' Hager and Guda Schrum Hager, my 9th great-grandparents and my grandchildren's 11th great-grandparents. Their son was Henry Hager (1644-1737), the Lutheran minister who came to Germanna in a "second wave" of German settlers from Siegen, Westphalen, Germany. Although advanced in years, he had determined to immigrate in order to serve the spiritual needs of the German settlement in the "New World." He established the first German Reformed Church (Lutheran) in America at Germanna. His wife was the former Anna C. Friesenhagen. When he died in Germantown in 1737, he was 93 years old and had ministered to his people in the New World for 23 years.

The Germanna colonists did not leave their homes in Germany without knowing their destination, nor were they compelled to do so. They believed they had been engaged by a recruiter to perform a specific job in Virginia in connection with a silver mining scheme hatched by the Board of Trade and Plantations with the approbation of the English Queen Anne. They came from the ancient iron-making capital of Europe, located in one of the most industrious provinces of Germany. Some were familiar with mining; others were farmers, carters, colliers, teachers, and clockmakers. Most were from Trupach, a village near Siegen. The Rector Family home in Trupach was still standing until it was destroyed by U. S. bombers during World War II.

But they had been led astray. When Virginia Governor Spotswood's recruiter arrived in London and found the Germans already there, he first told them to return to Germany since there were no silver mines in Virginia. Nonetheless, refusing to go back, the first Germanna Colonists arrived in Virginia in the spring of 1714 and then came up the Rappahannock River to Tappahannock, where they disembarked and made their way overland to the place where they would be settled, 20 miles west of present-day Fredericksburg at an old Indian encampment that would be called Fort Germanna. A second contingent voluntarily arrived in 1717.

The first written description of the Germanna Colony given by John Fontaine in his Journal describes a 1715 visit:

> *"found nothing to eat at the (Minister's house), and lived on our small provisions. . .There is but nine houses built all in a line, and before every house, about 20 feet from the house they have small sheds built for their hogs and their hens, so that hog-stys and house make a street. . . They go to prayers constantly once a day and have two sermons a Sunday. We went to hear them perform their service, which is done in their own language, which we did not understand, but they seem very devout and sing the psalms very well . . . This town (is) 30 miles from any Inhabitants. The Germans live very miserably . . ."* That minister was my ancestor.

The generations between the Germanna colonists and my great-grandmother, Mary Susan Rector Jennings, were prolific and adventurous. Still, I shall resist the recitation of such numerous "begats" and state simply that they included the English-born Wassons, one of whom married the Irish-born Nancy Means, born in 1717 in Fermanagh, Tyrone, Ireland, who was captured by Indians when her husband was killed while both he and Nancy had left forted safety to plant their crops. She was held captive for four years until she was finally released in a prisoner's exchange. When freed, she was described as "naked and nearly starved."

Landon Rector, my 3rd great-grandfather, married Mary Wasson (a granddaughter of Nancy) in Rhea County, Tennessee, in the early 1800s, and with three of their grown sons (John, Houston, and Landon Alexander) all came to Pope County, Illinois together in 1862, traveling by wagon and going north through the Cumberland Gap, then the long length of the State of Kentucky to cross over the Ohio River--probably at Golconda--in order to settle on yet another rocky piece of ground, close enough to the Jennings family for one of their descendants to meet and marry my great-grandfather George Jennings. It is evident from Rhea County and Rector family history that they left to escape having their sons fight for the Confederacy (*or* the Union).

Mary Susan Rector Jennings, my great-grandmother (wife of Joseph) was the 7th of the eleven children born to John and Melvina Barton Rector. She was born in Sulphur Springs (later known as Rhea Springs), Rhea County, Tennessee, on 10 Jan 1857, and was only five years old when her parents moved to Illinois.

The Stokes Family – My Grandmother's People

My maternal grandmother (Danty) was extremely proud of her Stokes heritage. The Stokes family was one of the first three families to settle in Union County, Illinois, coming to the area in about 1810

– a large family of Quakers from North Carolina who arrived in Illinois by way of what is now Christian County (Hopkinsville), Kentucky, where they had settled in about 1802-1804. When the Illinois territory opened to land purchase, three of the Stokes siblings, John Richmond Stokes, Young Stokes, and their sister Sarah (married to George Milton Brown) moved from Kentucky to Illinois by way of the Cumberland River, then down the Ohio and finally following Cache Creek north to Union County to what is now Mt. Pleasant, Illinois (also known as Stokes Precinct, and later still as "Lick Creek." John Richmond Stokes was my 3rd great-grandfather. At least one brother had remained in North Carolina; two stayed near Hopkinsville, where there is a Stokes Family Cemetery. John Richmond was born about 1778 in Virginia and died in about 1855 or 1856 in Union County. His parents were Capt. John Stokes and Margaret Young Stokes. Early family written history states that Capt. John was a native Englishman who emigrated to America prior to the Revolutionary War and was a soldier in that struggle. Relatives of the Captain's wife, Margaret Young, also participated in the Revolutionary War. The Young name was also carried down through subsequent generations.

Another of those "first three" families, that of George Evans, was near kin and almost surely the family of John Stokes' first wife, already deceased by the time they arrived in Illinois. The last name, "Evans" or sometimes "Evan," appears down through subsequent generations, evidencing the habit of naming a son by the mother's maiden name. (Danty's father's middle name was "Evan," and so she always called him.)

John Richmond built a house and a grist mill, and by 1818, his household consisted of two free white males 21 or older and 7 other white inhabitants. Since his family was one of the first three white families in Stokes Precinct, he is considered to be one of the "pioneer settlers" in that region. The Indians seem to have slipped away, and while the Stokes families owned no slaves, the Evans family did. John's brother, Young Stokes, moved on to White County at some point in time, but John stayed, married three times, and had eleven children: eight sons and three daughters. One of those sons was Matthew Stokes, my 2nd great-grandfather, who was born in North Carolina and died in Union County. Matthew was a prominent citizen of the County and, at one time, served in the Illinois House of Representatives.

My grandmother's parents were Samuel Evan Stokes (son of Matthew and Turzey Anderson Stokes), who was born and died in Union County, Illinois, and Almedia Jones Stokes, who was also born in Union County. However, she may have died in Williamson at my grandparents' home there. Samuel Evan and Almedia were married in 1873 in Union County and are buried there in the McGinnis Cemetery, as are my grandparents, as well as my grandmother's brother and his wife, Matthew Hubbard and Lucinda Keller Stokes, and four other siblings: Charles, Gary, Mamie and an unnamed infant who all died either in infancy or early childhood and are buried there in unmarked graves. Almedia's parents were John D. Jones, born in 1821 in North Carolina, and Esther Massey Carter Jones, born in about 1819 in Kentucky. It is believed that John, my great-great-grandfather, died of injuries suffered in the Civil War.

But now I must leave those distant ancestors and return to those I remember best: my grandparents, Miles Marion Jennings (Pa) and his wife, LeMaude Stokes (Danty). They were, in practice if not in fact, my first parents.

Pa was not cut out to be a farmer, and through the years he tried his hand at a little bit of everything. In about 1916 or 1917, he and my grandmother "sold out" in Union County, and he moved his young family to Pueblo, Colorado, to homestead. My mother was only 3, her sister Mary was just 5. He did some carpentering but apparently had what the family always described as a "nervous breakdown," and they were forced to come back home. He and Maude "kept store" in Buncombe, Illinois (a settlement just off the highway between Vienna and Marion) on their return from Colorado. Their youngest child, Maxine Lucille ("Maxie Lou"), was born in 1918 in a small house across the street from the store in Buncombe.

Sometime in the very early 1920s, Pa purchased a plot of ground on which a store was already standing in Fergestown (Williamson County), the little coal mining "burg" on the Johnson City/Marion to Herrin Road already mentioned. I suspect the location was chosen because one of his 14 siblings, Roy Jennings, lived just down the road with his wife and their four daughters: Chestina, Thelma, Alene, and Betty. Two other brothers, Frank and Otto, lived in the same county, as did two sisters, Lily and Amelia. Another sister, Sarah, lived in Vienna, 30 miles south. Rose and Della had married and moved away: Rose to California, Della to Arizona; Dewey married and moved to Oregon, where he owned an apple orchard. One brother, James Alvia, died in World War II. Three children died early: Emily, who was just 16; Thomas, born in 1896, who lived two years; and Alvis "Babe," the youngest, born in April 1900 and died sometime before 1910, perhaps at the same time as his mother, Mary Rector Jennings, who died in January 1904.

Pa built a five-room bungalow next door to the store (the house where I was born), and the girls went to school at the two-room school in "Fudgetown," and attended the nearby Methodist church, which was practically next door: down a little lane and up a slight hill to the northwest of the store and house. I often went to church there when I visited, and my mother and her sisters frequently came back for "Homecoming Sunday." Again, Danty "kept store" while Pa did carpentry work in and around Fudgetown. She was probably not unhappy with the task. Her father had always kept a hired girl to do the heavy work of housekeeping until he died when she was 16. Of course, Danty also had a "heart condition," angina pectoris, which could come upon her quite suddenly and often (I thought) quite conveniently. At least, it often occurred at times when the family considered it most convenient for Maude. The angina caused a tightness in the chest, palpitations, and shortness of breath, and while it was not fatal, it could be quite frightening to the afflicted and the audience as well. Nitroglycerin tablets were always close at hand.

I don't remember her being a meticulous housekeeper, though she was very particular that her family be "well turned out" when they left the house. Mom said that everything had to be ironed – handkerchiefs, sheets and pillowcases, even underwear. (I, too, meticulously ironed my first husband's boxer shorts.) In later years, Danty sometimes had her laundry done, both washing and ironing and I remember that in still later years, it was often Pa who did the family laundry.

In 1925, when Danty and Uncle Hubbard's mother died at Pa and Danty's home in Fudgetown, she was taken back to Lick Creek for burial. And it was my mother Evelyn, the seamstress of the family, although only 12, who made her grandmother's burial dress. One of her proudest memories was of trekking across the fields in the dark, carrying a lantern to light her way, to borrow the use of a neighbor's sewing machine to sew the dress in which her grandmother would be buried.

In later years, the family also acquired a piano: a big, heavy upright Kimball with a beautiful sound, though it took "four men and a boy" to move it. Mom learned to play it, and the piano was eventually moved to Mom's house, where my sister and I learned to play it, and later to the farmhouse in Massac County (my father's parents' homeplace) when I lived there. The piano burned, along with the house, in the 1960s.

Depression History - The late 1920s in "Bloody Williamson" County were not peaceful years. Efforts were being made to unionize the coal mines. The miners went out on strike to force the coal companies' collective hand, and the coal companies brought in truckloads of strikebreakers, many of them "foreigners" of Italian extraction, to replace the striking miners. Frank Mussa (who would become Aunt Maxie's husband) was the son of one of those Italians. The white-robed, gun-bearing members of the Ku Klux Klan marched to protest...and they marched past the little bungalow in Fudgetown while the family watched. One of the Jennings uncles was among the marchers, Danty once told me, but it was not something the family talked about publicly (or even privately, until years later). Secrecy was the very essence of Klan membership. When Danty imparted the information to me, it was in a near whisper as though someone might overhear.

When the depression struck in full force, people couldn't pay their bills, and Pa was unable to keep the grocery store open. Those years were a difficult time for everyone. My mother recalled that they were blessed to have family (Danty's brother and his wife, Uncle Hubbard and Aunt Cindy) who still lived on the Stokes family farm, and Aunt Cindy sent care packages of chickens and garden produce that were life savers. The families had always spent time together frequently, with Pa and Danty usually visiting Hubbard and

Cindy because there was livestock to be fed on the farm, and Hubbard and Cindy weren't very "venturesome." I doubt if either got past the Union County line more than once or twice in their lifetimes.

With the store closed, Pa rented out the bungalow he had built in Fudgetown (or perhaps left it unoccupied—I've never known for sure) and moved the family to Cypress, Illinois, where there was an overall factory. Pa had a truck that he used to carry the overalls to wherever a buyer could be found. Aunt Mary and my mother went to work in the factory, but the work was too hard, and the girls only lasted two weeks. I still have a doll-size "salesman's sample" of the overalls they sewed and Pa sold. Those little overalls are nearly a hundred years old. I've always been tempted to post them on E-bay--not to sell them but to see how much they're worth! Or perhaps the Antiques Roadshow would be a better venue.

There was a rayon factory in Metropolis (Massac County, Illinois), so Pa moved the family there, and Aunt Mary and Mom found work in the factory. My mother was not quite sixteen and hadn't finished high school. However, Aunt Maxie attended Metropolis Community High School, where I would later spend my senior year in 1950. The house where they first lived was on Sixth Street, a small square house with a "pointy roof" which Mom used to point out to me. Sometime in the next four years, Pa built their own house nearby, securing a loan from a local banker.

Pa took any work he could get during the depression and was often forced to live away from his family to find enough work to keep going. His health was not good, exacerbated by a mouth full of abscessed teeth, which he finally had to have pulled. Danty, on the other hand, still had her "own teeth" until the day she died. Well, most of them. She credited their sturdiness to always using baking soda and salt when she brushed them.

At some point, Pa even went back to Union County and tried working for Uncle Hubbard on the farm where he could at least plant a garden. He would hitchhike from Anna to Metropolis on weekends to be with Maude and the girls (and carry home those "care packages" from Aunt Cindy). His nephew, Herman Stokes, remembered "hitching" with his Uncle Miles once, and *only* once. It was a long, hard, hot trip. Even on today's roads and with far better vehicles, it's more than an hour's drive from Lick Creek to Metropolis.

Aunt Mary married Lewis Turner, a young man she had met while they were living in Cypress. My mother went north and lived with the new bride and groom for a time, but she soon returned to Metropolis – within a month, as she recalled – to live with her parents again and resume work at the rayon factory. In truth, she was needed there and was the main support of her family. In those hard times, Mom remembered, it was a treat to have butter on one's potatoes, and sometimes dinner consisted of potatoes and nothing else. But the Jennings family never "took charity." It was a proud thing to be able to say that; I suspect that Danty would rather have starved. She was a proud woman. I learned from the best: whatever happens, you hold your head high and walk through the storm as though it is just a mild breeze, barely enough to ruffle your hair. (And if you're a *real* lady, it won't matter. You'll be wearing a hat!)

Danty, I'm sure, had a hard time with life in the depression, and Pa's misfortunes in trying to make a living, although I never heard her say so. Her father Evan had been a farmer, a horse trader, and a man who loved company and sociability. He made a good living for his family, and it was said that he spoiled Danty rotten, perhaps because he and his wife had lost four other children. He died of a stroke when she was only 15, and she mourned him the rest of her life. He was not a poor man for that day and time. When Danty's mother filed for Letters of Administration, his assets were: 103 acres of land in Union County, unencumbered by debt, 6 head of horses, 7 head of cattle, 13 head of hogs, farming implements, household and kitchen furniture, one wagon and one buggy, 30 bushels old wheat, 15 acres corn in the field, $67.00 in money and one $40 note, all being estimated to be worth about $475. She listed as heirs herself, her son Matthew (always known as "Hubbard" to his family), and Maud. I'm sure it was Danty's inheritance that was "sold out" for that trip to Colorado. Six years older than his sister, Hubbard was 21 when their father died and thus became the head of the family. Ten years later he married for the first time, to Lucinda May Keller. They had three sons: Lowell Matthew, Timothy Evan, and Herman Lee.

My great-grandmother Almedia was midwife to the community for years and also "laid out" the dead. Danty often said that the reason she learned to make biscuits was that she just couldn't stand to eat the biscuits her mother had made after being out all night tending the sick or washing and "laying out" a corpse.

Pa was able to finish the house he had begun in Metropolis, and in 1933 the family was able to move into it – though not for long. They lived in Metropolis until (I believe) early 1934, when they were finally able to return to Fudgetown and reopen the store. When the house in Metropolis was finished, the local banker who had financed it refused to pay Pa for his work, and when they moved back to Fudgetown he simply took the house. It was, as far as I can recall, the only real resentment Pa ever expressed for anyone.

When they went "back home" I went with them, though somewhat incognito. I was concealed by my mother's pregnancy. Or, as she said to my brother years later when her memory was fogged by dementia, and she was trying to recall some event that had occurred before he was born, and he was trying to help: "You hush. You were *behind the door*."

It was during my mother's illness that I learned how dementia seems to demand that those afflicted speak in metaphors, a language that perhaps only poets really understand. On one of those occasions, she kept saying that she had lost her shoes. It was quite obvious that she had not; they were on her feet. But she kept insisting until I finally asked, "You mean your car is gone?" And she was so relieved that I finally understood that she was trying to tell me she had lost her means of getting places on her own. She did love to go places, and on one occasion, she actually walked out of Twin Oaks, the assisted living facility where she was staying in Metropolis and was discovered walking down the road. Where was she going? "Kay's having a party and they didn't invite me, but I'm just going anyway." *Of course* she was. (Kay was my younger sister.)

After Pa and Danty returned to Williamson County, Maxie finished high school in Johnson City and (after I was born) married Frank Mussa, son of the Italian coal miner. Danty grieved again (as she had when her oldest daughter married), but this time it was a "foreign" son-in-law whose parents spoke only broken English. Pa built a little one-room apartment attached to the back of the store for Frank and Maxie, and they "kept store" for a couple of years before moving to Chicago. I remember playing there -- the big wheels of cheese, the ponderous round wooden butcher block behind the meat counter.

When the store was finally closed, Frank and Maxie went to Chicago, where Frank worked as a welder in the steel mills in Chicago, and Maxie worked for a while as a secretary in a bank until their two sons, David and Daniel, were born. In later years, Maxie was secretary to the minister of a local church until she retired. Frank and Maxie both died of heart attacks: Frank quite suddenly after mowing the lawn, Maxie slowly and hooked to medical equipment in futile efforts to keep her alive. For a long time prior to her attack, she had suffered from chest pains, often soothed by applications of a heating pad. But she had refused medical treatment because she was afraid of "invasive" measures, even for tests. And then it happened, and she was alone and could not even reach her phone to call for help.

I thought of Aunt Maxie when I recently bought my "Dick Tracy" watch so that I could quickly summon help in the event I had a similar episode. I had one of those strange mystical experiences at her funeral. I was sitting with my sister Kay at the visitation, admiring the beautiful wildflowers in the casket spray and also wondering if Aunt Maxie was somehow present, when I noticed that one single thin twig that had been sticking straight up began to slowly bend—almost bow—toward the head of the casket. And then slowly bend back upright. I was so certain of what I had seen that I whispered to Kay what had just happened. But I don't think she believed me. And it didn't happen again, at least not while I was watching.

When Maxie and Frank moved to Chicago, the store was closed, and Pa eventually tore it down and made a landscaped garden with wandering paths and flower beds, lots of pine trees, and even two small ponds -- one with an island in the center. The ponds were joined via a narrow canal with a wooden bridge built across it. There was a rather large rectangular area, tree-shaded, flat, and well-grassed, between the highway and the ponds. I think Pa intended that section as a croquet court, but perhaps he just ran out of ideas for the space. The paths were lined with orange daylilies, and my cousin Jack and I discovered that when the lilies died and their stems dried to hollow tubes, it was possible to light one end and smoke it. However, it required a very long stem to keep from drawing in just smoke, without flame, and therefore you had to stretch your arm wayyyy out to "light your fire." Jack got sick on his. I never did.

It was at some point in those years after the family returned to Fudgetown that Pa began working in the coal mines, employed at the Jeffrey mine where my mother's best friend, Lona Rae Murphy, worked as secretary to the manager. I don't believe Pa ever worked underground, but he came home as covered with coal dust as if he had. His work there made him an admirer of John L. Lewis, the leader of the Coalminer's Union. He was also a fervent supporter of Franklin D. Roosevelt, who had--in Pa's and many others' views--saved the country after the depression with his Works Progress Administration and the CCC camps where many young men could earn a small living while they were learning a trade.

So, of course, my mother was a lifelong Democrat. She served as an election clerk in our local precinct for many years, at first (or so she said) because she was the only Democrat *in* the precinct. My father was born and raised a Republican. (At one time, Massac County was the second most Republican County in the state.) But they never argued their political differences, at least not in my hearing. Mom was also a Baptist, while Dad was raised Lutheran. I don't think they ever argued about that, either. Dad just didn't go to church. But he never missed casting his ballot at election time. Mom said it was to cancel her vote. But she might have been joking. (Or maybe not.)

My Father and His People – The Kortes and the Quints

My mother always told me that my father's grandfather, Henry Korte (1862-1942) was a "sheep-boy" in Germany, and I've learned that the story was true. A distant cousin told me that all the Korte boys who arrived in America from the old country were sheepherders, or "sheep-boys." They stayed alone in the pastures, herding sheep with only their dog for company, and were given a sheep of their own to raise. When the sheep was sold, it paid for their passage to America.

My father's great-grandparents, Conrad Korte and his wife Carolina (who both stayed in Germany) had nine children, and in order of birth, they were: an older son whose name is unknown to me, but who also stayed in Germany, inheriting the family farm; William, who came to the United States and married Mary Anna Brugger; Wilhemina "Minnie", who married Charles Kirchoff (of the Paducah Kirchoffs who owned and still own a Paducah bakery); **Henry (my great-grandfather);** Conrad (Jr.), who married Caroline "Carrie" Hasfelt, bought land and built a home next door to **Henry's**; Fritz, who married Doris "Dora" Struve; Maria, who married an Albers and stayed in Germany; Mieka, who married a Dunn and moved to Arizona. There was also, according to tradition, another daughter who left Germany for the United States but is believed to have either died en route or after arrival, never reaching Illinois. My grandfather and his siblings were the second generation to come to this country.

I remember many of them, and visiting their homes; they were a part of my childhood. Although my great-grandfather Henry died when I was seven or eight, I remember visiting his brother, Uncle Conrad (Daddy pronounced it Coon-rod) and Aunt Carrie often. They never had children, but their house is still standing beside the great open space where my great-grandfather's house once stood until, several years ago, a tornado tore it into bits and pieces and scattered the crumbs of shingles and furniture across their open fields and beyond.

We (my parents, my sister and I) often visited William's son Julius and grandson Waymond (just my father Raymond's age). Waymond's mother, Lottie Quint Korte, was the granddaughter of Dad's mother's grandparents, Henry and Lottie Niehouse Quint. You could see the log cabin where the Quints had lived when they first came to Illinois from Julius and Lottie's front porch. Julius wore a black glove on one immobile hand, and I never solved the mystery of what had happened and whether the glove held a real hand or shielded a fake one. I always yearned to touch it, but I never did. I also remember often visiting one of the Kirchoff daughters with my mother when I was quite small. I still occasionally have lunch at Kirchoff's Bakery when I'm in Paducah. Both the corned beef and the pastrami sandwiches are the best in town. (I've never asked for a family discount.)

Henry Korte, my "Little Grandpa" (so-called in later years because he was smaller than both his sons) had arrived in New York, together with his brother William, on September 29, 1881, on the ship General Werder. According to the ship's manifest, "Heinrich" was 18. His father's brothers had arrived some years before him, so he lived with his Uncle Fritz at first and went to work in his Uncle Christ's brickworks until he was old enough to take up land. Christ built a beautiful Victorian-style brick home next door to his own first home, a log cabin. I visited there when I was working on genealogy for the family; there is even a library! The whole house literally echoes history. Those earlier settlers were founding members of St. John's Lutheran Church in Massac County. Most of my German ancestors who came to America, as well as all the older generations of their descendants, are buried in the cemetery there.

In 1884, Little Grandpa married a local girl, Sophia Weseman. When I found their marriage license, I compared it to the birth date of their oldest child, my grandfather (of course I did!) and realized, with a smile, that the bride was already pregnant. Two years later, he purchased 140 acres of land about five miles north of Round Knob and ten miles north of Metropolis from a Mescher family, who had moved closer to Round Knob. He died there in 1941, in the home where he had raised three children. It was built on a knoll overlooking the low-lying croplands which, combined with hard work and ingenuity, had made his not inconsiderable fortune. I remember attending the visitation when he died, the hushed voices and overpowering scent of flowers in the parlor (we called it a "living room" at our house) where he lay in state. I had never seen a dead person before. I stayed very close to my mother's side and held tight to my little sister Kay's hand.

Two of his three children had died before him: a daughter in childbirth and his younger son of a heart attack during the great flood of 1937. My grandfather Charles Korte was thus the only child to survive him.

Little Grandpa was an authoritarian of the German variety: the man ruled the household, and to a considerable degree the households of his progeny. He grieved terribly when his daughter Louise ("Lulu") died. When his wife died, and then his youngest son in 1937, his daughter-in-law stayed on to keep house for him and raise her three daughters. His younger grandson, my Uncle Ernest, recalled him as a man of seemingly inexhaustible energy. "You didn't like to be on one end of a crosscut saw when he was on the other end," Uncle Ernest said. "He could just about work you to death when it came to sawing." And, "When cars came out, and he got one, you took your life in your hands if you went off someplace with him." He had a heavy foot on the accelerator and an utter disregard for roadway boundaries and the hazards of oncoming traffic. (Do you suppose one can inherit driving habits? I've been accused of similar behavior.)

My mother remembered, with something akin to awe, Little Grandpa's work methods when dynamiting stumps in the "new ground," where woodland was being cleared for cultivation. He would travel in his Model A Ford from stump to stump, stop, kill the engine, get out, set the charge and light the fuse, then crank the engine (by hand!), jump in the car, and only then, while the fuse was still burning down, would he put the car in gear and drive away.

My father Raymond was three years older than Uncle Ernest, but he did not often speak of the past—or perhaps I never asked. He may have been a naturally taciturn man, but I'm almost certain that he also suffered from depression and an almost innate shyness. Most of what I have learned about his family has come from my mother's recollections over the years, what I later gleaned from friends of the family, and what I learned from Uncle Ernest.

Dad's first-grade teacher, Edith Mescher, was still teaching school when my oldest daughter was in Ms. Edith's first-grade class 40-odd years later, and she remembered my father's first-grade experiences very well. He couldn't speak a word of English when he first came to school, for at that time most German families in Massac County spoke only German in their homes. (Ms. Edith also taught my brother Kent: thus, three generations of our family.)

When Dad came of age (13 or 14) he took his confirmation classes in German, the last such class taught in German at St. John's. Mother said that Dad refused to study until the night before but then stayed up all night "cramming" and, of course, passed easily. He was a smart man, a voracious (though not very selective) reader. But then, there had not been much "literature" in his life to choose from. There were no books or magazines in my Korte grandparents' home that I can recall, although I'm sure there must have been at least a Bible and perhaps a local newspaper. I have always believed that the last thing in the world Dad should have been was what he was destined to become: a farmer. (Destiny, I believe, is not so much *fate* as it is a *fact* of both time and circumstance.)

In later years, Dad's memory of his childhood tongue had diminished to the point that he would seldom even *use* a word of German, except when asked to say the blessing before a meal. Then he would pray in German. The only German word he ever taught me was from that prayer: It sounded like "b'dote," and I'm fairly certain the English translation is "bread," so it must have been the Lord's Prayer (though much abbreviated). Once, when a neighbor got a letter from Germany, Dad had to take it to Uncle "Coon-rod," who was perhaps one of the last of his family who could still read German. We sat on the back porch and ate Aunt Carrie's cookies while the men struggled to decipher the letter, written in "high German," because apparently Uncle Coon-rod only knew "low German," and Dad had forgotten most of the "high German" from his confirmation classes. It was then I learned there were two German dialects!

I did not spend much time with my Korte grandparents. Not from any estrangement or lack of caring, but because my grandfather became ill with Parkinson's Disease when I was quite young, only a year or two after Little Grandpa died, and he was an invalid for the rest of his life. My grandmother, Mary Quint Korte, was an almost inscrutably quiet woman. She seldom smiled, and then it was a bashful one, as though she had surprised even herself. It has only recently occurred to me that she had, at some point, lost all her teeth. But my mother also said that when a strange vehicle pulled into the yard at the farm, Grandma would always hide. So perhaps she had simply learned very early that there was safety in invisibility.

She had married Grandpa Charlie in August of 1908, and the newlyweds' first home was a two-room log cabin on a farm they were given by Little Grandpa that sat at the T-intersection of the New Columbia and Big Bay Roads. The cabin may have been-- at least it was almost certainly on the site of--the first trading post in northern Massac County, according to local historians. There was a "dogtrot" between the log cabin's two rooms. It was still standing when I was growing up, and I remember playing there under the shade of a pear tree in its front yard. Those pears never *ever* seemed to get *really* ripe.

My father was born, I believe, in that log cabin on March 9, 1910, although he may have been born at Little Grandpa's house. I doubt my grandmother would have gone to her own father's house to bear her first child. I simply cannot believe she would have trusted any child to the untender ministrations of her thoroughly disliked stepmother.

Grandma Korte's own grandfather was J. Heinrich Frederick "Henry" Quint, who immigrated to America from Osnabauck, Germany, along with two sisters, arriving in Baltimore, Maryland on the Steamer "Vint Shinklehame" in 1845, and traveling from there to Cincinnati, Ohio by train. In Ohio, Henry (my great-great-grandfather) married Amelia Charlotte "Lottie" Niehaus (1820-

1891). They were married on May 10, 1849, in Cincinnati, just seven days after Henry had purchased the property that would become their home in Massac County.

He bought eighty acres at $1.25 per acre for a total of $100. Their first two children were born in Cincinnati, which may have been the reason it was not until 1855 that Henry and Charlotte loaded their belongings on a flatboat (really just a very large raft) and began their journey down the Ohio River to what must have seemed to them to be, if not "the promised land," then certainly "a land that promised."

My only published novel, *Down River*, was inspired by stories of those westward-bound settlers' journeys down the Ohio, and I also attempted to reconstruct it it in the lengthy Quint history that appeared in my genealogy of the Kortes and Quints several years ago. The site of their new home was a log cabin in which Henry and his wife lived those first years and perhaps longer. I have a photo which, I was told by a Quint relative (second half-cousin), is a picture of Lottie, looking near middle-aged, sitting in the doorway of the cabin. It was in a picturesque setting, apparently on the western incline of a hill, facing the sunset and overlooking a good portion of the surrounding countryside after (I imagined) the timber was cleared. It occurs to me now that much of my "creative" writing has been my attempts to turn history into fiction. In my professional life, I must admit that, at times, my writing seemed like an endeavor to transform fiction into historical fact.

Henry and Lottie had seven more children in Illinois; the second from the youngest, Ernest Quint, was my great-grandfather. Ernest grew up and married (first) Emma Gieseke, the girl next door. Her mother had died of "weakness" and her father had died just nine months before Ernest and Emma were married. They had three children: my Grandma Korte was the oldest; her sister Amelia

"Melie" next; then an infant, Effie Sophia, who died just days before her mother. Three months after Emma's death, Ernest married Annie Reineking, whose family lived on the next farm over and who had come to care for his ailing wife and the older two girls. *Their* first child was named Emma Bernadine Sophia Quint (apparently named for Ernest's first wife and their deceased child); however, the child lived for only nine days. They had four more children, two sons and two daughters. I remember Aunt Melie well, but the half-aunts only slightly; one half-uncle (Jesse) lived practically next door to Little Grandpa (though around the corner and down the hill). I haven't figured out the exact logistics. Still, I believe Grandma probably lived next door to Grandpa when they were growing up, for my (Great)-Uncle Jesse's house was (I believe) built on a portion of the Quint/Gieseke property, which was just east and adjoining that of Little Grandpa and his brother, Uncle Conrad ("Coon-rod").

Grandma was six years old when her mother died, but when I was growing up she still spoke with longing of a mother she had barely known, as though life would have been different, somehow "better," if her mother had only lived. Grandma always remained very close to her sister Melie, although it is somewhat difficult for me to know what "close" meant to my grandmother. She was not one to openly show her affection, which I suspect may be a common trait in German families (a trait I also seem to have inherited). She may also have suffered from what we would today call depression. In most photos and my own memories, she has her arm cradled across her slightly protruding abdomen as though shielding something--or perhaps simply holding her feelings tightly inside, almost as though in terror that they might erupt.

Until her death, she wore her hair in the style of her youth: a waist-length coil of graying hair twisted into a round bun on the back of her head and anchored with long, thick, brownish-colored celluloid pins. Her hair was thin and straight, like my father's, like mine, although mine has turned mostly white; neither her's nor my father's ever did. Before going to bed at night, she would let her hair down, bring its whole length around and down over her shoulder – always her left shoulder – and comb out any tangles (there were none, of course), then form it into a long loose braid. Closing my eyes, I can still see her twisting the strands into place.

How many times had she done that, I wonder. She would surely have learned how to braid her own hair when she was seven or eight. She was 80 when she died. Over 26,000 times in her lifetime, she had performed those same familiar gestures. Her sister Melie never cut her hair either, although photographs indicate that both their half-sisters did. Family photos picture Mary and Amelia separately from their two half-sisters. The two boys, Willie and Jesse, are also pictured separately but *with* their father and mother. Those old photographs tell us almost more than we want to know about the family dynamics (and the importance of females).

Their stories are important to my own story because they bear an almost subliminal acknowledgment of the "roots" from which I was "propagated" and seem tangled in my own. And perhaps because Grandma Korte's father, my great-grandfather Ernest Quint, one day closeted himself in the family outhouse with a shotgun and, in Uncle Ernest's words, "blew the top of his head off."

His suicide was not exactly a secret, though it was never mentioned when I was growing up. I can't remember when I first learned about it. My mother may have told me. Of course, I wondered, "Why?" But no one seemed to know. Had he learned he had some fatal illness? Had he suffered financial reverses? (He died in 1930 when the Great Depression struck down many proud men.)

Was he perhaps a "drinking man"? I asked my Uncle Ernest (only 17 when it happened), who was named after his grandfather Quint, and in his 90s when he himself died, sane and sober, and he said, "Well, he drank some. But then, everybody did."

Beer, wine, whiskey: homemade fermented and distilled beverages were always close at hand in Germany, and the "old country ways" were brought to America, where they found close kin. Fritz Korte, one of my family history sources, told me that he himself once did a thriving wine business, peddling much of his product in Paducah, driving across the Ohio River Bridge at Brookport. (There was also still a ferry in Metropolis, west and downriver from Brookport, when I was growing up.) Fritz once had a bit of trouble with his corncob stoppers, losing wine because the mice in the barn where the wine was stored chewed the cobs out of the bottles. He said that switching to cork stoppers "probably saved us from starvin' to death."

Some people handled their liquor better than others. Some couldn't handle it at all. And so the mystery of why my great-grandfather found it necessary to end his own life died with him. Yet the ripples of his death still lap gently across the lives of even his great-grandchildren. Some of us still wonder, as though the ghost of that death might someday creep into and through our own veins and turn us against life and living. At least I do.

Of Charlie and Mary Korte's three children (my father, his brother Ernest, and sister Clara), my father was most like his mother, I think. Certainly he inherited her dark complexion and her deep-set, shadowed eyes. In group and the many individual, and very professional, photos taken when he was just a little boy, his dark skin—he tanned so easily—and deep-set "haunted" eyes set him apart from the other children. I think he inherited her shyness and tendency to depression as well. Perhaps both of them dealt with it by self-medicating with alcohol. Grandma Korte always had a bottle of wine on the shelf in the refrigerator of their house in Metropolis. Dad's whiskey bottles were secured in places not so easily found. Mom spent considerable time looking for them when I was growing up. But she kept one at the bottom of the flour bin in the kitchen. She said it was to pour over the fruit cakes she always made at Christmas time. (That was true; I recently found her recipe.) But I've always wondered if she also kept it handy in case Dad just *had* to have a drink.

Fritz also told me about Arnold Riepe, who was skilled in working with copper and much in demand by the moonshiners who plied their trade in the Brookport bottoms along the shores of the Ohio River. But Fritz also said that, every once in a while, Arnold would "just get wild." (Could it have been the moonshine, I wonder? Or was it "in the blood?") He ended up confined to Anna State Hospital for a number of years and, by the time he was declared cured and discharged, everything he owned was gone. (My father was once confined there for a few days when he too became uncontrollable from the effects of alcohol. That story later.)

Family stories, handed down, say that bottled beer stored in the attic once started "popping its corks" during a family gathering at my (paternal) grandparents' home. But I didn't find any empties in the attic when I lived there, only a beautiful blue hand-blown and hand-painted pitcher and four glasses (one slightly chipped). They were remnants of my grandparents' wedding gifts. The pitcher sits now atop a bookcase in my living room, over 100 years old and waiting for whoever chooses to inherit it. I don't remember what happened to the glasses. (And I am absolutely certain that beer would never have been allowed in my *maternal* grandparents' house!)

We often hold tight to family keepsakes like Grandma Korte's pitcher as though they were keys that would (or should) unlock the secrets of deaths, births, and marriages, loves found and lost. But we can only ask questions of history. We search church records first written in German but now translated into English, spend hours peering at the blurred microfilm of ancient newspapers, and pick our way around and over moss-covered tombstones in old cemeteries (such lonely, lovely, silent places) where we strain to decipher nearly obscured names and dates. We handle gently the crumbling obituary clippings, turned brown with age, that we find tucked into the pages of family Bibles and the musty-smelling scrapbooks containing photos that no one bothered to label. They had no reason to bother. *They* knew who *they* were.

So it is that over and over again we unbraid the past, separate the strands of fading memories, comb them out, then braid them back again. But we can't always find the answers to the questions we ask. Nor can we always plait the answers we do find into a tidy braid to be twisted into a ball and pinned neatly away somewhere at the back of our mind.

"I need to know my story . . . all of it.

- *Anne Wilson Schaef*

My Own Story - THE EARLY YEARS

I'm supposed to "claim the events of my life to make myself mine," and I've already claimed quite a few. Some of the facts may be repeated as I continue, although perhaps in a slightly different form, but we "old folks" tend to do that. Since I still haven't stated exactly *when* I was born, here are the very first facts *as they were told to me*:

I was born on July 21, 1934, in the front bedroom of my maternal grandparents' house, the house my grandfather had built in Fergestown (aka "Fudgetown"), in Williamson County, Illinois, next to the little grocery store I believe he'd bought with the land. A Hallmark paper my mother gave me in 1987 as a birthday present chronicles the events of the day and year I was born. I've kept it, of course. I've kept a lot of things. And given a lot of things away. Perhaps wisdom comes from just living life and learning what to keep and what to throw away.

In 1934, the United States faced a severe drought that gripped much of the country, while in the West, Dust Bowl storms wreaked havoc on the land. During the same month, there was a strike of longshoremen in San Francisco. John Dillinger, also known as Public Enemy No. 1, had been killed by G-men in Chicago, and President Franklin Roosevelt was going on a cruise to Hawaii with his sons, Franklin Jr. and John. (John Nance Garner was the Vice President, in case anyone needs to know.)

At the Oscars, *It Happened One Night* won Best Movie, Clark Gable and Claudette Colbert were best actors and actresses; St. Louis beat Detroit to win the World Series, and Columbia won the Rose Bowl over Stanford, 7-0. Shirley Temple was in Little Miss Marker and sang *Baby Take a Bow*. When Shirley grew up, she became the U. S. delegate to the United Nations. That's quite a bow!

The population of the United States was 126,485,000; a three-bedroom home could be purchased for $2,925, a new Ford for $535. Gas was 19 cents a gallon, a loaf of bread 8 cents, and milk was 44 cents. Average income was $1,237 a year. Just for the sake of comparison, in 2020 the U.S. population was 331,000,000, my 4-bedroom house sold in 2019 for $140,000 (in a small town in Kentucky), new Fords were cheap at $25,000, I paid $3.39 a gallon for gas last week, $2.98 for a loaf of bread and $3.98 for a gallon of milk.

I didn't learn until I was 15 that for those 15 years I had been, legally at least, "*Leona* Rae" and not "*Lona* Rae," as Mom had intended. We discovered the error when Mom and I went to the Williamson County Courthouse to get a copy of my birth certificate, which I would need to obtain a driver's license. The doctor had either misheard or misspelled the name and might even have been "under the influence" at the time, according to Mom's recollection. I had been named for my mother's best friend, Lona Rae Murphy, and *not* my father, Raymond Korte, as some have since believed, unless that was her subconscious intention. (I had a second cousin, once removed, who told me in a rather haughty tone of voice that illegitimate children were often given their father's middle name in order to "claim" him.) But I was *not* illegitimate, no matter what stories she had heard to the contrary. My parents' marriage license was prominently displayed, framed, and neatly centered above the headboard of their double bed all their lives together. A quaint and ancient custom that seems to have become culturally obsolete, along with the marriage rites the license affirmed. However, I'm also sure those stories my cousin heard had included tales of a "legitimately illegitimate" half-sister whose middle name was *also* Rae. But I do not intend to pursue those "alternate facts" down that particular rabbit hole. That's not *my* story. But it certainly could have been.

My mother filed the necessary affidavits and legal paperwork to correct the mistake about Leona/Lona. Still, it occurs to me that it was perhaps the very first time in my life that it was necessary for me to "reinvent myself." I seem to have been doing it periodically ever since. But I like my name and am glad we made the correction. It's an old name and rather unique; I have seldom actually encountered anyone else named Lona and certainly no one else whose name was "Lona Rae" (except, of course, my mother's friend). And I've always liked being *a bit different*, or at the very least *not quite ordinary*. So now that I've admitted it, we can go on from there!

The first thing I actually remember, not counting those events that were told to me and are just memories of memories, is of the house where I was born, the house my grandfather Jennings built. And I remember distinctly the little upholstered stool my grandfather made so that I could sit between him and my grandmother in their black Pontiac coupe and see over the dashboard. It was not built for safety reasons but simply so that I would be able to see out. In my mind, even today, it was not just a "seat" but evidence of love.

For those who may have skipped or perhaps merely scanned the first section of this Memoir (I forgive you), I called my maternal grandfather "Daddypa" at first, more than a nod to the fact that my father was not present in those early days. As I grew up and my "real Daddy" joined the family, Daddypa became "Pa." My grandmother was, always and forever, to me at least, "Danty." She had wanted to be called "Granny," but apparently I had a bit of difficulty with the guttural "G." I've no idea why we've always spelled it "Danty" with a "t." The names I called them are important because they describe so accurately a fact of my life I have since recognized. I have always had two sets of parents: Pa and Danty, and my biological mother and father, Raymond and Evelyn Jennings Korte, "Mom" and "Dad."

I am absolutely certain that Pa loved me from the moment I was born, as only a grandfather can love his first grandchild (and a girl grandchild, as well). Having had three daughters already and no sons, he'd had plenty of practice in loving girlchildren. And since one of those daughters, Maxine Lucille (her name shortened to "Maxie Lou" so long ago I think the original was forgotten even when they wrote her obituary) was still a teenager living at home when I was born, I became the fourth daughter for all practical and emotional purposes.

It is not at all surprising that Dad, when he appeared in my life for the first time when I was about three years old, had no idea what to do for, or even how to behave with, a daughter. He'd had no experience at all with children. But a three-year-old has a small comprehension of those facts of life, and so the two of us always struggled through the years that followed to learn how to love each other and then how to express that love.

My grandmother and my mother were such different women. Danty was a dreamer, a poet, a bit of a visionary; Mom was practical and down-to-earth. While Danty was writing a poem or reading a novel, Mom would have been baking a cake or sewing a dress. And so, of course, I have always tried to do both, often at the same time.

Striking a balance between doing what I desperately want to do while simply *having* to do what others believe I could and should do has been my lifelong dilemma. Of course, although they say "no man can serve two masters," I learned long ago that the most difficult thing I would ever have to do is serve ANY master, including God.

Bathtubs in Which I Have Bathed (and sometimes cried)

The story of my life could be told in bathtubs – beginning with one of the first pictures taken of me: Danty bathing me in a small tub or sink on the kitchen counter of the house in Fudgetown where I was born and lived for those first three years of my life. It must have been taken in the early morning because, although the picture is in black and white, it is obvious that the sun is shining through the kitchen's east window.

There were no modern conveniences in the house where I was born. I remember there was a cistern just off the screened-in back porch, and that vines covered the porch screens in summer until Pa replaced the screens with glass years later. A gutter system directed rainwater into the cistern, and water for drinking, cooking, bathing, and laundry was raised up via a bucket-and-winch system. The winch always creaked when in operation. There was an outhouse too, down a path toward the garden. And a chamber pot (usually called the "slop jar") for use by children or adults in the middle of the night. It was usually kept on the back porch. My grandmother was particular about the outhouse. There was always a sack of quicklime there for sprinkling on the waste to promote decay and also kill unpleasant odors. It may have been one of those "WPA" toilets built by the Roosevelt administration's Public Works Administration. More likely my grandfather built it. Pa was always building things. The scent of sawdust can still comfort me. So can the scent of honeysuckle.

When I visited, and I visited often, sometimes entire summers after my mother and I no longer lived there, my grandmother and I would stand on the concrete pad surrounding the cistern every evening, brushing our teeth with a mixture of baking soda and salt. A teaspoon of soda in a half-cup of water is also a good remedy for heartburn for those interested in homeopathic medicine. Rock'n'rye is supposed to be good for *anything*. That's rye whiskey with a stick (rock) of peppermint candy added for flavor). There was a bottle of that sitting on the top shelf of the cabinet over the refrigerator at Pa and Danty's. That was the only alcoholic substance, other than rubbing alcohol, I ever saw in their house. The rock'n'rye wasn't for social drinking. It was medicine. Never tried it, and probably now I never will. There are lots of things I've never tried, and more than a few I regret having sampled.

I did not meet my father, and I don't believe he had ever "set eyes on me" until I was not yet three years old—in any event, sometime late in 1936 or perhaps very early in 1937 when (I am told) he arrived at my maternal grandparents' home, suitcase in hand, with instructions from his mother to "go get your wife and child and don't come home without them." Danty was, I am quite certain, even less pleased with him than she had been with her other two sons-in-law, and she never made a secret of it in all the years that followed.

It was in Metropolis, of course, that my mother met Raymond Korte, a Massac county farm boy, the man who would become my father, the man who would become her husband (and yes, in just that order). Sometime in 1933, Evelyn went to a dance in Metropolis with some girlfriends and saw a young man who stood out from the rest, although he didn't have much to say and didn't seem too fond of dancing. Ray Korte was a tall (well, kind of tall – about 5'11") handsome man with deeply tanned skin from working outdoors and deep-set blue-gray eyes swept by long dark lashes. Old photographs indicate that a girl of that day might well have seen a resemblance to the sleepy-eyed Rudolph Valentino. He drove a good car--his first brand new one had been a gift from his Grandfather Quint–perhaps drove it a little too fast, and always had money in his pocket. If he drank a little too much in those post-Prohibition times, so did most of the boys. His family was of good, solid German stock, and they had a big farm in the northern part of the county. If he was a little wild – if he'd even wrecked a car or two – well, all he really needed was a good woman to settle him down! More than one young woman would have liked to, and *did*, set her cap for Ray Korte.

Mom remembered that the day after their first date, which was apparently a double date arranged by mutual friends, Ray had to go searching for someone who could tell him where "that girl I was out with last night" lived. The family had just moved into the new house Pa had built, so it took a little sleuthing. "But," she said, "after he found out where I lived, he came around pretty regular."

Ray Korte already had a reputation for being, to put it kindly, a "bit of a rounder," and despite that, considered a "good catch." But what would you do with him after you caught him? His first wife (a girl named Margaret Woodward) certainly hadn't known. They had been married less than a month when they got into an argument and his bride drank carbolic acid, which is a dreadful and painfully slow way to die. She may have only intended to scare him or teach him a lesson, but it scared her to death on April 1, 1934. (And yes, I know that is now called April Fools' Day. Purely a coincidence, I'm sure.) It is also, if you're prone to counting such a thing, three months and 20 days before my own *birth* date.

Though I had known the "secret" of my father's first marriage for a very long time (Danty told me), I found a face to go with it when Uncle Ernest discovered for me, in a shoebox he lifted down from the top shelf of a bedroom closet, a picture of Margaret. "She was a good-looking woman," Uncle Ernest said, with perhaps just a hint of a possible teenage crush lingering in his voice.

But in a strange and perhaps unkind way, I should be grateful that she died. Otherwise, I would have been born a bastard—a shameful thing in that day and time, to be born to an unwed mother. Shameful for the child, shameful for the mother. And my life would almost certainly have been entirely different. Not better, not worse, just different. (Destiny again: time and circumstance.)

My genealogy mentor, Chesalyn Krueger Quint (married to one of my second or third Quint cousins), told me that when Margaret died, my Grandma Korte grieved terribly, saying over and over again, "Why, why, why did she do it?" It must have struck Grandma particularly hard when her own father had shot himself a bare four years before.

My mother once told me that Dad's "first wife" – she never *ever* called her by name -- had been addicted to laudanum, a not uncommon habit in that day and time. Chesalyn also told me that Margaret was "laid out" at home and then taken directly to the cemetery, but not because she was a suicide (only Margaret could know if her death was intentional) and thus forbidden a Christian burial. It was simply because the minister at St. John's, the family church, was in a dispute with the congregation and, in a fit of pique, had locked the doors of the church against its members. But there was a visitation at my grandparents' home, and Margaret was laid to rest in the family plot, and there she remains. (Although there was a time in my life when I came close to my own breakdown and was quite certain that she haunted the house where she had lived with my father, where she was "waked," and in which I was then raising my small children.) But that is still another story for a *much* later place in this history. I did include Margaret's story and her picture in my book on the Korte-Quint families. By the time I wrote that, I had learned that "we are only as sick as our secrets," and I was done with hiding them.

My mother, already pregnant with his child (me) even before his first short-lived marriage began and so suddenly and tragically ended, still managed to marry him on April 21, three weeks after his first wife's death and exactly three months before I was born. (It has always been my understanding that her parents had moved from Metropolis, where she had met my father, back to the family home in Fudgetown, perhaps (?) before she realized she was pregnant. And absence had obviously not made my father's heart grow fonder, or at least not fond enough to track her down (or perhaps respond to her pleas and/or demands to come and get her). I am well aware that, while I may know almost all of my own story, there are probably details of my mother's which she believed it unnecessary to reveal to me. Being raised in a "don't ask, don't tell" culture leaves huge gaps in many stories. Sometimes those gaps are chasms into which people fall and never really return to solid ground.

But I do know that when my mother learned that my father was again single, she was determined that her child would not be born "out of wedlock" if other arrangements could be made. So she visited his mother and told her that she was having a child, that Raymond Korte was unquestionably the father, and he knew it, and she wanted to make the paternity of her child legal. After suitable instruments were signed assuring that neither she (nor me) would demand a share in the family fortunes--documents which Danty would take great pains to show me as soon as I was old enough to read them--on 21 April 1934, they were married in Johnson County. I am confident the location was chosen to assure that news of the nuptials wouldn't appear in the only newspaper in Massac County, where the Korte family all lived. Their only witnesses were my father's sister Clara, and her boyfriend and eventual husband, Reuben Copley. Once the legal formalities were over, they all got into their respective vehicles and returned to their respective homes.

One of my mom's favorite stories was of a little boy who had been listening to his older brothers talk about their dating experiences and decided it was time to start his own excursions into the world of courtship. There was a little girl he liked, and he offered to take her for a ride in his little wagon, but first she had to promise him that after the ride was over, she would "give him anything he wanted." That, he had heard from the "big boys," was the way the dating game was played. She agreed, so he took her for a wagon ride down a long, steep hill, and when they had coasted to a stop at the bottom, the little boy demanded his payment: "Okay, now you have to give me anything I want." And the little girl said, quite cooperatively, "O.K." And the little boy said, in honest puzzlement, "Well, what do I do now?" Mom once told me that when she "set her cap" for Ray Korte and finally married him, she too sometimes wondered, "Well, what do I do now?" But it would be nearly three years from the date of that hasty marriage before Evelyn actually joined Ray–with their daughter Lona Rae (that's me) – on the family farm.

It was not an auspicious beginning. But single parenthood was not easy in the 1930s, and divorce was almost unheard of in those days. (Suicide, I've learned, was sometimes the only available option.) My father was always his most charming when he was also contrite. When he suddenly appeared in Fudgetown three years after that marriage, I'm certain that my maternal grandmother was less than hospitable. Danty would have been appalled at the idea of allowing my father to sleep with my mother in her house, marriage or no marriage. She once told me that even after 50 years of marriage her own husband had never seen her completely naked. She got ready for bed by putting a long flannel nightgown on over her clothes and then undressing beneath it. I'm certain she told the truth because I've watched her do it. I've never found it necessary to try it myself.

I can only imagine the family conferences that must have ensued before my mother packed up and went home with my father to the big two-story farmhouse where he still lived with his parents and (perhaps) his sister and her husband. Aunt Clara and Uncle Rube had married in January of 1936, and they had one daughter, Mary Ethel. Uncle Ernest, Dad's brother, and Aunt Dorothy married in February of 1936. They had two children: Billie Lee and Donna Sue. (Only Bill and Donna Sue are still alive.)

The recently reunited couple lived at first with his parents in the big two-story house. They were given one of the two upstairs bedrooms, the one directly over Dad's parents' bedroom (the downstairs bedroom, years later, would become my own husband's and mine). Mom often said she could hear them talking at night, always in German. I can only imagine the difficulty of consummating a marriage directly over your in-laws' bedroom with the knowledge that any noise above a whisper could and probably would be heard. But I have to imagine ith because my mother certainly never specifically discussed that aspect of the situation.

While I am unsure of the exact date of Mom's exodus to Massac County, they must have united just before the flood in January of

1937, which inundated the entire farm, forced everyone out of the house, and nearly ruined it forever. Water came up to the eaves of the front barn and was deep enough for them to be able to climb into the upstairs windows of the house from a row boat to get dress clothes for a funeral after Dad's uncle, Harmon Korte, died of a heart attack during the flood. More about the flood in just a bit.

I also know that, during the flood, I was living with Pa and Danty, perhaps temporarily, because Mom also recalled that Dad went to Marion to get flowers for the funeral (Metropolis and Paducah were also flooded) and went to Pa and Danty's house to see me. I was either still living with them or had been sent to stay there when the flood came, and Marion was only a few miles from Fudgetown. It's a "memory of a memory" that brings tears to my eyes even now. It took me a long *long* time to believe that my father really loved me. (First, I had to change my definition of "love.")

My parents did not set up housekeeping until sometime after the flood, and then in a very small, barely livable, four-room house on a small farm the Korte family had either bought for them or already owned, located on top of the New Columbia Bluff, twelve miles or so north of Metropolis and perhaps a mile and half north of the farm. (The little village of New Columbia was another half-mile or so east of our house.) Mom said that when they first moved in, she had to set the legs of the bed in little cans of kerosene to keep out the bed bugs she had acquired along with her new home, a most unwelcome "house-warming gift" from the previous tenants.

The road up the Bluff from the farm to our house was a steep and winding one, and even after it was straightened and blacktopped in later years it could be "hard-sledding" in wintertime. The Bluff also represented an invisible line of demarcation between the English-Scotch-Irish population atop the hill and the German population below it. I didn't recognize that fact for years. I did know that Dad was often awakened in the middle of the night in winter to pull someone up the hill with his team or, in later years, with his tractor. He eventually had a gasoline tank and pump installed in the driveway by the garage (built in the early 40s), and he was known as a "soft touch" if a young man needed a couple of gallons of gas so he could go see his girlfriend on a Saturday night. My sister Kay was, I believe, born in our house there in late May of 1938, born at home, as most children were back then.

Dad built a big barn (still standing) sometime in the years right after Kay was born. I remember the barn raising—a community event--and the big party and dance that followed. I didn't know until the years just before Mom died that she had really loved to dance. "But I gave it up," she said. "Drinking seemed to go with dancing, and I never liked drinking, but your daddy did." It went without saying that what she *really* didn't like was the drinking *Daddy* did.

My father's drinking was always a source of contention between my parents. It was not an everyday affair, but periodically he would (I believe) find himself in a situation where everyone else was drinking and he would think that, just possibly, he too could have "just one." And almost inevitably discover once again that, if he started, he couldn't stop. But he was also a hard worker, and he had a lot of work to do, so he often had a "hired man" to help out on the farm. I especially remember one, a cousin of Dad's, who lived with us, probably that very first year. I was not yet four, I believe. One Saturday night, Dad and the hired hand came home from town after consuming more than their share of alcohol. Sometime that evening, either Dad or the hired hand emptied a pocketful of change on the floor, perhaps accidentally but, as I remember it, on purpose, and then wanted me to pick the money up. It's not a pleasant memory. It felt embarrassing watching grown men engage in what seemed like a mocking act as if I were a small toy meant solely for their amusement. (Pa wouldn't have allowed it; Danty would have reached for her nitroglycerine tablets.) They laughed; I might have cried. To this day, thinking about it still stirs a queasy feeling in my stomach. I've never been fond of teasing, not then, not now. It took me many years to realize that this "queasy feeling" could also be described as "fear." I've heard some people refer to it as a "God-shaped hole."

Daddy built the chicken house all by himself, or at least he put the roof on, because I watched him from the kitchen window, swinging up through the rafters and nailing the long sheets of tin on. But he had to call for Mom to bring him a ladder because he couldn't get back down the same way he went up. There was a brooder house, too. Mr. Burris, the mailman who delivered our route, brought baby chickens every spring. The back seat of his car would be filled with big flat boxes that had holes all over the top, the baby chicks sticking their heads through the holes and cheeping away like mad. If I close my eyes, I can still remember the scent and sound of baby chickens. When the chicks got too big for the brooder house, which didn't take very long, it made a fine place for Kay and me to play.

There was also a coal shed because the house was heated in winter with a Warm Morning coal stove, which took up a good share of the living room. And an outdoor privy, surrounded by hollyhocks in summertime. Ours was a "one-holer," and it didn't have one of those silly cutout moons on the door, either. Seems to me that was like inviting peeping toms. I have no idea why people always planted hollyhocks around privies, but they did. Maybe because hollyhocks grow to a concealing height and come back up every year as sure as summer, but a little girl will never forget that the flowers are like baby dolls with fluffy colored skirts: tiny ballerinas.

There was also a cistern at that house, which my mother once threatened to jump into during one of her many fights with my father. (His drinking often made him a hard man to live with.) I didn't know until half a century later when I began genealogical research that several local women *had* committed suicide by jumping into a cistern or a well. It was quick, convenient, and fairly certain, depending on the depth of the water and whether or not you went in head-first (breaking your neck) or feet first in water that was well over your head, preventing either rescue or a change of heart. But perhaps it seemed a better alternative for ending one's life than drinking carbolic acid. At least it was quicker.

But Mom was sometimes combative, too. On at least one occasion she hit Daddy over the head with a cast-iron frying pan, which is a formidable weapon. It didn't seem to "faze" him much, though. While he might not have been a "*flat*-headed Dutchman" (a common epithet for German men) he was definitely a *hard*-headed one, especially when he'd had "a few too many."

During those first years, my mother did all her laundry by heating water in an iron kettle over an open fire in the backyard, scrubbing the clothes on a washboard, and then rinsing them in a tub of clean water. All the water had to be "drawn up," a single bucket at a time, out of the cistern. The only modern convenience on wash day was a hand-operated wringer fashioned of two rollers between which the wet clothing was fed and squeezed dry. The wringer was situated on a stand between two tubs, one for washing and one for rinsing, so the feed had to be reversed when the clothes came out of the rinse. When I got tall enough, I was allowed to turn the handle of the wringer. (Sometimes today, you'll see one of those contraptions on the front porch of a Cracker Barrel Restaurant—an antique curiosity.) At some point, someone did install a hand pump on the back porch, which required priming with cups of water to create the necessary suction to draw the water up from the cistern some three or four feet away.

The clothes were dried outside on two lines strung between the coal shed and a pole at the west end of the yard, where a row of iris formed a natural barrier between the lawn and an untended field that was an extension of our yard. I did not have access, and that only briefly, to an automatic washer and clothes dryer until I was 20 years old, married, with one child and "another on the way," living in an apartment building in Chicago.

Dad was the first man in the Korte family to buy a tractor, but he never lost his love of the horses he had grown up with and worked with all his young life. He still had two or three stabled in the barn when he died. A local boy, speeding around the curve in front of our house, once ran over one of Dad's horses. He never forgave the boy or the boy's father, who owned one of the grocery stores in New Columbia, the "three stores and a blacksmith shop" which was the commercial center of our community. He wasn't so mad because the boy had struck the horse (which was, after all, supposed to be behind our fence) but because he'd left the animal to suffer, not bothering to stop or call for help. And the fact that the boy had the nerve to call my father a "flat-headed Dutchman" at some point in the dispute didn't hasten Dad's forgiveness. That and the fact that the boy's father didn't even *offer* to pay for the horse.

When I was old enough to be trusted on that tractor, a yellow Minneapolis-Moline, I usually pulled the "side (de)livery" rake, which swept the mown hay sideways into long straight rows to be picked up by the baler. Farm kids learn early to drive the farm vehicles and to "keep it between the lines," or the rows, as the case may be.

Life on the Farm - The big two-story house where my grandparents lived, and where I lived when my husband Jay and I came back to the farm with our three very small children in early 1957, was built in 1913 after a flood *that* spring had also decimated the log cabin and its contents, and three years after my father was born—thus about the time my Uncle Ernest came into the world. The new house was of white clapboard, with a long porch on the north side facing the *old* Big Bay Road, which was moved after the later flood in 1937 to its present location along the levee that raised the banks of George's Creek to hold back future inundations. By the time I came to live there, the *old* road was just a dirt lane leading east to the back barns and the woods that separated the Korte farm from the Foss farm next door. It now borders the pond that was dug for fill when I-24 bisected the farm (north to south) in the 1960s. Two doors opened onto the porch; one led to the "old" living room (the "master" bedroom when I lived there). The other opened to what had been the huge dining room when I was small (and became our children's bedroom). There were only two closets downstairs-- the space under the narrow stairway to the upstairs and a tiny corner closet, barely larger than a china cupboard, by the back door that faced the main barn.

When I was a child, there were three pecan trees in the yard, spirea bushes in front of the screened-in side porch, and a saucer-shaped concrete goldfish pond my Aunt Clara had created when she was a teenager. My brother lives on the farm now, although the old house is gone. The cabin where our father was born 112+ years ago is also just a distant memory. My brother's home stands where the old house used to be, and the old windmill by the front barn still turns. And if someone has torn it down since the last time I was there, it still turns in my memory.

Mother told me a man had died in one of the upstairs bedrooms in that house, and when I researched local newspaper archives I discovered it was actually a local teenage boy who had suffered fatal injuries when he was caught in a threshing machine during the fall harvest. He had been brought into the house and died before he could be moved or a doctor summoned. The incident merited only a small paragraph or two in the local paper.

Before the 1937 flood, the house had some surprisingly modern conveniences. There was a hand pump right in the kitchen – no need to go outside for water. A shallow well had been sunk (or drilled) only three or four feet from the south wall of the kitchen. The water, however, had an extremely high nitrogen content (as I discovered when I had it tested in 1957) and would have probably caused diarrhea or, as it was sometimes politely called, "summer complaint." Mother recalled that my sister Kay (four years younger than me) had that problem after she was born. Perhaps she was born there rather than in the home atop the New Columbia Bluff, where Mom and Dad moved after the flood. Mother never spoke of the births of any of my siblings, although I believe both Molly Lou (who died in 1945 when I was 11 and she was a year old, a Downs' syndrome baby) and my brother Timothy Kent were born in hospitals. Kent was born in 1949 while I was on a 4-H trip to Chicago. He is still living and, to all appearances, robustly healthy and happy.

There were no fireplaces in the new house – no doubt they'd had enough of fireplaces in the drafty and inconvenient log cabin. But there were chimneys in every downstairs room for heating stoves and stovepipe holes in those same chimneys in the two upstairs bedrooms. I'm sure the original kitchen later became my living room because when I lived there, the actual kitchen was the smallest room in the house, very nearly a lean-to tacked onto the east side of the house with a screened porch on the back of that addition. I'm sure Little Grandpa, or some man, designed that, although the barns were huge and most probably built long before the house. In Germany, the accommodations for livestock were often on the ground floor, and the family lived on the second.

When Delco systems came in (before the flood), one was installed, its batteries powered by the big windmill, which also pumped water for the livestock into a huge concrete trough. When telephone service became available, a line was run to the house. Grandma and Grandpa were on a "party line" with at least two other families: one ring for the first party, two quick rings for the second party, three quick rings for the third. You weren't supposed to listen in if the call was for someone else. But I'm pretty sure everyone listened anyway. (I just realized that party lines were probably a forerunner of Facebook!) The main switchboard was in Round Knob. But when I lived there in the late 1950s there was no telephone at all. I was very, *very* isolated in the midst of acres and acres of corn and soybeans, with a line of trees far away in the east, behind the back barns.

Fritz Korte told me that Arnold Riepe (of moonshine fame) had the first radio in the county. "He built it himself," Fritz said – and added that "the neighbors just about wore Arnold's mother and sister out, coming over and staying until after midnight to listen to Arnold's radio. It was mounted on a board, and you had to use a stylus to tune in the station." The technology has been explained to me several times, but anything with moving parts or "waves" of any sort is beyond my comprehension (quantum physics excepted). I still consider electricity a kind of miraculous gift from God, akin to grace, both of which only God *really* understands.) "They could get one station down in Arkansas someplace real clear," as Fritz recalls. "And it was especially clear late at night." This explains the midnight visits to the Riepe family.

The radio story reminds me of going to Tom and Pearl Pullen's house to see the first television set that came to New Columbia. People were so crowded in the doorway between the glassed-in front porch and the Pullens' living room that we had to take turns staring at a very small window full of snow – and listen to the static that often accompanied it. But I'm getting ahead of my story.

The 1937 flood rose to the bottom of the second-floor bedroom windows at Grandpa Korte's home, and the entire contents, as well as the Delco system, were destroyed. The water came up very quickly. Horses and cattle were driven to higher ground. Uncle Ernest recalled being told that the flood in 1913 had also come up quickly – so quickly that the family had fled to the nearby New Columbia bluff (surely in a wagon?) and climbed high enough to escape the rising water.

In 1937, the men in the family tried to save Grandpa's hogs by carrying them up into one of the barn lofts. (Hogs are *very* difficult to herd anywhere, even under normal circumstances. I have hands-on experience and, believe me, it's almost as bad as trying to herd cats. Hogs are just bigger and dumber.) But the burden of the animals' weight was too great, and the loft floors collapsed, plunging the hogs into the water below. Those hogs proved to be the death of my great-uncle Harmon, too. An article in the Republican Herald reported:

> "Mr. Korte was driving hogs out of the backwater with his brother, Charlie Korte. He reached up with his arms, when at the barn, and fell forward on his face, dying almost instantly. . . He had been in good health until March 26, 1926(?), when he was shocked by lightning while doing his morning chores. Since that time, he had been under the care of a physician of Mayo's hospital, Rochester, Minnesota. He was told by his physician that he must retire from work to prolong his life because of his heart. But the great disaster that had befallen his brother and neighbors by the flood had so concerned him that he had exerted his strength more than he should, this causing his death quite suddenly." (The newspaper was dated January 28, 1937.)

The whole family was staying at Little Grandpa's house, which was at a much higher elevation than Grandpa Korte's. Uncle Ernest (only 14 at the time) remembered he was at the barn when "Uncle Harm just kind of gave a sound like he was grasping for air, and then he went down, and he was gone."

There is a heart condition to which Korte men are predisposed genetically. Both Uncle Ernest and my brother Kent had it, and both have had surgery. I've sometimes wondered if Great-Uncle Harm's heart condition was also inherited. Kent's valve was repaired. Uncle Ernest's was replaced, and Uncle Ernest, who was always extremely careful with a dollar (and I may be understating the degree of his caution), was appalled at how much that replacement valve, taken from a cow, was costing him. When I visited him in the hospital, he said, "I never got that much in my life for a WHOLE cow, much less a little bitty piece of one." But he was grinning when he said it, and he survived another 15 years with a piece of a cow's heart beating strongly in his chest, so I'm sure it was worth it. (Even to Uncle Ernest!)

After the flood, the family shifted gears into low but went on. Still, things were very different. Grandpa and Grandma Korte's home was never quite restored to what it had been before the flood, and the cleanup alone took considerable time. The return of electric power waited until REA (the Rural Electrification Association) came through sometime in the mid-40s. I remember distinctly when, at about the same time, the lights came on at our house on the Bluff, bringing civilization: an electric cookstove, a refrigerator that made its own ice, water piped up from the spring to the house and the barns, an electric washing machine (square-tubbed, stored in a corner of the kitchen), an electric iron replacing the gas iron that smelled funny and hissed 'til you were done using it. (The gas iron had replaced flatirons, heated on the wood cookstove.) But no bathroom. That would have to wait until our own new house was built in 1949. Just in time for Dad's first and only son to be born. But I'm sure that was just a coincidence.

I can just barely remember what my Grandpa Korte was like before he became ill with Parkinson's in the mid-40s. On Wednesdays, he always took cattle to the stockyards in St. Louis for farmers in the area and, when he came back, there were always Baby Ruth and Butterfinger candy bars (the extra-large size) in the glove compartment of the truck for his grandchildren. He always wore a hat, a brimmed fedora like a Chicago gangster might have worn.

The Korte men have always worn hats whenever possible; they lose their hair early. Dad switched to Stetsons for "dress-up" as he grew older and began to ride horses as a pastime, so of course my brother Kent did too. And they also traded regular shoes for cowboy boots, Sundays *and* weekdays. Mom made Western style shirts for both of them. At one time, Kent also raced trotting horses, even won the DuQuoin Hambletonian. My full-time partner for several years, Dave Kingsley, always wore a Stetson and cowboy boots. I would be the last to deny that my initial attraction bore just a faint hint of *déjà vu*. He looked like he came from "home."

Parkinson's disease is an illness that takes over the body slowly, beginning with hand tremors and progressing to the point where the patient becomes virtually immobile. It moved fast with Grandpa; there was no treatment available in the 1940s. When he first became ill to the point that someone needed to stay at night to help Grandma, Dad and Uncle Ernest took turns. But when it became evident that it was going to be a long-term job, my grandparents broke up housekeeping on the farm and bought a small bungalow on McCrory Street in Metropolis, just a block over from the house Dad's sister Clara and her husband Reuben had either bought or built sometime after they were married. Within a year or so, Grandma and Grandpa bought a larger and newer house across the street from the first one. One of the two bedrooms (the back one) had twin beds, one for Grandpa and one for his full-time attendant. (There were no nursing homes in those days, though there was a "poor farm" for the indigent.) My sister Kay and her new husband rented that first small house when they were first married and lived there until they bought a home of their own in a new subdivision on the north edge of Metropolis (and later built a still larger house outside of town, backing up to the Massac County Country Club). Kay's husband Don had gone to work at a local bank after a stint in the Army and stayed till he retired.

I was having an overnight visit with my cousin Mary Ethel, Aunt Clara's daughter, on (I think) September 2, 1945, when news came of V-J Day, the end of World War II. I was 11, just going into eighth grade. The Copleys had quite a party. I had never before been present when grownups were drinking, at least not socially. I've never forgotten how much fun they seemed to be having. But, of course, wars don't end every day. I remember two other things about the War. Danty took me with her to Herrin one day (actually, Pa took us, because Danty never learned to drive). We went to a Red Cross meeting and rolled bandages. The ladies were cutting up their old (and perhaps new) white sheets into strips 2-3 inches wide and rolling them up for bandages. I felt quite grown up sitting with all those ladies working for the war effort. I must have been 8 or 9. The other thing I remember is not having butter, which was replaced by margarine. Except the margarine was as white as lard. So the package included a little red capsule, about the size of a "red hot" candy, which had to be broken and kneaded into the margarine.

The year after the war was over and new automobiles became available, Dad bought a brand new Hudson Hornet, silver gray and low to the ground—very different from our old black Hudson with its boxy cumbersome chassis. Unfortunately, Mom was coming back from the store and, perhaps unfamiliar with the new car, slid it sidewise into the ditch just 50 yards from our house, banging up the passenger side. I really think it hurt her pride as much as it hurt the car, although Dad was considerably more upset because he hadn't yet gotten insurance on the Hornet. Life is full of small tragedies and larger ones that can't be fixed, even if they *are* covered by insurance. Aunt Clara died of a malignant brain tumor in 1972. She was only 56 years old.

When Grandpa Korte died, the farm was divided between my father and Uncle Ernest, with Aunt Clara taking her one-third share in money—the custom in those days. Uncle Ernest built his new house closer to his portion of the farm, and my father bought the home place, taking on a substantial mortgage (to pay his one-half of Aunt Clara's share). He didn't, however, take out life insurance to secure it (despite his experience with the Hudson Hornet). Mom told me much later that he didn't want anyone wishing him dead so they could collect. And Mom and Dad didn't move to the farmhouse when Dad purchased the farm. It was used for tenants, usually Dad's hired hand's family, until I moved there with my family for a few years in the late 50s, after which it was again occupied by tenants until it burned, sometime before my brother married and put a home of his own on the site of the old one. The tenants weren't home at the time of the fire but, as already noted, the big Kimball piano perished with the house.

Uncle Ernest and Aunt Dorothy had two children: Billie Lee and Donna Sue. Billie and Mary Ethel were two years older than Kay, and Donna Sue was six years younger. Kent, of course, was 15 years my junior, so he doesn't appear in early photos. He was, as my Mother once said when dementia locked her memories away and she began to speak in metaphors, "still behind the door." I love that simple but profound phrase; it writes a whole book on the world of Spirit. I remember when Aunt Dorothy's father died at her house-- most people died at home in those days--there was talk about the "feather crown" that was left behind in the pillow when he died. There is a suggestion that the crown was formed by heat as the soul escaped to make its way to heaven, or so I either remember being told or fancied for myself. I thought that must be the most wondrously mystical thing I'd ever heard of, but I still haven't seen a feather crown, though I'm quite certain they exist. So few people sleep on a feather pillow these days that I guess I never will see a crown. I do have two feather pillows on my bed. I use them as decorative bolsters. If I knew in advance that I might die in my own bed, I think I'd try to stick one under my head so some curious descendant could check out the "feather crown" business. Somebody do that for me (without telling me, of course) if I start looking like my time is near. It may well be part of my final chapter in that "book on the world of Spirit."

More of Life on the Farm - I remember the days when big threshers powered by steam went from farm to farm harvesting the wheat crops, and the big dinners served in the dining room at the farm when 20 or more men—family, friends, and threshing crew--sat down to eat. The first serving was always for men only, with perhaps a side table for children. Women didn't eat until after the men were finished and had gone back to work, a practice that was not reserved for threshing dinners; it was a general custom with farm families when I was growing up. Daddy liked to tell a story about going to a threshing dinner at a local family's house where a pot of chicken and dumplings, one of his favorite dishes, was passed around. But it had apparently been *cooked*, and was certainly *served*, in a "chamber pot." Daddy said he just couldn't eat anything that had been cooked in a slop-jar, and had difficulty eating the rest of the dinner as well.

When the big threshing machines were phased out by the introduction of tractors and, as I recall, less wheat was planted, and much of the ground was turned to corn and soybeans, my father bought a hay baler, a corn picker, and finally a combine, equipment that became a source of additional income in the fall as he went from farm to farm harvesting neighbors' crops after his own crops were in, and sometimes before.

The newest farming equipment has enclosed cabs, air conditioning, stereo, and GPS to guide you down the rows. But I remember going with Dad to the "new ground" (that same new ground where Little Grandpa dynamited the stumps) when I was quite small, and Dad still picked corn with a team and wagon. In the "old days," children were useful for picking up the corn from the "down rows" that were pushed down by the wagon as it passed over the middle row. I was far too young (and a girl) to pick corn, although I could sit on the wagon seat and tell the horses when to "giddyup" and when to "whoa," while Mom and Dad walked along picking corn from the stalks on either side of the wagon. Uncle Ernest recalled that picking the down rows was a particularly onerous job when he was a boy, especially since his Uncle Harm had only daughters, and he and my father were always pressed into service when it was time to harvest Uncle Harm's corn. (He was, remember, only 14 when his uncle died.)

In the late fall, when it was cold enough to keep the meat from spoiling before it could all be "put up," it was hog-killing time. Butchering was also usually a multi-family (sometimes a community) affair when three or four hogs would be killed, scalded to loosen the bristles, then hung while the hair was scraped off, and the carcass finally cut apart into hams and shoulders. The fat was trimmed off the cuts of meat and then rendered out in big iron kettles over open fires in the yard, with crispy chunks left behind as "chitlins." The tenderloins were canned for winter, and the entrails were cleaned and then stuffed with seasoned ground meat for sausages. Neighbors and family who came to help were always sent home with fresh meat.

There was a smoke house just steps away from the kitchen at the farm, still standing when I lived there. The walls were lined a foot thick and also floored with sawdust. Canned goods were stored there, as well as apples, pears, and root vegetables (potatoes and turnips). Attached to the back side of the smoke house was a long room with a separate entrance, slat-sided so smoke could escape, where the hams, shoulders, sides of bacon, and sausage were cured. Houses built on a hill often had storm cellars, dug into the hillside. But there were no hills on the farm: the land was all pancake flat except for farm ponds. It had, in fact, once been the bed of the Ohio River before an earthquake in the far distant past had moved the river several miles south to where it now curves around the narrow tip of Southern Illinois.

Nothing was wasted. Pigs' feet were pickled in vinegar and canned; the head was boiled and the meat separated from the bone for head cheese and souse meat (a pickled version of sausage). Grandma Korte made "blood pudding" too. I don't believe I ever tried it; even the name of the thing kind of turns my stomach, but it was a German delicacy and only available at butchering time. Doesn't keep well. (And where is a wry-faced *emoji* when you need one?) Brains were also cooked soon after butchering, usually for the next day's breakfast. They didn't keep well either. Brains and eggs scrambled together were, in fact, a breakfast treat, with or without homemade biscuits and gravy. My sister-in-law Ethel Bullock Crabb cooked pork brains for breakfast the morning before my first child was born, as we all counted minutes between birthing pains. Why I still remember the brains and eggs, I have no idea!

Butchering stopped for most folks we knew some time after the Massac County Locker plant opened for business. The locker plant also made it possible to keep beef through the winter, so steaks, hamburgers, and beef pot roasts became family staples for the first time. Roast beef was usually Sunday dinner's main course at our house then, cooked on low in the oven so it would be ready when we got home from church. For many years, Allen Rottmann (father of my sister Kay's eventual husband, Don) operated the Locker Plant, and most Saturdays when our family went to Metropolis to shop, we would stop by the locker plant to visit "our" locker, one of 200 or so large locked boxes in the huge freezer room where the meat was stored. It was bone-aching cold in the freezer room, and it had a memorable odor – not bad, just memorable.

When the REA brought electricity to the rural areas, and home freezers became available and affordable for more and more families (including ours), the Locker Plant went out of business. The fixtures were auctioned off, and Dad bought a whole wall of the old lockers–20 or so–and installed them against the south wall in the basement of our new house for storage. The old lockers were one of the last things we cleaned out when Kay, Kent, and I (with help from Kent's wife Donna, Kay's husband Don, and my friend Dave Kingsley) got the house ready for an auction of its contents and eventual sale of the property after Mom went to assisted living.

Auctions were always a big deal for our family: a source of entertainment, a social occasion for visiting with friends and neighbors, and an opportunity for a bargain. The first one I remember attending was for the sale of my Korte grandparents' possessions when they moved to Metropolis. They were leaving the big two-story house for a much smaller home, and there was also a lot of excess and some badly outdated farm equipment. Billy Dameron was the auctioneer. He owned a livestock auction barn in Vienna and also auctioneered for Tom Pullen's livestock auction in Metropolis (just off Route 45 and across the road from what used to be the Massac County Fairgrounds). When my brother Kent was born and became Dad's sidekick, he started imitating the auctioneers almost as soon as he could talk. Although he earned a Bachelor's Degree in agriculture at Murray State University, auctioneering has always been his first love as well as a big part of his bread-and-butter. Like our father and our mother's father, Kent wasn't really cut out to be a farmer.

Mom loved auctions, too; it's either a family disease or a family tradition. Kent still gets a kick out of telling about one sale where he was auctioneering, and Mom and I were bidding against each other (both unaware, of course). He just kept urging us on, enjoying the joke. When Jay and I came back to the farm to live, ready to begin housekeeping in the big empty farmhouse, nearly everything in the house except family hand-me-downs was bought at auction. And I still have some furniture and many accessories I acquired the same way over the years. At one time, when we moved from Chicago to Kentucky in 1990, I spent so much time at auctions that I finally had to rent a couple of booths in local antique malls to get rid of the excess. It was fun while it lasted, and I still have bits and pieces of what remained after I had to close up shop when my third and last husband, Bill, became terminally ill and died in 1995.

In winter, Dad logged the woods that surrounded the cropland in the bottoms behind the farmhouse, first with horses and later with his tractor. Like most farmers, then and now, he always kept a big truck, and in winter, he'd take off the siderails that he used when he was hauling livestock, creating a flatbed that was more suitable for hauling logs. When we lived there, our son Johnny watched his father and grandfather load logs onto the truck one winter and, in the spring, he rigged the truck he had gotten for Christmas with cord so that he could load his own logs: long, straight twigs he'd picked up in the yard.

It was then, too, that I realized one day I might have inherited a bit of my maternal grandmother's psychic power. Jay was logging alone in the woods with the tractor, and I was working inside the house at the kitchen counter (which faced a blank wall) when suddenly I "saw," in my mind's eye, the tractor Jay was driving turning over. I was so certain it had actually happened that I put the three children in the car and drove along the road that led to the back barn and the woods. We had gotten just past the barn, nearly a half-mile, when Jay came walking out of the woods. That was the first time I can recall "seeing things" that I shouldn't have been able to see, but it would not be the last.

There were lots of outbuildings on the farm: three barns – one in front and one in back of the house, another in the far back field. There was the old Delco shed, where equipment for the electric system had been stored before the flood, and a rowboat still hung from the rafters (perhaps in anticipation of another flood?). The chicken house was lined with nests for the hens and a roost (not *just* for the roosters). A machine shed was added in later years, first with a gasoline pump alongside and later propane tanks when farm equipment manufacturers switched to that fuel from gasoline. And there was always the windmill. Kay wrote a poem about the windmill, but I can't seem to find it anywhere. I remember the day when I went with the three children to visit a neighbor who also had a windmill. Mary, the youngest, was not much more than three years old. I thought I was keeping an eye on everyone when she called me, and when I looked, I had to look UP. She'd found the rungs on the windmill and climbed halfway up but couldn't figure out how to get back down. I had to climb that darned windmill and figure out a way to get both of us back on the ground. Never a dull moment when you have three children in three years.

Growing up on a farm taught me so many things about life and living and "making do" that I could never have learned in books: cooking, baking bread, sewing, milking a cow, churning butter, raising and then killing chickens, gathering eggs, quilting, gardening, canning, wallpapering, painting, upholstering, cleaning and fileting fish, dressing and cooking wildfowl (quail, duck, geese and an occasional pheasant) and game (deer, squirrel, rabbit), and once – **only** once – frog legs. Those darn things will jump right out of the pan.

There's a trick to killing chickens that my mother taught me. First, you have to grab them by the legs and lay them down to force them to be still. Then, take a broom handle and place it crossways across their neck. Put a foot on each side of the broom handle, right on the chicken's neck, and press down. While doing this, don't just pull, but YANK the chicken out from under the handle. The body will stay with you, but you have to throw it quickly to one side to keep from getting all bloody when the chicken flops around long enough for the body to forget it's lost its head. The head, of course, stays behind, under the broomstick. Grandma Korte used an axe and a big round stump as a chopping block, but I never could get the hang of it.

Jay (the kids' dad) always skinned and gutted the squirrels and rabbits he killed, but I had to dismember them. I never did the rabbits if I had a scratch on my hand, and I always washed my hands with alcohol afterward. Rabbits were supposed to sometimes have "rabbit fever" that you could catch and die from. And we always cooked the squirrel's head and ate the brains, but I've heard people don't eat that part anymore because squirrels sometimes have some kind of brain disease now, too. I might have cooked a 'coon, because I remember eating it, barbecued. But on second thought, it was definitely Mom who cooked the 'coon. And she always wanted somebody to kill a rabbit when she was planning to make homemade hot tamales. She'd use corn shucks to wrap the tamales, boiling the shucks to soften the fibers. She'd only make tamales in the fall, perhaps because, at that time, the corn shucks were dry (not green) and thus "in season." Or maybe it was because rabbits didn't get "sick" at that time of year. I'm very nearly a vegetarian these days. Can't think why. But once again I've jumped into the future instead of staying in my childhood as I had intended.

When electricity came through the countryside and finally got to us (I think I was ten or so), Dad eventually installed an electric pump in the spring located at the bottom of the hill below the barn and piping that brought water up from the spring to the barn and the house—a long, long way, and most of it uphill. The clothes-washing operation was then moved to the screened-in back porch in summer and to the kitchen in winter. And the water was heated on the new electric range. (The iron kettle eventually became a huge flowerpot in the front yard of our new house, built in 1949, and stayed there for the next 50 years.) A square-tubbed Maytag electric washing machine was added to the laundry equipment, but piping was never extended to a bathtub or commode, and we had no hot water heater until we moved into the new house in the fall of 1949, just before my brother Kent was born. I was 15 years old, a senior in high school.

The washer was in the basement in the new house, but Mom still hung her clothes outside, climbing a 5-foot sloping hill out of the basement to get to the lines on the far side of the house. It was not a particularly well-planned arrangement. Years later, not too long after Dad died, she went to Vienna one day and bought a stacking washer and dryer and had the pair installed in the kitchen in place of one of the cabinets. She was nearly 70 years old, but she was finally in charge of all the money. And as proud of those new appliances as if she'd created them herself.

She'd been in charge of her *own* money for quite a while, although she was pretty quiet about it. She'd started making wedding cakes after she made one for my wedding, and then she began catering the whole wedding. And since she had to buy supplies and hire helpers, she opened her own bank account. But she didn't tell Dad exactly how she was managing her catering finances until they were out one day and Dad started to buy something, reached into the pocket of his bib overalls where he kept his checkbook, and realized he'd left it at home. Mom didn't say a word; she just opened her purse, pulled out *her* checkbook, wrote out a check for the correct amount, and handed it to the cashier. Dad didn't say a word either. And I'll probably never know when or how or even *if* he paid her back! (Just kidding. Dad always paid his debts. As soon as he could, which sometimes took a while. Farming is a gamble, and two good crop years out of three is practically a bonanza.)

All that talking about washing reminds me again of bathtubs --Until I was ten or twelve, round zinc washtubs sufficed for bathtubs. In the house where my parents set up housekeeping in the summer of 1937, that would be our mode of bathing until, at some point in time, my father created a little room off the kitchen (borrowing from either the kitchen or the back bedroom) and installed an old-fashioned clawfoot bathtub which drained out under the house and down the hill. A small submersible electric heater warmed the bathwater. In the summer, though, Dad would often go down to the creek which ran through the little valley behind the house and take a bath in a hollowed-out place floored with flat sandstone rock where waist-deep water collected, along with tadpoles and water-bugs.

When my sister Kay was born, I was two months short of four years old, so I'm pretty sure I would have been sent to Pa and Danty's to ensure that I wouldn't see or hear anything that might have provoked questions. I just barely remember **not** having a sister. I don't think I was ever jealous. After all, I had been told all my life that I was a beautiful and precious (or maybe it was precocious) little girl whose Aunt Maxie had once announced, "I'm not taking her on any more of my dates. She tells everything she knows, and she talks so plain you can understand every word." I am sure she was telling the unvarnished truth, and I haven't changed much in that regard in these 89 years. I've taken more than a few skeletons out of family closets and carried them around to be rattled for the edification and amusement of the entire neighborhood. But admittedly, most of *that* talking has been since I left home for the wider world. (I've been told by people who should know that I was "slow to talk" because I was handed anything I might conceivably want before I had to ask for it.)

My baby sister Molly Lou was, I'm pretty sure, born in the hospital in either Metropolis or Paducah on Valentine's Day of 1944. I was nine then, not ten until the end of July. She died in March the following year, a Down's syndrome baby, and my mother rocked her that whole year. Molly died of the enlarged heart that so many Down's babies suffer, and for which there was no correction 75 years ago. Mom said her arms ached for months after Molly died; she had rocked and carried Molly in her arms through that short and difficult life. My father drank. It was perhaps his only way through. I know from later confidences that he and my mother were told that Molly's condition was a consequence of his drinking. I don't believe that is true since I've learned that the condition is caused by a missing (or perhaps added?) gene. But I believe *he* believed it was. (I'm reminded of that old axiom which states that "It's not what you *don't know* that kills you; it's what you *know for certain that just ain't true*."

At one point, when Dad persisted in haunting the corridors of a hospital in Marion in a not nearly sober condition—the hospital where they had taken Molly shortly before her death—Mom found it necessary to have him confined for a few days to Anna State Hospital, an institution primarily for the treatment of the mentally ill. That's what people did in those days to sober someone up when they refused or were simply unable to do so on their own. There were no "recovery centers." It was at least more comfortable, and with far fewer legal consequences, than jail, the only other alternative. And I didn't learn about the "confinement" until years later. There were always things that should never, ever, be spoken of again. Those *damned* secrets!

My little sister Molly's death was my first close encounter with life's cessation, except for my great-grandfather's death when I was seven. I don't recall anyone explaining what was happening or was going to happen. In those days, loved ones were brought from the funeral parlor back to the family home and neighbors "sat up with" the deceased all through the night before the funeral. Our house was very small with a living room, the adjoining bedroom (no door) where my parents slept, and then a step down into the tiny bedroom where I shared a double bed with my sister Kay, another open doorway into the narrow kitchen which took up most of the rear of the house. There was only one actual door, a closet door in Mom and Dad's bedroom inside that whole house. While everyone was crowded into the living room, Kay and I were kept out of the way during the "sitting up" and visitation, often on the screened-in back porch. At least that's where I recall the two of us were when an older neighbor woman told us we mustn't bother our mother because "she's having such a hard time." I remember, once again, the overpowering scent of flowers, but I don't remember the funeral or if I even went. But I do remember that someone decided my sister Kay and I should not go to the cemetery for the burial.

And so, in the weeks and months that followed, I had a persistent dream that no longer haunts my nights but that I do still occasionally recall in safe daylight hours. I would dream that my mother, unable to accept her loss, had somehow managed to bring my baby sister's body home, wrapped in a blanket (or sometimes it seemed to be her coat), and secreted it away on a shelf in the only closet in the house – a boxed-in corner of my parents' bedroom. Kay and I slept with the head of our double bed against the back wall of that closet, and in my dreams my mother would get up in the middle of the night and go to the closet so that she could once again hold and rock her baby: the child who would never wake or cry again. That is the first dream I have never forgotten, though there have been others that I try very hard never to remember, and just a few that I have remembered long enough to change the entire course of my life. I believe, you see, in synchronicity, and I have finally learned that dreams can teach me lessons, that they are another of God's ways of guiding my steps through life if I can only interpret their symbolic language.

My sister Kay was always more forgiving than I of our father's frequent bouts with John Barleycorn (a euphemism for alcohol for those not so familiar with archaic jargon). When, years later, I wrote a poem about another incident in our family history and included it in a chapbook I wrote for my last year in college (I graduated almost exactly 50 years after I started), Kay declared that the story wasn't really true. At first I hesitated to include poetry in my story, but

Stephen C. Rowan, in his book on creeds, says, "Poetry is not a *less* exact, but a *more* exact form of language." . . and that to truly appreciate creeds we should "sing them. . . dance them. . . print them in iambic pentameter" for (as it is also written *some*where): "The letter kills, but the Spirit gives life." So, creed or no creed, here's the poem. More poetry and song will probably follow eventually. But iambic pentameter may be a bit of a stretch.

The Tree

Momma spent the whole day getting Christmas started,

decorating the tree that

Daddy brought home from the woods,

tying on the shiny gold and silver balls

you could see into, like funny mirrors,

the dangly icicles that hung down

in shivery ribbons of twisted steel, catching the light,

making the tree alive.

She helped me put our angel on the top,

lifting me up until I got the Christmas lady straight

and puffed her skirt out even all around,

smoothed down her shimmery gold hair.

Mama gave the angel one last touch

after she put me down – a finger kiss, I think.

Then Daddy came home

smelling of the cold and something sad:

beer, the barn, wet leather, sweat, stale cigarettes.

(I knew that smell – it made my stomach jump.)

And he was mumble-singing underneath his breath,

just half above a whisper:

"Won't be home 'til morning…

'n' maybe not at all."

Breathing hard, walking unsteady,

he stumbled coming in the door –

or his boots might've tripped him –

somehow he fell, against and then across

the Christmas tree.

("But all have sinned and fallen short of glory,"

Was what the preacher always said.)

The angel lady tumbled off.

Daddy stepped on her with his muddy boot

and broke one of her wings,

tore her skirt off at the waist.

Her beautiful gold hair covered her face.

The tree punched in the wall, making a hole,

then leaned over and fell, so slow,

taking an hour, taking Daddy with it,

'cause he held to the tree to keep it up.

Or maybe save himself.

After forever, Daddy did raise up,

but all that Christmas Eve our tree just laid there,

stretched out long and finished,

its stiff needles poking into all our presents.

Some of the ornaments broke in pieces.

Some rolled off and lost themselves in dark safe corners

where they found me.

While Mama laid in the bedroom crying,

and the angel laid broke and dirty on the floor

and Daddy laid out in the stable

finishing the bottle

he'd hid underneath the hay.

And that was not a Very Merry Christmas. But you suspected that, didn't you?

"School days, school days, dear old golden rule days,

Reading, and writing and 'rithmetic, taught to the tune of a Hick'ry Stick..."

(Lyrics of an Old Song)

In My School There Were No Hick'ry Sticks!

It's time to turn from "morbid reflection" and tell about New Columbia, where I lived for all the first 18 years of my life, except those three years or so after I was born and two years of college. But first, I'll include a bit of local history for context.

The first actual commercial building of any record in the area which was also known politically as "George's Creek Precinct," was south and east of the foot of the New Columbia Bluff, probably on the south side of George's Creek, where a bridge crossed the creek and a store was built known as the "Nance Wilson Bridge Store," according to the book *Massac County Illinois History*. It is my belief, previously mentioned and supported by several historical records, that the Nance Wilson Bridge Store was built on what is now a part of my brother Kent Korte's property (the Charles and Mary Korte homeplace), land which has been in our family since at least the early 1900s. The log cabin in which I believe my father was born and in which I remember playing as a child sat somewhere at or near the location of Wilson's Store as it is described in the *History*. It may even have *been* Wilson's Store.

The cabin would have been built in about 1820-30 when that part of the county was being settled. Log cabins last a long time. This one had survived at least two floods, 1913 and 1937, the last one completely inundating it.

In the late 1860s, just after the Civil War, there was a racetrack laid out near the store, perhaps where Dad planted soybeans the years I lived there, a flat and level place that had once been the site of an Indian village. (My first husband, Jay, once had a collection of arrowheads he had picked up there. He let a professor at SIU look at them and never got them back, though they did attach his name--John Crabb--to the site.) The racetrack attracted quite a crowd in post-Civil War days, but there was a family of Confederate veterans and another of Union persuasion who persisted in settling disagreements with "fisticuffs." A "fight-off" had to be staged to settle the matter once and for all. Nobody died, and referees gave the decision to the Union side, which suggests a politically expedient decision upon which peace was declared in Massac County.

My mother also said that the first post office for New Columbia was located atop the Bluff behind our (new) house, where another log cabin also stood all the years of my young life and where, perhaps, its crumbling remains can still be found. It was accessed only by a dirt road that wended its way above and along the shallow creek that ran between deep banks and cut through our property on the east.

When I was growing up, that log cabin behind our house and its few acres of ground were owned and occupied by two Burnham brothers and the daughter of one of the brothers. They had neither car nor horse and walked to and from the main road--about a quarter of a mile--to go to the grocery store in New Columbia. There was also a cemetery there, where a "Dr. Wilson" was buried, according to local lore. My father purchased the property when both Burnham brothers died and Nellie, the daughter, moved to a house on the main road. Nellie's mother was a McBride, and the house was (I believe)

Arthur and Mae McBride's former home—Mae was the lady who died while she was praying in the church, if you read the Prologue. After she was buried and a respectful time had elapsed, Arthur married a rather well-to-do widow and moved to California with the widow's son and his wife (who was a second or third cousin of mine). Nellie, whose mother was a McBride, never married. I mention her because I have always wondered how, exactly, she survived. But she had five living siblings, who most probably assured her survival, and she was past 81 when she died.

When a part of the Burnham land was excavated for fill dirt as I-24 was being built (a highway that, continuing south, also intersected the farm where my father was born and which would later become my brother's property) old bones were unearthed, and work was temporarily halted to determine exactly how old the bones were, but I've never learned the results of the examination. My husband Jay (John) Crabb excavated at least one grave along the road that led back to the cabin, hoping to find Indian relics, and found the brass button from a military uniform. I don't recall if it was Union or Confederate, but I strongly suspect he may have dug up the few remaining remnants of Dr. Wilson.

The actual settlement of the present *New* Columbia, so named because there was already a *Columbia* Post Office in Illinois, was once the second largest in the county. The village is described in some detail, and many of its first residents are listed in a booklet I produced for the 150th Anniversary of the New Hope Baptist Church, the first church established in the area and the church my mother attended as I grew up. My father only came on one Sunday a year, the last Sunday in May, which was Homecoming Sunday. He had been confirmed in the Lutheran church and had attended confirmation class in German, part of the last class to do so. Perhaps he thought that was enough church for him.

But the communities "on top of the hill" were settled by those of English, Scottish, and Irish descent, while those "below the hill" were often of German ancestry. And there was still, in those days, a distinct cultural difference in both religion and social customs. More than likely, the fact that we lived "on top of the hill," rather than in the German "bottoms," gave me an entirely different perspective on life than my cousins, especially those raised in the Lutheran church. And my "Korte cousins" all were.

I was just a month or so past my fifth birthday when I was enrolled in the New Columbia Grade School, which was situated perhaps a bit more than a half-mile west of our house, south of and behind Cagle's Grocery Store (owned by the family of the horse-killer). There were two other stores in New Columbia: Otis Nutty's Grocery, which was located just west of Cagle's Grocery and also on the south side of the road. Down a steep hill behind the school, there were sand pits, leavings of a former brickyard. There was a narrow gravel road between the Nutty and Cagle stores leading to the school and on to the sand pits.

Across from Nutty's store was Richardson's Store, which housed the post office in those early years. Richardson's store closed when the post office was discontinued and mail began to be delivered by a rural mail carrier, as it still is today. They had a daughter named Doris, who was a year or two older than me, and I got one of the few spankings I remember from childhood when I stayed after school one day to play with her without permission and scared my mother half to death.

Just west of Nutty's store was a blacksmith shop owned and operated by Vanis Travis. The next closest blacksmith was Rube

Cash at Round Knob, five or six miles south and halfway to Metropolis. Both had old-fashioned forges and did a good business shoeing horses, as well as repairing and maintaining iron farming equipment. There is a distinct ring to an iron mallet hitting a red-hot iron horseshoe as it rests on an iron pedestal. That was the way horseshoes were shaped to fit a horse's hooves. Once you've heard that sound and the reverberation that follows as the mallet bounces two or three times, you'd know it anywhere. (When I read or hear, "Under the spreading chestnut tree, the village smithy stands. . ." I think of Vanis and Rube. Or perhaps it's the other way around.)

When horses became nearly obsolete except for pleasure riding, Vanis closed up shop and he and his wife Fanny went north to become house parents in a facility that housed either delinquent or disabled youth. I don't think Rube Cash quit blacksmithing until he died. I remember when one of Vanis and Fanny's daughters had a baby boy, and I went with Mom and Kay to visit the newborn. I stood up close to the bassinet and waited till everyone else was in the kitchen so I could pull the baby's diaper down. I'd heard rumors that boys had something "down there" I didn't have, and I was determined to discover the truth for myself. The rumors were true! But despite Freud's declaration that girls are afflicted with "penis envy," I do not recall "wanting one of those." My mother had a favorite joke about the little girl who found out that boys "did their business" standing up and why that was physically possible. And the little girl said, "That would be a handy thing to have on a picnic." I was considerably older before I was told that such male attachments had "alternate uses."

Once daily mail was assured, Dad subscribed to the *St. Louis Globe-Democrat*. My grandparents subscribed to the *St. Louis Post Dispatch*, so of course I preferred the *Post*, which had a larger and, in my opinion, a better comic section, especially on Sunday. Pa picked it up at the little Texaco gas station just down the road from his house every Sunday morning. Though Pa was one of fifteen children and had only finished three years of public school, I'm sure Pa read that paper from cover to cover. And there was always radio. He would sit by the radio in a heavy oak rocker with a thick padded leather seat and listen to Edward R. Murrow and other newscasters, soaking up the news and smoking Camel cigarettes. Though largely self-taught (I have no idea how or when he learned to build houses) he was a well-informed man. Danty was far less politically inclined. She was a dreamy gentlewoman who wrote poetry with a distinctly melancholy flavor and took out novels from the lending library in Herrin. I often read them along with her. *Gone with the Wind* took up a good part of one summer visit.

But the Sunday paper was not delivered until Monday at *our* house. Dick Tracy was in one of the comics, and he had a watch that he could actually talk on. Little did I know that one day I, too, would have a "Dick Tracy" watch, one that worked even better than his. Mine gets the weather report, daily news, emails, texts, and even moving pictures. It will also tell you when to stand up, count your heartbeats, remind you to meditate and criticize the amount of time you spend goofing off on the Internet. I am quite certain that Dick Tracy's watch was not so intrusive. Or so entertaining.

My watch's movies are very small ones, even smaller than the ones in the "big-little" books that had pictures in the upper right-hand corner of every facing page and, if you "flipped the book" by running rapidly through the pictures back to front (or was it front to back?), you'd see a movie. Some of them (I've been told) were pornographic, with drawings that depicted sexual activity in a cartoon-like fashion. When I finally got my driver's license and was allowed to have the car in the evening, I often went to Reevesville, a little village that had grown up next to railroad tracks where the trains stopped to take on water for their engines and where there was a restaurant with a jukebox and local teenagers gathered. One night I took a bunch of friends for a ride somewhere. Several days later, Dad produced a big-little book and asked where I'd gotten it. I swore I'd never seen it before, and I hadn't. And I never saw it *again*, either. I've always wondered whose book it was and why they never asked me if I'd found it. And, of course, I also wondered what really happened to that book after Dad confiscated it.

But now to school: My elementary education was acquired (perhaps not solely) in that one-room schoolhouse where a single teacher conducted classes for all eight grades. There were five or six rows of desks, five or six to a row, the seats in every row linked together so that the back of the head of the person sitting directly in front of you was only a scant two feet away. This was distracting and also extremely unhygienic in the event that your neighbor did not bathe regularly or, in a worse-case scenario, had head lice. I speak from experience.

The west wall was all windows, also distracting, although there were heavy shades that could be pulled down if the afternoon sun created problems with heat or vision. Front and back walls were lined with 3-ft tall blackboards, beginning at about waist height (for a grownup), with a gutter running along the bottom to hold erasers and chalk. That was a bit high for a 5-year-old. It was considered an honor to be given the job of dusting the erasers by beating the chalk out on the concrete steps outdoors. The boys competed for the privilege—anything to get outdoors. But the girls usually didn't want to "mess up" their dresses. (We always wore dresses to school, with long cotton stockings in winter and sometimes "snow pants.")

I was a girl, and I really wanted to dust erasers. But it was a long time, and I was all grown up before I would dare fight a man for a privilege he deemed his by right of gender. And longer still before I would learn that it was often just not worth the trouble.

When I first started school, the room was heated by a large coal-burning stove in the northwest corner of the room, but one summer, a couple of years later, a furnace was installed *under* the building, and there were floor registers that spread the heat more evenly. There was an especially large register in the floor in the corner where the stove had been, almost directly over the new furnace, and on really cold mornings it was a wonderful place to stand and warm up. Think about the pictures (now almost iconic) of Marilyn Monroe and her skirts blowing up as she stood over that sidewalk vent.

One of the most embarrassing moments of my entire life was one truly frigid morning when my father had driven me to school and, always the good neighbor, stopped to pick up the man who lived across the road from our house and was walking our way (he had no car). The minute Badger (that was his nickname, and it fit him) got in the car, you could smell him. Skunk! And, of course, that is an odor that permeates everything. When I got to school, took off my coat and hat, and walked over to stand on the radiator to warm up, the smell of skunk billowed up and out, and I was soon standing alone on the radiator. The rest of that day has been erased from my memory. And I am grateful. As Nietzsche said, "That which does not kill us makes us strong." I have yet to die of embarrassment, although I have come very close to fainting on several occasions. In Dad's defense, I'm sure he had no idea that he was inviting a skunk, or at least the odiferous remains of one, into the car when he stopped to pick up Dodger.

The east side of the school had two cloakrooms (boys' and girls'), each with an adjoining toilet, and the wide corridor separating them led to double exit doors opening to the playground. There was no indoor plumbing, however. The toilets simply opened over deep pits, and the commode-styled seats were lidded. The girls' was a "one-holer," and I assume the boys' was, as well. A boy and a girl could go at the same time to their separate accommodations, but two children (even of the same sex) were not allowed out of the room together. I suspect *that* practice, at least, is still customary. However, the fact that there are now so many genders, or at least so many ways of *expressing* gender, suggests that the matter of "who goes, where, and when" has become hopelessly complicated. I really don't care where and when anyone else "goes," but personally I prefer to "go" alone.

The teacher was in charge of making sure that the "conveniences," as ladies referred discreetly to such places whose purpose was beyond mention in polite society, were sprinkled with lime once a day. She was also in charge of everything else except carrying the coal to stoke the furnace. That was a job for the older boys. And, if memory serves, the New Columbia High School (built in the mid-20s) which I attended for three years (1946-1949) had the same type of accommodations. Indoor plumbing was added at some point, most likely when it became a consolidated elementary school in the fall of 1949. That was also the year I got a new brother, our family got a new house, and we had an indoor bathroom for the first time, with a door that closed. And actually *locked*. I think there is a possibility, already mentioned, that the new house and new brother are somehow related to the fact that my father finally had a son, but I cannot be certain that connection is accurate since I have to question my perspective.

Our audio-visual aids in that one-room school consisted of a series of maps on rollers mounted atop the center blackboard at the front of the room and usually utilized only during history and geography classes. Between the teacher's desk (centered under the geography maps) and the rows of students' desks, there was a long bench referred to as the "recitation bench." Classes were conducted in age order, and usually subject order, with the students of whatever class or subject was being taught simply called forward to sit on the long recitation bench for the duration of their class.

There were certain advantages to the one-room schoolhouses that dotted the countryside in those days. They were located close to their pupils, always within easy walking distance, although "easy" might be a mile-and-a-half. They were economical as well: only one room required heating, and only one teacher was employed. But in retrospect, I realize that the teaching methods were equitable as well. The students were from every social and economic strata of the community, and all received the same instruction. And if any student was "slow," that student would have eight years--and sometimes more--to absorb the subject matter.

One drawback was that a student with a natural aptitude for learning could become bored. However, in that instance, the student could also be advanced by being allowed to "skip" a grade. Of course, they did not really miss the intervening year of instruction because they would absorb it eventually, along with work they had "skipped up" to. However, the arrangement sometimes resulted in the 7th and 8th grades having only two or three students. I skipped the second (or perhaps it was the third) grade, which meant since I had started school when I was five, I graduated two whole years earlier than most students my own age.

We did not have to purchase our own textbooks. They were supplied by the school district and handed down from year to year until the pages were dogeared and the covers separating from their spines. The subject matter was pretty basic, but repetition and frequent spelling "bees" and other competitions drilled those basics into our young brains. When we were not "reciting," we were doing homework or reading one of the books from the meager library, but the teacher or an older student was available for assistance.

I don't recall ever actually taking homework *home*. We did have workbooks, and one was for penmanship, which is "cursory" writing in modern parlance. (I understand that cursory writing is now considered archaic.) The style I learned was the Palmer Method. But anything I learned in Palmer was somewhat ruined when I took Gregg Shorthand my senior year in high school. And I would surely have flunked shorthand if my mother hadn't made me practice. "You'll need it someday," she'd say. And, of course, she was right. It made my work far easier when I became a reporter, and it came in handier still during those years when I had to rely on secretarial work for my "bread-and-butter."

But the books I really loved and still remember are those that lined a set of bookshelves in a front corner of the schoolroom, over by the windows. They were the books of my childhood: *The Bobbsey Twins*, *Nancy Drew*, *Five Little Peppers*, and so many other childhood classics of that era. I remember wondering what on earth "watercress sandwiches" were made of. The Bobbsey twins seemed to eat them for lunch at least once a week.

Every year in the late fall we would get a few new books, and they were treasures to be read and re-read. There was a poster pinned to the wall above the bookcases where every student's name was listed with a long line of boxes following the name. When you had read a book, the teacher would add a gold star to your line. I always seemed to have more gold stars than anyone. I don't think I was competing. I just loved to read. Books were my first escape from life, my first addiction. Unfortunately, they would not be my last.

Our teachers were not always "properly" educated. My husband Jay's mother had begun her teaching career at 18. I believe she had graduated from high school and perhaps had a year at "teacher's college," but not much more. She had to stop teaching when she was married at 20 to a 17-year-old coal miner, a marriage that lasted 63 years until his death in 1988. Female teachers in those days were required to be either single (and chaste as nuns) or widowed. My first teacher had to "retire" when she became pregnant out of wedlock. The next teacher had to resign when she married, perhaps in anticipation of the possibility that she, too, would become noticeably "great with child." The next one was a widow, Irma Goddard, who lasted three or four years, and the teacher for my last two years was a man, Jack Rice.

I had known Jack (although I called him Mr. Rice then) all my life: his wife was a registered nurse and one of my mother's best friends. His children (Mike and Nancy) were born perhaps 10 years after my sister and I, so he was probably newly married when he became my teacher. He was a good man and a good teacher with, I believe, a university education and I recall him fondly for his patience in explaining several times to a stubborn 11-year-old the complicated (at least to me) method of calculating the area of a racetrack. (For the uninitiated, you simply "cut off" the two half circles at either end, combine them into a complete circle, leaving a rectangle, and then add the area of the circle to the area of the rectangle and *Presto!* you have the area of a racetrack.) I've never really liked math, anyway. Today I read a great many books on quantum physics, but I must confess I still simply ignore the math. I suspect some physicists do as well. They seem to go directly from concept to conclusion, which is a bit like going from dream to reality. (Or is it from reality to a dream?)

Jack's wife Francis was an extremely well-read woman, and many years later she told me about the historian Josephus, and his chronicles of life in Israel during the early Christian era. Jesus Christ, I would discover, was barely mentioned (if at all). I'll have to check. My copy of *Josephus* is still on the top shelf of one of the six bookcases I have devoted to spiritual matters and the holy books of so many religions. The books on philosophy, psychology, history, and quantum physics go on the bookshelves on the other side of the room. However, I've noticed lately that it is sometimes difficult to decide which side of the room a new book should "go."

One of the local high school teachers boarded with Josh and Eunice Teague, an elderly couple who lived within walking distance of both the high school and grade school. I don't recall the teacher's name, but I do know that she played the piano and, since the Teagues had a piano, she gave lessons. We also had a piano (which I've mentioned before), transported at some point from my maternal grandparents' home. It was a tall, lumbering thing with a beautiful tone, its music stand slightly defaced by a giant X painted into the wood (with iodine, by my Aunt Maxie, I was told). I must have been eight or nine when I began taking lessons. When that teacher either married or moved on, my mother took both me and my sister Kay to Metropolis every Saturday to take lessons from a young unmarried lady, Roberta Dollar, who lived with her parents. I think she charged either 25 or 50 cents for each of our lessons. When I advanced to classical music, Dad bought, from a traveling salesman, a complete set of the 11-volume Scribner Music Library, for which he paid (I think) $50. I have always suspected that he might have done so partly because the salesman told him that Otis Nutty had bought a set for his daughter Diane.

But then, I have also learned to suspect my own tendency to question my interpretation of my father's motives and actions, perhaps because I have learned that there is more than one way to express love when you just *can't* speak it right out loud. Most of that Library was well beyond my abilities even after many lessons, but I treasured the books because I knew (or at least hoped) they were a gift of love from a man who found it difficult to express affection. I suspect I am more like him in that way than I am willing to admit. I have described it this way:

> *I once thought many, many things to say.*
>
> *Finding myself speechless then, they went away.*

Though I have never been able to memorize music (as it is played), not even a single song, I am a fairly competent sight reader and music has been a pleasure all my life. (That does not apply to lyrics; the lyrics haunt my days and sometimes my sleep.) I have a huge collection of sheet music since I don't play by ear or from memory, and for many years I have had either a piano or an organ, and sometimes both, in my home. So did my sister Kay. Her practice ran almost exclusively to hymns and religious music. Mine is far more eclectic, just as my life has been. I love the music of the 30s and 40s and all the old standards from the Big Band days. Mom had also learned to play at some point in her own childhood and had sheet music for songs like *My Alice-Blue Gown* and *Down the River of Golden Dreams*. I played them for her often in those last days of dementia when music was the only way we could communicate. I play them sometimes when I'm thinking of her. If tears threaten, I stop. They blur my sight, and so I can't continue. At least that's what I tell myself.

I bought my first organ because I so envied a woman who played the organ in an Italian restaurant near Wheaton where Jay and I went for dinner frequently when I was the editor of the *DuPage County Times*. The lobster was good, the cream garlic dressing for the salads pungently memorable, but the main attraction was the singalong that we always had for "dessert." We both loved to sing, and I yearned to play the organ as well. (I didn't even have a piano then.) So I bought a used Wurlitzer, took lessons from Midge, the organist, and when she had to go out of town to a family wedding, she invited me to substitute for the weekend. I came well-prepared but discovered it was not nearly as much fun as I had expected it to be. I wanted to play what I wanted to sing, and *they* wanted me to play what *they* wanted to sing. I have since learned that one of my shortcomings is that I do not "play well with (or for) others." I have suggested to my children that particular statement as an appropriate epitaph for my tombstone.

It gave me far more pleasure years later when I played for my mother and her neighbors in the assisted living and nursing homes where she spent her last years, venues where no one really cared what you played or how well you played as long as you just kept on playing. My last organ, a Hammond, caught fire from a faulty electrical condition. Fortunately, my grandson Raymond and his two sons were in the family room, eating popcorn after an afternoon of sledding, and he unplugged it and scooted it out the nearby door.

I gave my piano to Raymond when I sold that house four years ago, perhaps as a reward for saving the house from burning down when the organ caught fire, perhaps because his son William was taking lessons. I had already downsized to an electric piano with a full 88 keys. It's easy to play and portable. I'm told that playing an instrument of any kind is also a good mental exercise to keep dementia at bay. It's also good for the soul. But I have gotten sidetracked again and wandered far afield. Forgive me. I must go back to school now.

Back to school: I don't remember at what time we began the school day or at what hour it ended, but there was always a morning and an afternoon recess and a rather long lunch hour, which was spent mostly on the playground unless it was far too cold, or raining. Everyone brought their lunch to school. My first-grade teacher (and please remember I was only five) told my mother that I asked her one morning: "Guess what I've got for lunch today?" and answered myself, "Same old thing, sandwiches." According to the psychologist Jean Piaget, five-year-olds talk about absolutely anything to get attention; if no one is there to listen, they talk to themselves. According to my personal experience, 89-year-olds will do the same. Perhaps it's second childhood?

Some kids carried their lunch in a sack, some in a "lard pail" (a small half-gallon-sized tin bucket with a handle and lid). Those whose families could afford it carried lunch boxes with compartments for a thermos to hold soup or milk or even hot chocolate, the contents dependent on a mother's creativity, her culinary accomplishments, and the family budget. (I *always* had a lunch box. Mother would have been mortified to send me to school with my lunch in a paper sack.) Everything was homegrown or homemade, except perhaps "store-bought" bread. Fruits, of course, were seasonal. Oranges and tangerines were reserved for Christmas treats in those days, bananas were considered almost too exotic for ordinary people, strawberries nonexistent except for a couple of weeks in late May and early June, and grapes were summer fruits best turned into juice or jelly (or wine, if you were so inclined). But, of course, Mom made grape juice and jelly. I remember there was one very poor family who lived in a one-room shanty down the hill behind the schoolhouse with the old sandpit for their front yard. Their kids went home for lunch every day. At least they said they did.

My father's mother (Grandma Korte) was raised by a stepmother who had four children of her own who survived infancy: two boys and two girls. Grandma said that she and her "own" sister went to school with cold breakfast biscuits smeared with lard while her half-siblings' lunch buckets held "yeast bread with bacon or ham, and sometimes real butter and homemade jelly." She might have been exaggerating just a bit, but I doubt it. Cruelty can sometimes be familial as well as social. Mom was far more accommodating. If we'd had pie or cake for supper and there was any left over, it would be in my lunchbox. We could have pie or cake even for breakfast. (Aunt Maxie was absolutely scandalized when she brought her two boys to visit and discovered the breakfast menu might be last night's dessert until Mom pointed out that cake wasn't all that different from donuts.) I am recently trying a gluten-free diet and cannot have cake or donuts for either breakfast, lunch, dinner, or a late-night snack. If any reader has ever eaten one of those huge, round, tasteless "rice cakes" which are mostly crunch and air, perhaps they will sympathize with me. I say "thank you" every night to whoever is listening for ice cream (lactose-free, of course).

The games we played: There was plenty of time for games at recess and lunch, some of them involving the whole school and others that were somewhat segregated by age or gender. In those days, that preliminary was not as complicated as it would be today. There were, of course, only two genders then, or at least only two were socially acknowledged. We played tag and hide-and-seek (though there were not many places to hide). There were no ball games that I remember, except "Annie-over," which involved throwing a rubber ball over the schoolhouse for someone on the other side to catch. I don't believe anyone owned either a baseball or a bat, and certainly not a ball *glove*. I don't recall ever seeing a basketball goal or a basketball until I got to high school. But we played circle games: ring-around-the-rosy (favored for grades 1-3); Simon says, which involved a leader making hand or foot movements preceded by verbal instructions, such as "Simon says raise your right hand" for the rest to mimic, with those failing to correctly respond retiring from the game until the last one became the winner (or the leader of the next game). You could play "Simon Says" inside, so it was favored on rainy days.

"Follow the leader" was similar, except the players had to line up behind the leader and follow his (or her) chosen course and shouted directions. And there was "run sheep run" and "prisoner's base," but I've completely forgotten their rules, though I'm sure they did involve "choosing up sides" and often resulted in hurt feelings. I know about things like that. For the first two years, I was usually the smallest and frequently the last chosen. I wanted to grow up *so* bad and *so* fast.

London Bridge was another favorite, especially for the younger girls. But I distinctly recall it being repurposed as a kissing game in later years when "post office" and "spin the bottle" were also in vogue. I think the verse for that was something like, "Take a key and lock her up, lock her up, lock her up; Take a key and lock her up, my fair lady." "Locking her up" involved escorting the young lady to another room for a moment of privacy when the kissing took place. I was either never allowed or never invited to play post office.

(One is allowed some regrets for both adventures and misadventures.) However, when a certain politician recently urged his fans to chant "Lock her up, lock her up" with regard to the opposing party's female candidate (*for president*!) I found myself remembering that childhood chant. I had always *wanted* to be locked up when they were playing post office. Life, I've learned, is inevitably about perspective.

I was given a set of "jacks" when I was seven or eight and spent most of that year becoming expert at bouncing a tiny ball and scooping up little six-pronged metal objects singly and then with varying hand and ball and pickup maneuvers required as you advanced in difficulty. You could play either singly or with others in competition. The game required a hard, smooth surface, so a linoleum or hardwood floor was ideal. Concrete could be extremely hard on your knuckles.

Jumping rope was a favorite activity for most of the girls and could be enjoyed either singly, in pairs, or in a group. The boys rolled hoops, played and traded marbles (if they had them), walked on stilts (homemade of two sturdy 2 x 4s with bracketed stirrups nailed on), wrestled (behind the coal shed, out of sight of the teacher), pitched washers (an antique version of the modern "cornhole" played with the holes dug into the ground and metal washers (circles of steel 2 ½-inch in diameter with holes in the center instead of beanbags). Empty Vienna sausage cans were handy liners for the holes and provided a satisfying "clink" if you scored the washers' equivalent of a "hole in one."

Even grownups pitched washers, at least until they became strong enough to pitch horseshoes. Horseshoes is *not* a woman's game. There was almost always a washer game going on in the open space between Otis Nutty's store and Vanis Travis' blacksmith shop. And Otis had gas pumps while Cagle's and Richardson's did not. There was also a wood burning stove in all the stores during wintertime, and a cold drink dispenser year around, one of the old-fashioned kind, flat-topped with cold water and ice in the reservoir, and a metal partition just above water level with drink-size holes for the Coca Cola and Nehi bottles. It wasn't coin-operated, but it *was* self-serve; you just had to pay Otis or his wife, 'Letha, before helping yourself. Drinks were a nickel a piece.

Which is a somewhat sly way of introducing one of my first lessons in ethics. Dad did his Sunday loafing at Nutty's store (everybody did their loafing there, rather than Cagle's—*they* weren't "loafing" people) and Mom, my sister Kay and I would pick him up on the way home from church. (He didn't go to church.) One of the most embarrassing episodes in my life occurred one Sunday morning when we stopped to get Daddy and, while my mother did some shopping or talking or something, I went to the cooler and helped myself to a soda.

Daddy didn't say a word until we were halfway home and then he asked, with a sidelong look in my direction, "Did you pay for that coke?" I hesitated for a few seconds before whispering, "No," realizing in that pause that I was guilty of stealing the soda, although perhaps (in my defense) expecting that Daddy would notice and pay for it himself. I must have had an allowance, although I was probably only 6 or 7, because I also realized I was now supposed to pay Mr. Nutty a nickel the next time I was in the store. I can't recall if I actually did. But I must have, because if I hadn't made my amends, I would surely never have dared show my face in his store all through high school, when I also recall often walking down to the store for a grilled baloney (that's the hillbilly pronunciation of "bologna") or cheese sandwich at lunchtime. But I had learned a lesson about the "wages of sin" and a bit about repentance and remorse. And it just occurred to me to wonder: when did I stop calling my father "Daddy"?

I was never very athletic, but one summer we went to visit Aunt Mary in Kankakee and stayed for nearly a week. And they had sidewalks. The greatest thing about sidewalks was that you could roller skate on them. I spent most of that week blissfully skating up and down the sidewalks of South Main Street in Kankakee on my cousin Jack's roller skates. I was probably nine or ten. The skates clamped to the edges of the wearer's shoe soles and extended or retracted so that "one size fit all." The sliding mechanism that extended or retracted the skates had to be tightened into place with a "key" and roller skaters wore their key around their neck because the screw would loosen while skating, and adjustments had to be made frequently. If it was raining in Kankakee, you were allowed to roller skate in the Turner basement. There were, needless to say, no sidewalks on the farm where I grew up. We didn't have a basement either until the new house was built in 1949. But by then I was much too old to be roller-skating in the basement. In the fall of 1950, I went away to college; in the summer of 1953 I would be married.

We never played cards in school, not even Old Maid. But I learned to play pinochle at Pa and Danty's house. After their own children were grown – but during the time when I was still spending a lot of time with them – she and Pa would play two-handed pinochle, although all card-playing was frowned upon by good Baptists. I remember one time the local preacher came to call in the middle of the afternoon, and when Danty saw his car pull into the driveway, she got all flustered and said, "Miles, we've got to put the cards up." And they did. They picked up the card table – cards, unplayed hands and all – and carried it into the front bedroom *and* shut the door. In utter innocence, I asked Danty, "But doesn't God know you play cards?" To which Danty answered, somewhat short of breath from all the hurrying about, "Yes, but God doesn't care, and the preacher does." Perhaps that was my first inkling that religion might have a great deal more to do with what the preacher (and other folks) thought and said than what God considered appropriate, because that incident sure stuck with me!

My favorite activities at school were of the educational variety: spelling contests and geography challenges. I still like word games (Scrabble) and logic puzzles (Sudoku). On the last day of school, when our parents often joined us to pick up final report cards, they sometimes joined the games as well. At least my mother did. Dad wasn't much for games. I can recall distinctly the heady triumph of once "out-spelling" my mother, who was no slouch. And tears still well in my eyes when I recall that, after her death, I opened her Bible one day and found a sheet of notepaper on which she had tried, over and over, to spell the days of the week. She would do so well on the first three days, but when she got to "Wednesday," she just could not get it right no matter how many times she tried. But she somehow knew instinctively that all her attempts were wrong. Aging dementia, of whatever cause, is tragic. Difficulty with spelling "Wednesday" is only a little bitty problem compared to the magnitude of the rest of it. (Then why, I ask myself, is it only those long rows of misspelled Wednesdays that still bring tears to my eyes these long years later?)

Every year at Christmas, there was a Christmas program for which we practiced for weeks. We sang songs, played characters in little skits, and even the youngest had a "piece" to say. One poem I still recall, so I'm pretty sure it was once assigned to me:

Old St. Nick is short and thick,

So I've been told by Ma.

But I've seen him, he's tall and thin.

And looks just like my pa.

There were treats: sacks of candy and always an orange *and* an apple. The songs included those from our songbooks: Up on the Housetop, Jingle Bells. At church there was also a program with a more religious emphasis, with piano accompaniment. We didn't have a piano at school, so all singing was *a capella,* a phrase I would not know the meaning of until years later.

We never ever danced at school (ring-around-the-rosy doesn't count), although sing-alongs were almost daily activities. I've found a copy of the yellow-backed songbook we used with its so-familiar Christmas songs and very old-fashioned favorites like *Up on the Housetop*, the *Spanish Cavalier*, *Yankee Doodle Dandy*. However, when I was old enough to join the local 4-H club we played games there as well, and square-dancing was considered a game. I loved it! Dancing has always been one of my favorite things to do. As my long-time friend and partner Dave Kingsley would say, channeling his father, who had been the leader of a local country band for many years, "Why wouldn't you do something that gives you permission to hold a girl in your arms for at least three minutes, and maybe even hold her cheek to cheek, and know you're not going to get your face slapped?" Dave's dad was right, of course, and it has also been my personal experience that an entire courtship, from meeting a stranger to beginning a long-term love affair, can be conducted in that not-so-simple three minutes. It's kind of like this:

What Mama Didn't Know

I was gone long before we'd even said "Hello"-
You looked so darkly dangerous, and Mama'd told me
when I met a man like you I'd know to run
'cause men like you were hard to hold.
I must have left a hundred times before
you wandered close enough to touch or kiss me;
But somehow never quite got out the door
'cause I kept wondering if you'd miss me.
I suppose I had a chance when we were dancing
close to say, "Just one, and then I have to go."
But I couldn't say a word, 'cause I was chancing
Mama might be wrong, or maybe Mama didn't know:

When a darkly dangerous man whispers, "Please stay."
there's no running fast enough to get away.

Mama knew, of course. She'd met Daddy at a dance, and never could get away. And never really wanted to, I suspect. At least not for long.

There were many social divides in the community where I grew up: political, educational, religious, economic, and even that division by status that is sometimes described as being on the "wrong side of the tracks." There were no racial or ethnic divides for the simple reason that almost everyone was "WASP" (white, Anglo-Saxon, and Protestant). But there were still "tracks" which, though invisible, were well-maintained. When the New Columbia

High School was dissolved, and I went for my senior year to Metropolis High School (class of 1950), there was still a separate high school for black students. I'm not sure when schools were finally integrated.

There were a few exceptions. The Cagle family was Jewish, and some people referred to the patriarch (Jesse) as "Jew" Cagle. I think I thought for a long time that "Jew" was the man's first name. But I don't believe I recognized the truth until, as I've already mentioned, one of the Cagle boys ran into and killed one of my father's horses and, in the disagreement that followed, called my father a "flat-headed Dutchman." It was apparently the ultimate insult to my father, and I had no idea what he might have said or done to deserve it. I do know that from that day on he would not set foot in Cagle's store, not even to buy a pack of cigarettes. (Though he would send one of his children.) And for the first time he used the epithet: "Jew" Cagle.

I had my own problems with one of those boys, but it had nothing to do with either his ethnic origins or religious background. Of the three stores in New Columbia, only one sold "dry goods," that is, sewing supplies and fabric. I went there alone one day to buy fabric for a dress, a home economics project, during my freshman year in high school. (I was, I remember, still only 12.) The boy minding the store that day (he was probably 16 or 17) waited on me, and as he spread the fabric out on the counter to cut it, he suddenly reached across and pinched my (very small) left breast, looking straight into my eyes with a slight smirk twisting his mouth, as though daring me to stop him. He then picked up the scissors and resumed work on the fabric that would become my new dress as though nothing at all had happened.

Nothing in my life had prepared me for a moment like that. I had absolutely no idea what to do. I paid for the fabric and took it home, and I will never forget the dress I made: maroon with a wide circular skirt and pink pockets—actually round gathered pouches. I loved the dress, but every time I wore it, I thought about that sly assault. And I simply could not tell anyone, for I was terrified of what my father might do if he found out. It had seemed bad enough that one of the boy's older brothers had run over Dad's horse, left it screaming (I'm sure it must have screamed!) in the middle of the road, and just left it for Dad to find. I don't believe I ever went into Cagle's store again, for any reason, even to buy cigarettes for Dad. It was as though another visit might be mistakenly construed as an invitation.

I was equally silent when a man who was a friend of my parents (as was his wife) asked me to ride with him to take ballots to Metropolis after an election and also became "familiar." He and my mother were both judges for the election, and I'm sure it never occurred to either of my parents that he could not be trusted with their daughter. I was then, in fact, still in grade school. But when, years later, after his wife had died and he was left to raise his own daughter alone, there were rumors that the daughter had taken his wife's place in more ways than one. I never doubted for a moment that the rumors were true.

And since we're speaking of horses (admittedly a paragraph or two ago) -- We always had horses when I was growing up – big draft horses to pull wagons and plows and even threshing machines, horses that responded to "giddyap" and "whoa", "gee" and "haw" (that's "go" and "stop", "right" and "left" –or maybe it's left and right--to those unfamiliar with horse talk). A light tap of the reins on a broad back was a signal to "get a move on," a gentle tug on the bridle bit would slow one down.

Even after Daddy bought his first tractor, he kept his horses, so I learned to ride bareback on a big roan mare, one of a matched team he used to haul logs out of the woods in the wintertime. By the time I was ten or so, I could slip a bridle over her head, lead her over to the nearest fence where I could climb up and slide over onto her back and walk her down the gravel road the three miles or so to my best friend's house. That seemed very close to freedom: just me and the horse under a summer sun with a light breeze blowing us on our way.

But late one Wednesday, which was livestock auction day in Metropolis, Daddy drove up in the truck and unloaded a little spotted horse whose name, he said, was Tony. Tony looked a lot like the horses the cowboys rode in the Western movies our family saw at the Royal Theatre on Saturday nights. Tony was, Daddy said, a quarter horse, assuring my mother that Tony was "very gentle." I did not know what a quarter horse was, but I was about to learn.

Tony had come with a saddle blanket, saddle (with stirrups, of course) and a bridle with silver conches. Daddy gave me a boost up into the saddle and walked Tony and me a few turns around the gravel driveway, instructing me in the art of "neck-reining" – a technique for turning your mount by sliding the rein upward along the horse's neck on either the right or left side until he turned in the direction his nose had been made to point. Mom took our picture with the Kodak Brownie camera, and then Daddy said the magic words: "Why don't you ride him up to the store?"

So Tony and I headed off to Otis Nutty's store about half a mile or so up the road, me fantasizing a hundred pleasant jaunts, Tony behaving nicely. When we got to the store, the men loafing on the front porch bragged on my horse, my saddle, and me. Feeling nearly grown up, I was sitting "tall in the saddle" as I neck-reined Tony in a semi-circle, heading him for home.

We started off the same way we'd come, in a nice slow walk, but in less than a minute Tony had moved into a slow trot, which rapidly accelerated to what seemed to me a gallop. He did not respond to my pleas of "whoa" or "stop." (Just maybe I was too scared to say either one.) Only sheer terror and a tight grip on the saddle horn kept me on Tony's back while we made a very fast quarter mile back to our barn. That's how I learned the reason Tony was called a "quarter horse."

Of course Tony stopped when he got to the barn (I still have no idea how he knew it was now *his* barn). But once I slid down off the saddle and was safe on solid ground, I vowed I would never get on, let alone ride, another horse, despite Daddy's insistence that "You need to get right back on." Naturally, Mom defended me, declaring that the whole affair was Daddy's fault. Since I refused to ride, Kay inherited Tony. My much younger brother became a barrel racer, which requires very fancy neck-reining and a very fast horse. My mother decided one Sunday afternoon years later that she would start riding with Daddy. He bought her a nice, gentle mare, and before long they became founding members of the Massac County Saddle Club. But I kept my vow, and I'm sure I missed out on a lot of family fun. But I still learned two important lessons that day. Daddy was right. First, if life runs away with you or even "throws you for a loop," just as soon as you catch your breath you need to get right back on! And the second lesson is: once you get on, nobody but you can ride *your* horse.

Families spent a lot of time visiting when I was growing up. There was no television and not a lot of money for other amusements. We did go to the movies when we went to town on Saturdays. The Massac Theatre was for first-run movies, and the Royal Theatre was for westerns starring Roy Rogers, Gene Autry, and Hopalong Cassidy (among others). I never dreamed that one day I'd marry too quickly, and just as quickly divorce, a man—my second husband--whose childhood playmates were Roy Rogers' and Dale Evans' children!

At both movies there were "Perils of Pauline" type serials, which always ended with the heroine in dire straits, so you had to wait until the next week for the hero to rescue her. Hallmark Movies today actually use the same plot line. (I binge-watched during the pandemic. I call them "lady porn.") At the uptown theatre you might also get a "Flash Gordon" serial – a futuristic forerunner of Star Wars. One winter Saturday, Mom took me to the Massac Theatre to watch *Gone with the Wind*. Years later, I wrote a poem that was quite literally true about that day:

Coming Attractions

It snowed all afternoon, almost a blizzard,
flakes falling thick as thumbs,
sticking to frigid ground,
slicking the long road home.

Oblivious to snow and other dangers,
Mom and I (Dad thought it was dumb)
went to see "Gone with the Wind."
According to the marquee, it was
PLAYING FOR ONE DAY ONLY.

We had to leave Scarlett standing
in hoopskirts, her shoulders bare,
alone on Tara's steps;
left her to remember Rhett Butler saying,
so frankly, "I don't give a damn."

Walked out into a wind so cold
it froze our tears.
Dad would be waiting for his supper.
We couldn't stay to watch
PREVIEWS OF COMING ATTRACTIONS.

We drove home slow, a long ten miles,
the road black-slick with ice, steep ditches
falling away darkly on either side,
in first gear for that last scary stretch
up the high and winding bluff –
almost slid home.

And I wondered all that heart-pounding way
why Scarlett could yearn hopelessly for Ashley
when it was so obvious that Rhett was twice the man.
And loved her.

I was so sure it would be far easier
  to love a man who loved you back.

And there was the radio, of course. I spent Saturday mornings listening to: "Grand Central Station, crossroads of a million private lives, gigantic stage on which are played a thousand dramas daily," and the spooky one that began "only the Shadow knows." Radio was great for the imagination: you had to visualize all the actors, the scenery, and the action. It's a long way from radio to today's virtual reality video games in 3-D.

Country music was also a big part of my life, especially when I visited Pa and Danty, mostly in the summertime, often the entire summer vacation. On Saturday nights, Pa and Danty always listened to the Grand Ole Opry on WLS out of Nashville, as well as the "Ernest Tubb Record Shop" and all the other programs that followed the Opry until late in the evening. Pa would sit in the rocker, his false teeth safely tucked away in his shirt pocket, and turn the air blue with smoke from his unfiltered Camels while I'd sit on the floor alongside his chair with my ear almost against the radio, listening to Ernest Tubbs, Hank Williams, Bill Monroe and the Blue Grass Boys, and Roy Acuff singing *The Great Speckled Bird*. In later years, Pa and Danty would make annual pilgrimages to the Opry, stopping at our house in Massac County on their way down and again on their way back. I sometimes wonder where they stayed while they were in Nashville. Or did they perhaps sleep in the car? Or just drive back and stop over at our house? Now I'll never know. Everyone is gone who might have told me.

And we went to the movies nearly every week. Another of my rites of passage occurred at the Royal Theatre one Saturday night. In those days, ticket prices were twelve cents for children and a quarter for adults, and the price changed when a child turned 12. I had just had the appropriate birthday, but as we were standing in line for tickets I heard my father say that he wanted "two adults and two children." He did not realize, I'm sure, that he had just insulted my newly acquired "adulthood." But he had, and I responded by announcing that he had to pay full price for my ticket. He, of course, refused. I suspect he had just forgotten, or perhaps as a matter of principle was going to exert his parental authority. (There I go, still doubting his motives.) However, I wasn't about to bend and so announced that, in that case, they could just go in without me. I would sit in the car. I would not go into the theatre with someone who was trying to cheat the theatre owners. Actually, ". . . STEAL from them" is what I think I said.

I have no idea what transpired between my parents once they got inside, but it wasn't too long before Kay came out with a quarter, which she handed me with the message, "Dad says come on in." And I did. I marched in triumph to the ticket window, paid my admission and went in. It was, I'm sure, difficult for everyone that summer I turned 12, just out of grade school and headed for high school, to realize that I would always be "a little ahead of myself."

It must have been about that time that I started getting an increase in my allowance to $1 a week. I spent most of it every Saturday afternoon, by myself, going to Humma's drugstore (the uptown Humma's--there were two and the other was closer to the river and didn't have a soda fountain) for a grilled hot dog and a cherry ice cream soda, then a two-block walk to the Massac Theatre where the first-run movies were played. It's hard to believe, with today's prices, that I got all of that for less than a dollar. Saturday evening, the whole family always went to the Royal Theatre and its Westerns. Daddy was a big fan of anything that had horses in it.

One Saturday afternoon my very first boyfriend, Donald Windhorst, came to the Massac Theatre and sat beside me and held my hand. He followed me to the Royal Theatre and once again sat beside me, in a seat far removed from my family, and held my hand again. Over Dad's objections, as I recall. Mom had to explain to Dad that I was growing up. Years later, when I moved from Chicago to Kentucky and was working at a law firm in Paducah, I got a call to come to the front office. And Donald Windhorst was standing there. He'd heard I was back in town and just wanted to say "Hello." (That's all, folks. Really. Honestly. Just "Hello.")

There was another totally (or almost totally) innocent encounter at the Massac Theatre, to which I always went alone. Kay was far too young for grownup movies, in my opinion, and no one made me take her so I've course I didn't. One Saturday an older boy (actually almost a young man) sat down next to me and he also held my hand. He was, I still remember, traveling through the country, putting up those Burma Shave advertising signs that were once a fixture along every highway. Every half mile or so, there would be three or four words on a sign, with the final one announcing: "Burma Shave." I remember I was wearing Blue Waltz perfume (which had been purchased at the Woolworth 5-and-10-cent store with part of my allowance), and for a long time the scent of that perfume (or Burma Shave signs, until they all fell down) would remind me of that exciting, though very brief, romantic encounter with a perfect stranger. (There's a poem about that, back several pages, admittedly only one Episode in a Series.)

Pie Suppers - There were other opportunities for courtship, innocent as they may seem today. One of those important events, memorable to me at least, was the pie suppers. They were held at the local elementary schools, but the participants included everyone from the whole community. The pie supper was ostensibly a fundraiser for schoolbooks and other education expenses, but it was also a deliberate excuse for romantic encounters for students of all ages, first grade up to and through "graduated from high school but not yet married." Girls brought pies in highly decorated boxes, and an auctioneer sold them off to the highest bidder.

The event was painfully exciting. Would the boy you really liked claim you for his own by buying your pie, the description of which you had previously made known (loudly) in his presence and, of course, sit and eat it with you afterward? Or would you be embarrassed to tears by having *none* of the boys bid on your pie and be reduced to the ultimate shame: having your father buy it to save your pride and perhaps even the honor of your entire family? The ultimate excitement, of course, was to have two boys bid against each other, as though fighting a duel for your hand. (Pies at ten paces?) I don't recall that particular exciting event ever happening to me. If it had, I am absolutely positive I would remember and tell you about it in great detail, blow by blow (or at least bid by bid).

Water-Witchin' – Even after things began to modernize, people around where we lived still had old-fashioned ways of doing things. Dad must have been getting ready to build the new house the year he cut the trees down behind the back barns in the bottoms (the woods behind the Korte "home place") and hauled the logs to the lumberyard at Karnak to have them cut up into planks and studs and joists. They needed to "season" a year or so before he started building. Unfortunately, when he went to get the lumber to build the house, "someone" had sold his seasoned lumber and he had to accept green materials instead. It was about that time that he also decided, for no reason I can remember, to look for water up on the hill behind our (old) house. Perhaps he first planned to build there, close to the border between our land and our next-door neighbors, the Browns.

He must have spread the news around because an old man showed up at the house one spring day who claimed to have the gift of water-witching. He said he could find a place where water would be found fairly close to the surface. There was a good-sized shallow pond back in the woods behind the spot where Daddy was thinking of building, and this man seemed to think that a place near the pond would be a likely spot to find water. So he cut a forked limb off a green peach tree and, holding one of the "handles" in each hand, with the longest and thickest end sticking straight up (think slingshot, reversed), walked around for a couple of days, waiting for the limb to start twitching and twisting until the point turned upside down and pointed to where water was supposed to be. He did find a place (or said he did) and Dad dug there, but when he got ten feet down--well over his head--the ground still wasn't even damp, so he quit. In hindsight, it doesn't seem reasonable that he would even try. Our spring was down in a hollow at least 30 feet lower than where Dad and the old man were digging. But I guess in the old days, there were old ways. Sometimes they worked, sometimes they didn't. One of my sister's brothers-in-law has made a living with a well-drilling rig. (Dad had tried to dig his well by hand). But I have no idea if folks are still water-witchin' to find the right place to dig in Southern Illinois.

The Light Theft - When electricity came through one fall, we had our first electric lights on the Christmas tree: little candle-like lights with colored water in them. When the bulb got hot the water would bubble up and down. We went to town one Saturday and came home that night to find the tree dark and the lights gone. But Mom knew where they had to be and marched over to the house across the road where her Christmas tree lights were burning and bubbling brightly on *their* tree and demanded their return.

I suppose they never dreamed that she would actually confront them like that, but she'd once found two of her dresses and her good winter coat under the culvert that crossed the road between their side of the road and ours, so she knew where her Christmas lights had to be. These neighbors had moved in after the *skunky* one, but they had even more children. People said the smaller boys slept in the storm cellar and the bigger ones slept in the barn. It's awfully hard to feel sorry for people when they steal your clothes out of your closet and the lights off your very first electrified Christmas tree. When the oldest boy, maybe 16 or 17, got bitten by a copperhead while fishing in George's Creek down by Grandpa and Grandma Korte's farm, he walked up the Bluff with his right leg swollen up past his knee. Mom put him in the car, along with Kay and me, and drove all the way to Metropolis to see the doctor. (His folks didn't have a car, of course.) You could consider it just being neighborly or maybe the Christian thing to do. But I decided there must be something to that "casting your bread on the waters" stuff because, the funny thing is, I don't remember Mom missing any of her clothes after that.

But those Christmas lights also remind me that, when I came home from college at Christmas my first year, Mom had already put up the Christmas tree. She wanted to surprise me. She did. I burst into tears. I just couldn't believe she hadn't waited for me to help.

With electricity came other conveniences. As I've already noted, Dad put a pump in the spring at the foot of the hill below the barn and built a springhouse around it so we could dispense with use of the cistern and have running water in the house. The water from the spring was sweet and soft, although it occasionally had a tadpole in it, and it kept the Korte house and livestock supplied until county water came through sometime around 1970, long after I was grown up and gone. With refrigeration, we no longer had to keep a cow in order to have fresh milk and butter; it was cheaper to buy it than to feed the cow, and we didn't have to go without between calves.

(There was always a brief dry spell when the cow was bred, had a new calf, and "restocked.") The cream separator was removed from the corner of the kitchen, eliminating one source of income (and a persistent sour smell in the whole house). We'd taken our surplus cream to town on Saturdays for years. Although it was fun taking our collie with me up to the pasture to bring the cows down to the barn in the evening, I never did like milking a cow. I wasn't very good at it, either.

My mother made nearly all my clothes from the day I was born, most of it on a Singer sewing machine, foot-powered by a pedal that turned a wheel that, via a belt that turned another wheel, made the needle go up and down. I learned to sew on that machine, and when electricity came through Mom had it electrified. When we held the auction to sell her house and furnishings, I just could not bear to see that old electrified Singer go to someone else, so I bought it. Mary Beth has it now, but it's more a decorative object than useful household equipment.

One exception to Mom's hand-made clothing that I especially treasured was a pair of jodhpurs which I got for Christmas one year, a gift I had begged for after Diane Nutty, daughter of the owner of Nutty's Store, wore a pair. It occurs to me that I may have mentioned that fact in Dad's presence several times before Christmas. (I have never been above manipulation of the male species when it suits my purposes.) My joy was tempered, however, by the fact that I had also gotten chickenpox for Christmas, and I couldn't wear my new jodhpurs until the pox had subsided and the scabs sloughed off.

As previously noted, I spent a lot of time with Pa and Danty during summer vacations from grade school and high school, even during the two years I went to college in Carbondale. I got in serious trouble on one weekend visit for having cigarettes in my purse:

Danty found them, saw they were Viceroy brand, and she was certain (by virtue of the name) that they were some kind of dope! When I was smaller, we would go visit one of Pa's brothers and sisters, drive down to Lick Creek to see Uncle Hubbard and Aunt Cindy or go to Giant City Park near Makanda, where Danty would sit in the car and read while Pa and I climbed over all the rocks. Danty had had blood poisoning in her right leg at some time, and it was always considerably larger than the left one. She usually wore an elastic stocking around the bad leg to keep the swelling down, and she definitely didn't do much climbing. She was very much the "intellectual type." I inherited my love of books from her, I'm sure, and my pragmatic nature from my mother.

I graduated from grade school in 1946, two months before my 12th birthday. It was a county-wide affair, with students from all the one-room schools in the county gathering in Metropolis, the county seat. I don't recall the location of the graduation. However, it was probably the Metropolis High School gymnasium. Still, I remember the dress (I have pictures!) my mother made me for the occasion, yellow and sleeveless, with a white organdy capelet to wear over my shoulders.

Somewhere I have my felted graduation diploma, but what I remember most are the telltale stains of another "graduation" that day. When I came back from the exercises, there were red stains on my underpants, and I knew I was growing into womanhood. That was far more momentous that an eighth-grade diploma for a not-quite-12-year-old.

Vows

I promised me, the summer I was nine,

and knew that all the world was mine

(as soon as I had breasts,
a driver's license,
and a wedding dress),
that somehow I would win fortune and fame –
that someday everyone would know my name.

I traipsed the sunny sidewalks up and down,
my head held high as though I wore a crown,
and learned to walk
in borrowed high-heeled shoes.
My gown of old lace curtains billowed in the breeze;
around me floated veils of make-believe.

I was a Princess nearly every day,
a woman dreaming through a child at play,
dizzy with the dust of August
I was queen of all tomorrows,
Slipping through the cracks of time,
That long summer I was nine.
Well, perhaps I was eleven.

"Now faith is the substance of things hoped for, the evidence of things not seen."

– Hebrews 1

The Little and Very White Church in the Vale

My mother was a practicing Baptist, so I did all the things a good little Baptist girl does: I went to Sunday school, sang duets with my mother and frequent solos on Sunday morning, and sat through church beside her until I was old enough to sit with my friends in the southeast corner of the church on the very last bench in the back and play "hymnbook games." The "games" consisted of choosing a phrase like "between the sheets" and matching it to a song title in the book and trying very hard to stifle the giggles that often resulted in the surprising—and frequently sexually titillating--results. I attended G.A. (Girl's Auxiliary) on Sunday nights, prayer meetings on Wednesdays, and two weeks of Vacation Bible School every summer. I learned all the books of the Bible by heart, memorized Bible verses (many of which I still recall), and practiced "Bible drills," competing to see who could find a particular book the fastest.

When I visited my grandparents in Fudgetown, Danty always required prayers at bedtime. And while it may be a falsity, I recall Danty stating quite firmly, "I may not always be right, but I'm never wrong." At least, that's a quote I have frequently attributed to her as a consequence of my occasional attempts to try to prove that her beliefs or pronouncements might be "wrong." One of the most heated arguments we ever had was in my early teens when I was beginning to question the doctrine of the Baptist religion in which we had both been raised. I tried to explain to her my belief that, if salvation was at the pinnacle of a mountain that represented (metaphorically, of course) the world of spirit that one must climb, then God must surely have made many roads to get to the top.

But she contended adamantly that "There's only one road to salvation." And she made it quite clear that if I wasn't on *that* road, I'd better do some serious reconsidering. Since, by that time, I'd been safely "saved" and, in Pa's hard-shell Calvinistic view of "born to be saved or born to be lost" was (at least in my view) obviously "born to be saved…and had been," I didn't see anything wrong with a little discussion on the subject. Some 55 years later I was advised by an Episcopal priest that my view of things would have met with *his* approval. But it took me that long to prove (to myself) that Danty was wrong, theologically at least, though I'm sure she'd have argued with the priest as well. He was, after all, *not* a Baptist. In fact, when my oldest daughter, who first joined the Episcopal Church (a tragedy of epic proportions!) and then married a man who *was* a Baptist, Danty was euphoric: Becky was finally going to get "right with God." I'm not sure what she would have thought when Becky, on her own spiritual journey, decided to become ordained as an Episcopal deacon. But since Danty's death preceded the ordination, with all its accompanying vestments, pomp, and ceremony, I do hope she looked down (or up, or out, or in, or through, or *whatever*) and gave the whole affair her blessing.

Religion was one thing Danty could get very emotional about. Despite her very ladylike demeanor on almost any occasion, she was not above "shouting" if the Spirit moved her. And it was most likely to do so when she heard certain songs. "The Wayfaring Stranger" was one of those. The melancholy strains of that old spiritual could move her as nothing else could, and she would raise both hands to the heavens, clench her fists, and let out mighty whoops of affirmation. Scared me to death the first time it happened and embarrassed me on every subsequent occasion! It sounded astonishingly like she was "howling at the moon."

I sometimes thought that Danty was a trifle egocentric, if not actually narcissistic, but I would have never dared to tell her so. Still, she reveled in being the center of attention, and she usually was! Even years after she died, her daughters would marvel at how much the strength of her convictions still governed their thinking, and reminiscing about their mother inevitably dominated the conversation when the three sisters were together.

It surely pleased Danty when I put on the formal religious armor of Protestant fundamentalism at the New Hope Baptist Church,[1] about 12 miles north of Metropolis, Illinois, when I was nine or ten during one of the revival meetings I was taken to every summer. Baptist revivals were fourteen or occasionally even twenty-one consecutive nights of preaching, praying, pleading altar calls accompanied by plaintive and repeated verses of "Softly and tenderly, Jesus is calling, calling 'Oh, sinner, come home,'" and whispered visitations by fervent men and women who pleaded tearfully, "Why not tonight?" (If my recollections are accurate, there was even an "invitational song" in which that phrase was repeated (repeatedly). Everybody else was getting saved, and I definitely didn't want to go to hell, so I got saved too--and I was baptized in Mr. Botts' farm pond just down the road from the church.

If I have sometimes said that they got rid of the cows who drank in that pond and had quite obviously defecated around it in order to hold the baptizing, I may have been guilty of exaggeration. I do remember that they sang *Shall We Gather at the River,"* not *Let's*

---

[1] The Church was founded at about the time the Civil War by an Americus Smith and/or his siblings, descendants of a Sylvester Smith. Sylvester was reportedly a Revolutionary War Veteran who came to Massac County from South Carolina in the early 1800s, probably soon after land in Illinois was opened for sale (about 1810). When the church celebrated its 150-year anniversary in 1860, I was asked to create a booklet for its history, and it was my great pleasure to do so.

Go Down to the River to Pray. I didn't hear *that* gospel song until the movie *O, Brother, Where Art Thou* was released.

If this little blurb was an actual sermon, I might choose as a text the verse from Corinthians (13:11) "When I was a child I talked like a child, I thought like a child, I reasoned like a child. When I became a [grownup], I put the ways of childhood behind me. " *(*We all know that the word in brackets is actually "man," but I seem to be unable to avoid occasionally introducing my long struggle against gender preferences in Biblical excerpts.)

I have since written a poem about those days, a kind of highly exaggerated expression (not factual) of how I later felt about those early experiences. Forgive the slightly overdone alliteration. Sometimes I get carried away with literary devices.

The Lesson

"Now I lay me down to sleep
I pray the Lord my soul to keep.
If I should die before I wake
I pray the Lord my soul to take."
(Anonymous Children's Prayer)

"Say this with me," she'd whisper soft,
her hand cupped hard against my head,
nailing my knees to the naked floor,
melding my mind with the mastery of hers.
Her wistful words, so winsome, so woeful,
shattered the silence, shuddered and soared,

seeking the ceiling like startled sparrows

raised from rude earth by a grim raptor's roar.

The feverish fear in her fragile fingers

was a palpable prescience, a pious pulse,

a timorous tympany, empty of empathy,

valiant but vacuous and void of hope.

We are weaned from the world while still wetting our cradles,

word-whipped with weakness away from life's wiles,

'til despair drags us down into destiny's dungeon

where love wets the whetstone for death's wicked knife.

The sword swiftly striking its blow for salvation

is the cleaver that cuts out the culls from the flock.

Threats curdle young courage as claps of thunder

clabber clean, warm milk into dry cold clots.

Death is the danger: the dread dusk Goliath

neither stone nor sling can slay or stay;

sleep makes a slippery slope into paradise;

those prim, proper prayers are still pushing my sleigh.

Perhaps my first period of spiritual growth was that of NOT accepting all of what my family and the people in a small rural community of not more than 200 souls, most of them devout Christians, believed. (The few outliers were either "unbelievers" or outright reprobates.) I began by subtraction, discarding ideas that were proving untrustworthy. People call such ideas "fake news" today.

I'd made my "profession of faith," but the only sins I could recall were once taking a soda from the cooler at Otis Nutty's store without paying for it and touching myself where I wasn't supposed to (in the dark and under the covers with the lights out, of course). And if Heaven was "up there" and had streets of gold and rivers of water and "many mansions," why didn't Heaven come crashing down? The clouds seemed entirely too fragile to keep all that heavy stuff "up there." And wasn't that against the laws of gravity? This is, of course, a scientific observation that doubters have repeatedly cited as evidence that Heaven cannot be "up *there*." (Or, more recently, as cosmology would state, "*out there*." It is also a conclusion that a very well-educated local minister publicly admitted to being true at a gathering of imminent theologians I recently attended (as, admittedly, a not entirely neutral observer). I did observe that nobody asked the local minister whether or not Heaven might possibly be "*down **here***," since it certainly could not be "*down **there***."

I was equally puzzled because the resurrection the preacher promised, when the dead would supposedly rise up from the grave, seemed completely unscientific. I have not been alone in my concern. Philosophers, theologians, and other religionists have puzzled over complications that arise in reconstituting physical bodies, including the confusion arising from such situations as cannibalism. (I doubt seriously if an actual cannibal would be concerned about such incidentals.) Personally, I was haunted for years by nightmares of people who were buried alive and "woke up" *before* the judgment day and tried to claw their way out of their coffins. Especially after I learned that, before embalmment ensured that the dead were "really *really* dead," people actually put bells above graves, with strings attached that led down into the coffin for the convenience of anyone who woke up too soon. I suppose they tied the string around one's finger so that even a mere twitch would sound the alarm, but I've never been able to learn if there were explicit instructions as to which finger was considered the most appropriate—ring finger, index finger, middle finger? And what about my third or fourth cousin Julius who quite probably had no fingers at all on his right hand? Would they use his left hand? His big toe?

*(I will pause here to thank the Munchkins in the Wizard of Oz for that comfortingly precise pronouncement on the demise of the Wicked Witch: the poor woman was proclaimed to be Really **Really** Dead, which I am sure has been a comfort to all the children who have watched the movie. I once met a woman who thought she was a witch, but she was not really wicked, just very confused and perhaps more than slightly psychotic. And the water-witcher who tried to find water on our farm by what some would consider occult methods was neither witch nor warlock, so he doesn't count either.)*

Still, when I was 14 or so and away from home at church camp at Dixon Springs, there was a revival meeting at the Dixon Springs Baptist Church, and I went down the aisle again, this time to dedicate my life as a missionary -- to something, or someplace -- I wasn't sure what or where. We often had missionaries visit the church and speak of their experiences in foreign lands, primarily Africa but occasionally China, and their work seemed wondrously spiritual and more than a little exotic. However, once again in hindsight, I realize that it may be a mistake to make God a promise unless you intend to keep it at some point in your life. But of course, I was caught up in the emotions of the moment, and I also realize in retrospect that, like many other decisions in my life, it seemed like a good idea at the time.

Upon my return home from camp, I was invited to speak at a meeting of the Women's Missionary Society, an organization specifically created to sponsor and support the Baptist Church's efforts in that field. My mother had been a member from the moment she joined the church. And I distinctly remember on that occasion using as a "text" some Bible verses about someone who kept hearing God calling his name until he finally answered. I'm rather certain it was Samuel, but that was a long time ago and my memories have faded with time. It certainly wasn't Job. Job had his own problems with God, and the Devil too. (I also had nightmares about *that* guy--speaking of the Devil, *not* Job.) In Colonial America, they hung women for less, and in Europe they burned them at the stake. Why, I wonder, was it almost always women who were accused and executed for "witchcraft." Am I alone in suspecting that men were simply terrified of a woman's power? Perhaps not. After all, women in the U.S. were not allowed to vote until 1920, when my mother was seven years old, and also only 14 years before *I* was *born*.) And when a woman tried to become president, her challenger kept leading chants to "lock her up." In a cage, as though she were a wild beast. I loved learning recently that the Benedictine nun and avowed feminist Joan Chittister has been known to sing, in karaoke bars: "I am woman, hear me roar."

However, the first really *wide* chink in my childhood religious armor, which was supposed to protect me from the Devil and, ultimately, an eternity in hell, cracked open when I finally was allowed to visit the Metropolis Public Library, alone and with a card in hand, and discovered that Mary, the mother of Jesus, was not the only virgin who had birthed a "son of God." I learned in that first foray about Zoroaster, and Google now tells me that there have been at least 32 other legends of virgin births in ancient cultures—so many, in fact, that the early Christian church was, I have come to believe, forced to imitate and/or incorporate the concept of virgin birth to encourage acceptance of this "new" Christian religion.

Even today "divine birth" is accepted in some cultures, giving power by birthright to kings, queens, and emperors. Queen Elizabeth used her own just a few years ago. Now she too, is Recently Really *Really* Dead and buried in a lead-lined coffin for reasons too unpleasant to contemplate. Current Bible scholarship indicates that Jesus was probably crucified because he was believed to be claiming a divine birthright with the intent to unseat Rome's own "son of God." The coin of the realm where Jesus lived and died too soon had an image of the Roman Emperor Caesar on one side, with an inscription that also claimed Caesar to be the Son of God. Apparently, there was not room for two Sons of God in Israel. So perhaps it's not surprising that today we often forget that Jesus said we are *all* Sons of God. Yes, he is supposed to have said that, according to the Bible. I hope he Really *Really* did, because it is a statement I've come to rely on.

Richard Rohr, a spiritual teacher who happens to be a Catholic priest, wrote a book, *Breathing Under Water*, on the 12 Steps of Alcoholics Anonymous (a spiritual path that he considers very much like the practices of the earliest disciples of Christ). A subsequent book called *Falling Upward* describes what occurs at that midpoint in life when many of us discover that we have chosen the wrong path, a path that has descended into darkness, and then have an experience that is often called a spiritual epiphany, leading us out of the darkness and into the light, a direction that he (good Catholic that he is) continues to identify as "up."

Since the day I knelt on a witch's carpet (oh, yes, I really *really* did) my personal spiritual journey has been upward, out of the darkness into the light, following a path that has been more search than discovery, first to learn what people of other faiths and cultures believe, and then to decide what I believe. I walk (or stumble along) this path in good company with ministers and mystics, poets and priests, the witty and the nitwits, Buddhists and Brahmans, scholars and skeptics, meditators and Methodists, Baptists and Trappists, and more recently the quantum physicists who search for the answer to my own long-ago question:

> *"I grant your theories of evolution and*
> *Those drops of water acting on the grains of sand,*
> *But tell me this, explain it if you can:*
> *From whence came water, and from whence the sand?*

But it's far too early for, as the newscaster and storyteller Paul Harvey always said in days long gone by, "the rest of the story." First I have to tell you about going to high school, attending college for a couple of years, getting married, having children and a career, and a great fall *down*ward. As another old song says: "Those were the days, my friend. I thought they'd never end."

"When the New C'lumbia Tigers fall in line,

We're gonna win this game, just give us time...

The New Columbia (Illinois) High School Fight Song

Moving Up to High School

When I began attending the New Columbia High School, just a quarter mile or so east of Otis Nutty's store—close enough to occasionally walk there at lunchtime and buy a grilled cheese and/or bologna sandwich--students from at least six of the local one-room grade schools were gathered together, and there were still just 17 juniors, no sophomores, 22 freshmen and only 2 graduating seniors in the Class of 1947. I can still remember the names (except one) of those in the freshman class picture in the school yearbook, the only one published in the three years I attended. The following year, a lone freshman simply began taking sophomore classes and the next year returned to become a "freshman." The personal result for me, which was either fortunate or unfortunate depending on your perspective, was that I would graduate from high school at 15, intellectually advanced (or at least as advanced as other people, places, and circumstances permitted) and both physically and emotionally very immature.

I have managed to hang on to that yearbook through the 75 years that have followed, during which I have moved at least 30 times and been married three. I finally unearthed it after searching nearly a day and a half and realized that I was the Makeup Editor. There were only four teachers (and four classrooms) for the whole school, and one of those teachers was Pauline Artman, my absolute favorite. She inspired me to become a writer simply by scribbling an extravagant compliment on an essay I wrote titled "A Conventional

Nonconformist," which I had every intention of becoming. And it was indeed prophetic. I've always rebelled at anyone's efforts to lay down rules or dictate terms while I was, at the same time, trying to appear compliant. I suppose that could also be called "passive-aggressive" behavior, but it was years before I had read enough psychology to learn the term and identify with it.

We all rode the school bus to school and to all the ball games; we could get the whole school, not including teachers, on the bus to out-of-town games. (The driver's youngest brother was my second "real" boyfriend.) Out of town meant schools like Joppa, Sesser, Karnak, and Rosiclare, the small schools where we would not be too outnumbered and outplayed. We had so few boys in the school that the boys on the "second team" were actually the only substitutes the "first team" had, and the "first team" were the subs for the "second team!" But the good thing was that *every*body got to play. Every year, Mom made the outfits for the cheerleaders: variations on the school colors, blue and gold. The skirts were always full circles, with matching bloomers (so they'd show when you twirled). I was never a cheerleader, but I can still sing the entire "school song" if called upon to do so. And the "bus favorite," which began: "One hundred bottles of beer on the wall. . ." continued a countdown until all the bottles had fallen. Mom finally made my own full circle skirt, complete with an appliqued poodle, when I was a senior. "Poodle skirts" were the fashion that year.

The bus chorales may have been the reason teachers seemed to prefer their own transportation to games. We sang all the way to the games and slept all the way home. Well, some "smooched" in the back of the bus. "Smooching" could mean any contact that occurred between a boy and girl from the waist up and occasionally (I've been told) other areas of one's anatomy, depending on how dark it was in the bus, how bright the moon was on a given night, and whether or not there was also a teacher on the bus. One or two of those bus courtships ended in marriage but, on reflection, I realize that most did not--with the possible exception of those that began with an unplanned pregnancy and *then* ended in marriage.

Sometime during my freshman year, I allied with two other girls, Dorothy Ellen Quint and Jane Staton. We called ourselves *The Three Musketeers*, although I don't believe any of us had read the old Alexander Dumas tale. There were only a few books in the high school's bookcases, and those seemed to be secreted away from students in a row of waist-high bookcases on one wall of the principal's office. I don't recall ever being allowed to borrow any of those books, but they were still there when I had a job as secretary to the director of an agriculture school for veterans the summer between high school and college. I admit to taking that summer, and never returning, one book: The Poems of Robert Browning. I still have it, and I feel absolutely no guilt. Perhaps because I don't believe anyone else had ever read it. Classic literature was not really unpopular in rural Massac County; it was just that most people who lived there seemed unaware of its existence. I've spent most of my life trying desperately to catch up to all the things I missed (most of which I never even knew existed) in that close, intimate, almost insular community.

Dorothy was a distant relative (she was, after all, a Quint), but I will not bore anyone with an explanation of the connection. The third member of our triumvirate, Jane Staton, was no kin at all and never married. Jane had a twin brother, who died when she was born. But I don't think that had anything to do with her not marrying, and I just find it interesting because she's the only girl I ever knew who had a twin brother. She became a nurse and then joined the Army and retired as either a Captain or a Major. Dorothy's husband Carl (the son of my parents' next-door neighbors) became the President of one of the local banks. And I fulfilled my own prophecy and became a "Conventional Nonconformist" over and over and over again.

However, the ties that bound the Three Musketeers almost ended completely when we three decided the school needed a newspaper. I think it was my idea, and of course I appointed myself the Editor. We had, after all, taken typing that year, and we had the necessary equipment to produce a professional product. We printed it weekly on one of those now obsolete instruments for reproduction that used a tray filled with some kind of jellied base, a purplish-colored ink on an original which, placed face down on the jelly, dissolved into the base, and could then reproduce additional copies as sheets of paper were, in turn, placed face down on the base. If I could remember the name of the darned thing (maybe a hectograph?), I would not have to go to such lengths to describe it. But it produced, quite literally, "purple prose."

Our little newspaper was an extremely gossipy paper and could have been described as an example of "yellow journalism," except that I've already colored it purple. It was just one step above passing notes in class, and we would probably have skated past any censors quite easily if we had not published a not-very-kind joke at the expense of one of the teachers (who was, I am deeply ashamed to admit, physically disabled and so very vulnerable). As a consequence, we learned early about the hazards of stretching the boundaries of "Freedom of the Press" which, while somewhat elastic, were incredibly painful when they inevitably snapped back and bit you. Our newspaper, the name of which has been lost to history, was discontinued at the request – actually, the demand – of the principal, a man who obviously had no sense of humor but perhaps more common sense than the three of us combined. But it was my very first newspaper. It would not be my last.

The alliance of the Three Musketeers held tight through those three years at New Columbia, perhaps because not one of us really dated the first two years. I do not count as "dating" the young man who came in as a freshman when I was a sophomore (he was a year older) and introduced himself by dropping a frog down the front of my dress. We did date later after we had both matured a bit, and though I'm not sure I ever completely forgave him for the frog incident, when I saw him many, many years later, I did write a poem about him:

Old Spice

The first thing I noticed
was how dull and gray
your hair had gone;
once it was shiny black
and fell across your forehead –
You were forever
tossing it up and back,
impatient as a young colt
shaking its mane.

The cab of your dad's pickup
always smelled of moon-warmed fields,
leather and smoke,
the shaving lotion you wore all that year,

and the sweet sweat of
youth and urgency –
And no one else's kiss
has ever tasted quite the same.

When you came in from all those years,
your jeans still falling off your hips,
but belly rounded now
and shoulders slumped,
I could not know –
'til you picked up that old battered guitar
and laid your fingers on its strings
and stroked the music out,
and sang,
your voice would sound the same,
that when I closed my eyes
I would still taste
          Old Spice –
              and lespedeza hay.

In our junior year, our class produced a play, *Aaron Slick from Punkin Crick*, which was all about the excursion of a country boy to the big city, where he meets a "lady in red" and becomes involved in some sort of indiscretion which I am sure the script allowed him to escape without permanent damage. I was the Lady in Red, and my mother almost certainly made a red dress for the occasion, but I don't remember what it might have looked like. I am quite sure there was no kissing involved in my role, seductress though I was supposed to be. I would *definitely* have remembered that. (I was, remember, only 14!) I do remember that Aaron Slick was played by a young man whose last name was "Foss," and not "Quint," negating the possibility that any public appearance of intimacy might have resulted in another of those Quint-Korte liaisons.

In those days we had "last day of school" picnics, almost always at Fort Massac State Park just outside Metropolis. And, again, the whole school could fit on the school bus. We had one of those picnics at the end of my junior year, and it was bittersweet, but I believe it was to a Lake somewhere. We knew that some of us would perhaps never see each other again since the school was being dissolved that year, some students going to Vienna, some to Metropolis. There was another life change in the summer of 1949. We also moved into the new house on the hill above the old house, just in time for the birth of my baby brother, Timothy Kent Korte, a month before Christmas in 1949.

Pa was 65 years old when he began to build Mom and Dad's new home on top of the New Columbia bluff in Massac County, just up the hill and in sight of the old one (but a much longer walk to the barn). He had retired from the mines and had sufficient income from Social Security and a miner's pension to support himself and Danty. The house was a labor of love, I'm sure. He truly loved to build things. He encountered one problem he had not expected: he had never before built a basement where concrete was poured from a cement mixer, all of it at one time. In fact, he had probably never built a basement at all. And his forms were not strong enough. Consequently, the walls bulged in places, and there was a slight crack in one. It was not his proudest moment.

He and Danty lived with Mom and Dad while the house was under construction, but he became ill (I think he was simply exhausted) before he could complete the interior finish work. I believe it was that aspect he enjoyed the most. Maynard Lindsey, who practically lived next door (his house was halfway between ours and Nutty's store, diagonally across from the Browns) handled much of the interior trim work. I'm confident his work wasn't as good as what Pa would have done. Of course, I'm prejudiced.

I think I learned to drive the summer after I left New Columbia High School and before I went to Metropolis (or perhaps it was before I left for college, after my 16th birthday in July). And, of course, it was Pa who gave me driving lessons, instructing me by providing a diagram of the "H" pattern of gears (I still see that picture in my head when I have to drive a stick shift) and finding back country roads where I could practice in his black Pontiac coupe. He drove until he died, nursing it along carefully with the aid of a friendly and skilled neighborhood mechanic. God bless him for his patience. (Pa's patience, not the mechanic's.)

Mom recalled that when she learned to drive, you had to actually "crank" the car to start it, turning the engine over manually by using a lever inserted someplace under the front bumper. She had broken her right wrist that way in the far distant past. I was never a good student when it came to anything mechanical. Moving parts confuse me, and anything that has more power than I have intimidates me. I like being in control. It's probably why I've always liked working with words: I control them, and not vice versa.

My senior high school yearbook indicates still another change. There were 88 students in our senior class at the new school, and only 12 of them were from the New Columbia High School contingent. The country mice met the city "hepcats," and they ate us up and spit us out. We had to wait until mid-year for officials to determine if we were actually entitled to membership in the National Honor Society (half of us were), but that was too late to be included in the Honor Society photo for the yearbook. Some of our boys who were farmers enrolled in FFA (Future Farmers of America). I can count those on one hand, minus my thumb. Four of the girls (me included) joined the Glee Club. My friend Dorothy joined the FHA (Future Homemakers of America) and did a good job of homemaking for the rest of her life. (She's the one who married the banker.) None of our students played an instrument, so we'd never had a band. (I played the piano, but that didn't count. There's no place for a piano in a marching band.) None of our boys had ever played football, so they weren't represented on the gridiron. Only one, Ernest Foss (a/k/a "Aaron Slick") signed up to play on the basketball team, although almost all the New Columbia boys had played all of the three previous years.

The MCHS Yearbook says that I was in Glee Club, so I guess I was. And my picture with other members of the Club confirms it, but I can't remember a thing about it. The gym class was awful. There had been no gym classes at New Columbia. Some of the girls had played basketball, but I had been too small to compete. So I was terrible at basketball and I hated exercise. Still do, in fact. I just didn't fit in.

While there were some compensations in Metropolis, such as more modern accommodations and the availability of showers after physical education classes, I despised the showers. They offered no privacy, and in comparison to the other girls, I felt skinny and flat-chested, especially during a year when "pointy" brassieres were in fashion – I felt hopelessly inadequate. I was genuinely surprised those bras didn't poke holes in the girls' sweaters; but such were the fashions of the time. It's fascinating how styles change. Today, it's common to see many girls and even women opting to go without any undergarments, including, I'm told, going without underpants. It's called "going camo." Why, I have no idea. I always thought the underpants *were* the camouflage. But I was recently informed that "camo" is actually short for "commando." I can live with that.

I'd taken a typing class at New Columbia, but I also took a shorthand and a bookkeeping class at Metropolis. The shorthand teacher, Mr. Highfill, was the husband of the woman who had taught Home Economics at New Columbia. (I can still make bound buttonholes if requested.) Shorthand is the only class in all of high school that I almost failed, simply because I would not practice. Everything had always come easy for me: read it, test on it, ace it, and move on. Shorthand required a bit more effort, sometimes called "practice." When Mom realized what was happening. she made me "practice" every single evening, reading lessons to me over and over until I could write quickly and accurately. She insisted because, she said, "You're going to need this someday. If you can type and take shorthand, you will always have a job." And she was so very right. Whether it was taking notes at a city council meeting, for a legal brief, or working as a typesetter in a newspaper office, those two skills were job-getters and keepers. I also took Latin for the first time, which was an eye-opener because I had not realized how much European languages were derived from Latin roots. (I also took two semesters of Latin in college, as my college transcript insists I did, though I do not remember attending those classes at all. My mind, by that time, was on other things.)

I enrolled in the Rhetoric Class because I liked to write, and I quickly discovered that the Rhetoric Class was comprised of students who enrolled simply because that was the class that always performed in the Senior Class Play. Elaine Munal taught the class and was also the Director of the play. I so looked forward to participating. I had, after all, practically "starred" in *Aaron Slick from Punkin Crick*. However, Ms. Munal (an old maid in her 40s who still lived with her parents and reeked of Taboo perfume, so THERE!) advised me that I could not be a part of the Play because I lived in the country and "I'm sure you would find it extremely difficult to attend all the rehearsals. They're held at night, you know." My assurance that my grandparents lived in town and that I could stay with them on rehearsal nights did nothing to persuade her. But I got an A in her darned class, and she apparently could do nothing about the fact that on the basis of my four-year grade point average (I finally aced shorthand, too), I won a Normal School Scholarship, which entitled me to four years at Southern Illinois University, tuition-free. I just wish I'd had the sense, and both the maturity and self-control, to stay for all four years. One of my favorite teachers, Dora Walbright (Senior English) wrote in my yearbook, "Wish we'd had you sooner." And I wish that too. I am reminded of one of the poems we studied in her class (from *Rhyme of the Ancient Mariner*, in case anyone needs to know):

> *Water, water everywhere*
> *And all the boards did shrink.*
> *Water, water everywhere,*
> *And not a drop to drink.*

The time in Metropolis (1949-1950) held a lot of other experiences. Some of my fondest memories of all those high school years had nothing to do with "school" at all but rather those in 4-H Club and (sometimes) church. I began attending 4-H club at about the same time I began high school, and since many of the other members were from the German settlements "below the hill," the boundaries and therefore the strictures of my life were widened for the first time to include the whole county. We met as a group, boys and girls together, once a month for at least four years of my life, ending only when I went away to college in the fall of 1950. My 4-H projects were of the homemaking variety: sewing and cooking. Although Mom was quite adept at both, she was so busy "doing" most of the time that she didn't have time for much "teaching." So I learned to bake, not really my favorite thing, and to sew, which has continued to be one of my very favorite occupations. I could follow a recipe if I paid close attention and didn't start daydreaming, but sewing was creative, and although I began my sewing lessons by following a pattern, I also learned quite early (from my mother's example) that the ability to take an old garment and turn it into something that appeared completely new was a kind of art form. I can't paint a picture to save my life, and I can't play the piano without sheet music in front of me, but I can create a picture of a garment in my head, make a pattern for it, and then make the picture a reality.

I should add (actually a confession of yet another addiction) that I've loved clothes all my life. I was still in grade school when I got a book of paper dolls. One of them wore a set of blue panties and a matching undershirt (she was obviously prepubescent) and I named her Dana Andrews (actually the same name of a then-popular *male* movie star, a coincidence which should not be misconstrued) and supplemented her very meager printed costumes with shoeboxes full of clothes designed by me from "fabric" cut out of old magazines and catalogs. Dana was, I now realize, my alter-ego. I carried the whole shebang with me long after I was married, and my daughters will probably remember that they were not allowed to play with Dana except under very close supervision. But Dana had been my best friend through a sometimes lonely and isolated childhood, and I was reluctant to abandon her to the untender ministrations of baby hands. I still "play paper dolls," but now it's with real clothes and shoes, and my daughters know that if I go on a shopping spree or start sewing, I'm probably dealing with some crisis, or at the very least feeling a bit out of sorts.

Our 4-H meetings always ended with fun things to do: singing, square-dancing, games and contests, and once a year there was Camp, usually held at Dixon Springs State Park, the only place around which had a real swimming pool, and thus where I took swimming lessons year after year and never EVER learned to swim. But there was also a jukebox in the little restaurant by the pool, and one year another girl taught me to jitterbug (that's "swing dancing" to younger ballroom types). I even remember the song that was popular that year, "Peg of My Heart," a nice and easy swing tune that was easy to dance to. I was hooked, and dancing has been one of my favorite things ever since. That attraction may have been part of what lured me away from classes during my sophomore year in college. But no matter how late I got in from a "night on the town," I would still get up for a ballroom dancing class that met two days a week at 8:00 in the morning. Dancing certainly lured me into my first marriage and one other long-term relationship.

Dixon Springs has been one of my favorite places since my earliest childhood. It is still an Illinois State Park and only five miles or so from "Rock," the little community where Pa was born and raised. I have a picture taken of me on my 2nd birthday, standing on a rock by the little creek that runs through the main park. I was dressed in a fluffy white dress, bathed in sunlight, and only needed wings and a halo to look like a little angel. (Any horns that may appear to be sprouting surreptitiously are quite obviously mere age spots on the photo paper.) Many of my birthdays were occasions for family picnics at Dixon Springs. Baptist Church camps were held there too, almost every year through high school, with services at one of the three churches up on the hill above the park.

The Park had mineral springs, heavy on the iron, and had once been a health spa where people came to "take the waters." There were a couple of long two-story buildings that had rooms that opened onto screened-in porches on the long sides, with cots along the porches. We slept on the porches (adults and chaperones slept in the rooms), and if it rained there were canvas shades on rollers that could be pulled down over the screens. I learned a lot about the "facts of life" from the older girls during gossip sessions on those long porches, but not all of it was accurate. I think that most of them were very nearly as innocent as I was. However, I was somewhat more advanced than simply looking up words that began with "f" in the big encyclopedia that rested on a pedestal in our grade school classroom. The day I bought one of those huge books for myself, I felt my personal library was at last complete! But of course, the Internet has made such books obsolete. I sold mine, along with many other books I still regret discarding, at a yard sale when I downsized and sold the house five years ago.

During my last year in high school and my last year in 4-H, the outfit I had made for my project won 1st place in the County, and along with a blue ribbon, I won an expense-paid train trip to Chicago with other kids from all over the state. I really should *not* have won because the garment (a three-piece outfit in Kelly green, with a cape lined in plaid satin) wasn't perfect. I remember distinctly that the placket, which ran down the front of the skirt from waist to hem, had to be pieced because I ran out of fabric. The judges must not have noticed or perhaps thought it was part of the design. I have since realized that I have a bent toward perfectionism, and that perfectionists, while sometimes "missing the mark," invariably expect others to hit it every time. In fact, I have also learned the actual meaning of the word usually translated as "sin." It is "falling short of the mark." I wish I had known that when I was 14.

We stayed at the Palmer House hotel, saw the sights, and sang part of the way home on the train. I distinctly remember that I conducted the singing. Dad met me at the Karnak train stop late that night (just a dark, lonely platform in the middle of a field), and it was only then that I learned my baby brother Kent had been born while I was gone. We still didn't have a telephone. It wasn't that we couldn't afford one; there were simply no telephone lines going as far out in the country as our house. The Round Knob lines stopped at the bottom of the Bluff in 1949.

Something also happened that year that marked me, at least in my own mind, as "different." The senior class was given an IQ test, and someone made the mistake of telling me that I had scored a 147 on the test and that the score put me in the "genius" range. It took me years to realize that the reason I scored so high was most probably because I read so much and consequently had an excellent vocabulary. But I know today that, without a doubt, I am not nearly as smart as I always thought I was. Still, I rode high on "147" for a long, *long* time.

Once more about bathrooms: I enjoyed the bathroom at the new house for the year before I left for college, so grateful that a scholarship had given me a reprieve from spending the rest of my life working as a waitress in some local restaurant until I found a husband. I "turned" 16 in July of 1950 and was far too young to get married. Also, no one had asked; I was barely old enough to date.

In fact, I almost missed my senior prom. The boy I was "seeing" (the Old Spice guy) told me his father wouldn't let him have the family car for the evening. His first romantic overture had been (you may recall) to playfully drop a frog down the front of my dress a year or so before. We had somehow progressed from there to "smooching" in the front seat of his father's pickup. Since neither of us had telephones and we lived in different counties (he'd gone to Vienna High School with the rest of the Johnson County contingent from our old school), I have no idea how we made arrangements for those rather innocent liaisons. I was left to find my own date for the prom. My first Sadie-Hawkins-style invitation to a boy who seemed a likely candidate was politely refused. He said he was "working the lights" for the dance. I still think he lied. But then, my motives may not have been romantic. He was, after all, the son of the editor of the local newspaper. Perhaps, subliminally, I already knew where I "belonged."

So I went with the son of family friends. Donnie was just my age but still a sophomore. He had to ask permission from his own girlfriend, who happened to be my "half-second cousin, once removed," that is, my Grandmother Korte's half-brother Jesse's youngest daughter. Since neither of us had a car or even a driver's license, my mother took us to the dance and brought us home. I wore the dress mother made me; it was pretty and pink, with a white eyelet yoke and puffed sleeves, a three-tiered skirt--each tier a little fuller than the last--all the way to the floor. It was also a heavy-weave pique that rubbed the sunburn I'd gotten that day, driving the side 'livery rake ahead of Dad's hay baler in the field behind my grandparents' house (then occupied by a hired hand). I would live there myself, with my husband and three small children, not quite ten years later. It's funny how you remember the small things, like the sunburn.

While I had learned to dance, Donnie hadn't, so we held each other loosely and walked around the dance floor a couple of times. If anyone spiked the punch, I wasn't offered any. So I did attend my senior prom, but I don't recall that anyone else from the old school did. Some of the couples that had been close while at New Columbia were separated by the Massac/Johnson county split, and time and distance made the separation permanent. Most of them just weren't the prom-going type. They were more the smooch-in-the-back-ofthe-bus type. But I figured this might be the only prom I'd ever have a chance to go to (it was), and I sure wasn't going to miss it.

"If God is a fly on the wall, Nanny, hand me a flyswatter."

Gaby Brimmer

"In the waning days ahead, I gotta look back down the road.

    I know that it's not too late.

All the stupid things I've said and people I've hurt in my time,

    I hope it's not my fate

To keep defeating my own self and repeating yesterday.

I can't keep defeating myself, I can't keep repeating

    the mistakes of my youth.

    - Song by the Eels (Jeffrey Scott Lyster/Mark O. Everett)

College – For What It Was (and Wasn't) Worth

I was the first person in my entire family (both sides) to attend college. If friends and relatives gave me a rousing sendoff, I don't remember. I do, however, distinctly recall a particular going-away gift for my 16th birthday, just before I left for Southern Illinois University in late August. Aunt Maxie (privately, I believe) slipped me a small package that contained a safety razor and extra blades. She had apparently learned that I was still, though without asking permission, using my father's. I seem to remember the oddest *little* things and overlook those that are really of momentous importance. I had a scholarship, and I was going to college. But what I most remember is that I had my own razor and would be able to attend without the embarrassment of hairy legs and dark fuzz under my arms.

In my first year at SIU I lived in Johnson Hall, the Baptist dormitory which was affiliated with the Baptist Foundation. Since I could type and take shorthand (thank you, Mom) and came well recommended both by a scholarship that paid all my tuition and the flattering comments of various members of New Hope Baptist Church, I quickly found a job as secretary to the president of the Baptist Foundation, (Dr.) George Johnson and he dictated his weekly sermons to me, which I then dutifully typed. I remember nothing from the sermons he preached first in the confines of the presidential office to an audience of one (me), nor do I recall ever attending a service where he read one of them. My salary, a mere 50 cents per hour, although meager, covered my room rent, which included three meals a day and incidentals. In essence, I was self-supporting.

In the dorm I shared a bathroom (shower, no tub) with three roommates. One was a junior and the daughter of my mother's best friend, and also the older sister of the girl I used to visit while riding bareback on my father's big roan mare. My old playmate was still in high school, though two years older than me. Her older sister was an ideal chaperone for an immature and incredibly naïve 16-year-old girl away from home for the first time. A second roommate was a 20-something girl from a small town in northern Illinois who was coming to college rather later than the rest of us, with the intention of completing the requirements to become a teacher. She seemed shy to the point of introversion, and I cannot recall anything about her other than the fact that she existed (perhaps her name was Dorothy?). She vaguely reminded me of my Grandmother Korte (who, you may recall, hid from visitors). She was engaged to a boy back home, or at least she said she was. The third of my roommates, Phyllis, was from East St. Louis, a tall, busty blonde with a Jewish last name (which I remember but won't disclose lest she be charged at this vast lapse of time for contributing to the delinquency of a minor). Phyllis wore a girdle, used Merle Norman cosmetics, and smoked Pall Mall cigarettes (in a cigarette holder!). Her St. Louis boyfriend was, she said, a bookie. On Christmas break, when my hometown chaperone left school to marry her boyfriend, Phyllis took me to John's Buffet for my very first beer. I felt, finally, but entirely too soon, "all grown up."

I had spent a good portion of that first semester learning some rather unpleasant facts of life. No matter what my high school IQ test said and what my scholarship implied about my intelligence and abilities, there were a lot of people in this school who were smarter than I was, and that *included* the students. Both students and teachers came from different ages, colors, nationalities, cultures, and religions. I was intrigued, but I was also intimidated. And I also discovered that my mother hadn't supplied me with such practical knowledge as getting myself up for school on time, doing my own laundry, cleaning a bathroom, even picking up my clothes from the floor where I had dropped them.

When my roommates noticed the growing pile of clothing on the floor at the back of my closet and suggested I should either hang things up or wash them, I experimented with the laundry equipment located conveniently at the end of our second-floor hallway and promptly discovered that if you washed a purple cotton pullover with your white undergarments (the only color I owned), you would wear lavender panties and bras for the rest of the year. Perhaps the rest of your life. How could I *not* have known that before? Today, as I load perhaps the 15,000th load of laundry in my lifetime, I bless hot water, automatic washers, and dryers, but especially colorfast clothing.

(Note: 52 weeks x 72 years x 4 loads = 14,976!)

The dorm boasted a dining room and an excellent cook whose meals were heavy on calories and could be supplemented with an ample supply of free snacks. I believe she had formerly cooked for the rooming house of the college football team. I discovered the allure of heavily buttered raisin toast and gained 10 pounds while I lived there. I only recently discovered that I have become both gluten- and lactose-intolerant and cannot have even a donut without internal repercussions. I find myself sometimes craving raisin toast with lots of butter. And razzberry-filled donuts. I cannot even speak of butter pecan ice cream without feeling tears forming in the corner of my eyes.

But I also found the university library and spent hours in the stacks exploring books I had only imagined in my dreams. It was a feast never forgotten, a feast of words that has been called "The Great Conversation." I wanted desperately to learn to speak it. Even now, so many years later, the yearning lingers and hopefully remains as long as I have eyes to see and ears to hear. Of course I wrote a poem about that:

First Fruit

I wander in a forest of the past
And, hungered, choose the fruit from off a tree
Some other traveler has left for me.
A word, a verse, some message left behind
bears fruit and leaves its seed within my mind.

Somewhere, within the mind of living man,
a knowledge grows and wisdom quickens, then
and only then can truth be given birth,
kick free, scream to the world, "Hear me!
I have the secret. Let me live."

And this one, too, is added, grafted on,
To some old withered specimen until
A whole new species has been born.
Perhaps, someday, urged forward by that need,
I too will till the soil and plant a seed.

Yet I barely remember actual classes, except that English was "business as usual," history was interesting, Latin a challenge, and I came very close to flunking chemistry. Even that particular classroom was akin to entering a foreign land where people spoke a strange language, and the smell of chemicals turned your stomach. The formulas for elements seemed meaningless gibberish, and who cared, anyway? When in the world was I going to need to know the chemical formula for water? (Ah, but I *do* still remember it. Just in case! Because, you know, in 2022 we were in the midst of a drought nearly as serious as the one the year I was born. And while there's still enough oxygen to breathe, they're planning to use all the hydrogen to run the cars.) I'm joking. Or maybe not?

I have a yearbook from my first year at SIU, but strangely, not from the second. I have often wondered why I've held onto it. My picture doesn't appear on any of its pages, and I didn't engage in any extracurricular activities nor receive any awards. The second semester marked a significant shift to an entirely different college experience: keg parties, countless evenings spent at John's Buffet, and exciting excursions to Murphysboro and Culp, where nightclubs, music, dancing, and once-forbidden pleasures awaited. When I was discovered sneaking into the dormitory through a window over the basement coal bin late one night in the last week of my freshman year, I was not asked (or possibly not allowed) to return to either my job at the Baptist Foundation or residency at Johnson Hall.

I do remember that my "exit interviews" included a committee of fundamentalism-inspired dorm mates who held an informal meeting where I was confronted with a litany of my suspected indiscretions and obvious spiritual inadequacies and warned that I might very well have committed or was at least skirting dangerously close to the commission of the "unpardonable sin." The contents of the 62 books of The Great Books of the Western World, which occupy the bottom shelf of the bookcase behind my favorite chair, are sometimes referred to as "The Great Conversation. My college exit interview was a "Great Conversation" of another type. Today it would be called an intervention.

However, none of my dorm mates seemed sufficiently knowledgeable about what *exactly* constituted an "unpardonable sin" to frighten me into discontinuing my new excursions into the fascinating alternate reality I had discovered, so I departed Johnson Hall without ever confessing anything more heinous than disobeying curfew. I'm sure my parents had to be told of my failure to thrive in the Baptist milieu, but I had learned long before that there were some things one never talked about, even though *every*body knew.

That summer, between my first and second year of college, I went home for the holiday and dated a young man who lived on the second farm over from the Korte family farm "below the hill." One of my friends—the one I had visited on horseback years before and also the sister of my former college roommate--was dating his brother, so we double-dated. I don't think we were ever actually alone. However, the young man in question was in the Air Force, stationed at Scott Air Force Base near St. Louis, and ended up at some point being hospitalized for something–I don't think I ever knew what--at Walter Reed Hospital in Washington, D.C. We wrote back and forth for a while, but by the time he came home, at about the same time he was discharged from the Army, I was involved elsewhere. Years later, when Jay and I went to live on our family farm, he and his wife lived just down the road on *his* family's farm and visited at least once with their own children. I suspect once was enough for his wife, and I know it was more than enough for my husband.

When I went back to school for the first term of my sophomore year, I was able to get a job as secretary to Margaret Pulliam, the widow of a former president of the university and the present housing director. She was probably never informed about my curfew violations. It hardly mattered since I was now living off-campus at the "Spider Web," which was actually just the second floor of a large family home a couple of blocks from campus where eight of us shared three bedrooms and a bathroom (which lacked the privacy to actually take a real bath unless everyone but me was gone for the weekend). There was no housemother; the family seemed to ignore our presence upstairs if we didn't make too much noise. And there was no curfew! If anyone had wanted to make a movie of "Girls Gone Wild" (though very quietly), that might have been a good place to shoot the film.

I don't recall whether I also worked for Mrs. Pulliam the second term and lost that job for reasons that now escape me or if I simply found myself unemployed at the end of the spring term when my services were no longer required. The Spider Web was not open in the summer months, probably because the owners' children were home from school and most of my roommates went home for the summer, so I moved to "Club 16," a converted garage that housed 16 girls and had, on the first floor, a huge living room and a tiny kitchen--apartment sized stove and very small refrigerator--which shared space with shower and toilet facilities (not a particularly hygienic arrangement). All 16 of us slept "military-style" in single beds in the long second-floor bedroom. It was very much like a barracks or, I sometimes thought, an orphanage. I don't recall there being any closets or laundry facilities, and I cannot remember when or where we ate our meals. But then, I wasn't there very often, except to sleep, and again, there was no housemother keeping track of anyone's comings and goings.

I got a job for the summer off-campus, working as a waitress and occasional grill cook at a chili parlor downtown (Bob's Grill, I think it was called), where I became much involved with a local crowd of people my own age, most of them still in high school. (I was *still* only 17.) There was a married man who told me he was single and reversed his first and last names so I wouldn't learn the truth. Someone eventually told me that he had a baby son and was a truck driver for Kroger (or perhaps it was Jewel Tea). But he was cute, with black curly hair, reminding me of one of the bit players in the old Western movies we used to see at the Royal Theatre in Metropolis on Saturday nights. He drove a green Studebaker convertible and had a motorcycle on which we took long rides in the moonlight. On my 18th birthday, he took me for my first plane ride in a Piper Cub (he was also a pilot) in which we "buzzed" my home in Massac County and then went to a pornographic movie at the drive-in. The movie proved to be the film they show GIs to acquaint them with the dangers of sexually transmitted diseases! It was far from titillating, but I finally learned about what everyone had always warned me of and also discovered what was hiding behind the flies and zippers of the "big boys."

I could go into great and confessional detail about my "lost year," but it would be pointless. I did *not* commit the unpardonable sin, as far as I know, but I had discovered booze and boys at the same time, and the combination came to a foreseeable conclusion when the school authorities advised that I could not continue enrolling for classes which I apparently had no intention of attending. Shortly after my 18th birthday, I went home in complete disgrace, having spent most of my second year in college learning to drink, dance, and skip classes for what seemed much more fun. I had managed to get up two mornings a week (most of the time) for that 8:00 class in social dance. But my college transcript shows indisputably that almost all the rest of my classes were marked "Incomplete." I did not "fail," I simply did not show up for real life. Which is practically the same thing as failing, but by this time I had become pretty good at rationalizing the unacceptable.

Mom came up and got me, with my (not quite) three-year-old brother in tow, for a thoroughly shaming meeting with a psychiatrist I had been required by the university to consult. I still remember his name, "Dr. Noble," and that he asked me one question I have also never forgotten: "Lona, why do you drink?" The only answer I could think of then was, "I want to find out how my father feels when he drinks." (I've since learned and can produce better and more honest answers to similar questions.)

I went home, having lost my reputation, my scholarship, and a few other personal possessions that could never be replaced, including but not limited to my brand-new gray spring coat, which had disappeared somewhere the evening of the coal chute escapade. Years later, one of my friends from high school told me, "I was so glad when you got kicked out of school. All my life you'd been held up as an example: 'Why can't you be like Lona Rae?' And for the first time, they were scared to death I *would* be!" I still contend that I was not "kicked" out; I was "yanked" out. Or perhaps just quietly went "slip-sliding" away. (I finally got my degree 50 years later from Murray State University, and I am still contemplating the possibility of finishing my Master's. I think I lack 12 hours.)

The first couple of weeks home were of excruciating penance, comprised chiefly of stoic silence on the part of my mother (she was afraid to ask questions) and a meeting with my father, who had to get more than somewhat drunk in order to talk to me about it. I have often believed, however, that it was my first one-on-one meeting with another alcoholic. He, too, wanted to know why I drank, but I don't think he confided the reasons why he did. I don't know whether he ever went to an actual AA meeting. But I did, 25 years later.

The only bright spot in the whole situation was that I was never forced to make a public confession some Sunday morning to the entire congregation at the New Hope Baptist Church. In less than a month, I went to work for F. H. McGraw and Company, the prime contractor for the construction of what would become the Martin Marietta plant in Kevil, Kentucky (just outside Paducah), and I was soon caught up in what has since become known as the "Atomic Years" of western Kentucky.

My job was secretary to the McGraw paymaster (thanks again, Mom), and sometime that winter one of the other girls in the office, Rosetta Crabb, introduced me to her brother John David (also known as J. D. or Jay). We dated through early spring and summer, danced a lot to the music of Jack Staulcup's Orchestra at Spur Inn, a nightclub down near Cairo, and married on July 9, 1953. He was nice-looking and a very good dancer, we were both from Baptist families. His parents seemed to like me, and he said he loved me. We learned that we were sexually compatible (he'd been married twice before and was very experienced), and he also said he could not have children. I am not sure which of those many factors were the deciding ones.

My children have sometimes believed that I did not want to have children, and that's not true. Like everything else in my life, I wanted to be the one who either chose to do something or chose *not* to do it. At that point in my life, having just failed myself, my family, and everyone else in some very important ways, I think I was afraid that having and raising a child might result in another failure. Jay's declaration that he could not have children might have seemed like a perfect solution to what could well have been a temporary problem. I've made many decisions in my life based on little more than that.

"Success in marriage does not come from finding the right mate but from **being** the right mate."

Anonymous

John D. and Lona Rae (Korte) Crabb

July 9, 1953

Of Love and Marriage

When I think of my marriage now, through the perhaps faulty filter of the intervening 70 years of living (yes, it has been exactly *that* long!), I am always reminded of a sentence that comes directly from the AA's *Twelve Steps and Twelve Traditions*, which I eventually discovered: "Not one of us had learned to be a true partner to another human being, just one of a family, a worker among workers; we had either tried to rise to the top or hide underneath." That sentence aptly describes my first marriage. It also describes what I have attempted to learn to do during a good portion of those next 70 years.

Those first efforts were fragile indeed, but they are a part of my spiritual story, my "stumbling toward God," which had started some time ago in the New Hope Baptist Church where I learned lessons that were engraved on my heart, perhaps too deeply to ever be entirely erased. Emmet Fox, whose meditations on Biblical passages I have read every morning for many years, says: "You form certain beliefs, for one reason or another—and then you have to live with them. When you were growing up, well-meaning people told you many negative things by way of warning, thereby implanting fears and these fears are with you today, consciously or subconsciously. Other problems you brought here with you when you were born. . . Thank God it is not necessary as a rule to delve into the recesses of the subconscious and dredge for these things. . . we learn that by beating the symptoms spiritually (not, of course, covering up symptoms, but beating them) the fear or false suggestion that caused the symptom disappears too, and the patient is free." I believe Fox speaks truth. In many ways we were alike, if only superficially. We were both the oldest children in our families and doted on by our maternal grandparents. We each had two living siblings (and both had one sibling who had died as a baby). We had both been raised in the Baptist church. We both liked to sing. Jay had been a member of a local quartet, I had sung solos at church for years, and some of our happiest moments would be singing as a family with our three children. We both liked to dance, and we were, or at least I was in the very beginning, very much in love (or perhaps in love with the idea of being in love?).

But the *meaning* of "love" to me, even after all these years, is still a mystery. Like "God" (and we are told by those who claim to know that "God *is* love") love seems too large, too deep, to ever be fully understood or measured or limited by words. And it means different things to different people. One spiritual teacher, Scott Peck, defines love as "The will to extend one's self for the purpose of nurturing one's own or another's spiritual growth." And, further, that "love is an act of will, both an intention and an action." Well, my intentions were good, but my actions? Maybe not so much. (Imagine a wry-faced emoji right about here.)

Both Jay and I fell into marriage with good intentions and very little experience in how to take the actions that would allow us to either continue "loving" or learn to *be* loving. Both of Jay's previous marriages, one while he was in service and a second to a girl who almost immediately left for college, had ended when his wives were unfaithful. And the marriages had been so brief that he had never had the responsibility of a full-time wife. When we started dating, he was 26 years old, still living with his parents and driving the family car on dates. And I was 18 years old, still living at home and driving our family car as well. (Just a year before, as I have already disclosed, I had dropped out of college after two chaotic years and come home in disgrace.) His most valued possession was probably a shotgun. He used it as security for a $100 loan from a friend of his who owned the local Dairy Bar, and that $100 was the down payment on our first car. I believe it was a two-door Ford. I owned a bedroom set (which certainly came in handy), and we bought a couch and end tables (on the installment plan) from Pansing's

Furniture Store in Metropolis, from which I had previously purchased the bedroom set. The bedroom set was already paid for.

Mother made my wedding dress, a lovely cream-colored satin buttoned all the way down the back with hand-made loops. I could not get either in or out of it without assistance. She also made our wedding cake, perhaps the first of the two or three hundred others she made over the ensuing years. Jay's younger (and only) brother Joe was his best man; my younger (and only) sister Kay was my maid of honor. We were married at the New Hope Baptist Church, but only after the Board of Deacons finally agreed to allow us to be married there, in spite of Jay's two previous marriages and subsequent divorces.

Friends and family brought gifts and best wishes to the wedding reception, which was held on the front lawn at my parents' house on a beautiful and pleasantly warm July night, twelve days before my 19th birthday. We were gifted with pots and pans, linens, sets of fragile but lovely crystal goblets and sherbets (gifts from Mom's sisters, which I do not recall ever actually using), and most of the necessities of housekeeping. I think the only wedding gifts I still have after nearly 70 years are a few pieces of Fostoria, two Corningware bowls (green with white flowers and matching covers--one cover has a chip), and an ironing board.

We were chivareed on our wedding night, a quaint custom in Southern Illinois in those years, which involved tying old shoes and tin cans to the newly married couple's car and then following them to their new home (surreptitiously, and after a bit of time had elapsed and there were no longer any lights on in the house) and then serenading them with loud noises (honking car horns, beating on a galvanized washtub and firing off several volleys from a shotgun were not unusual). Jay was spared another local wedding night custom, which involved kidnapping the groom and taking him to some remote location where he would be abandoned and left to find his own way back to his bride.

Our marriage lasted nearly 20 years before it broke apart under the weight of the expectations and demands we each placed upon it, and then crumbled into a thousand pieces. The sets of crystal had already disintegrated when a faulty shelf in a kitchen cabinet broke and fell, raining shards of glass all over the kitchen floor. The ironing board was made of steel and has held up remarkably well. Since drip-dry clothing has made ironing optional, I seldom use it, and it will probably last until I die since I seem incapable of either giving or throwing it away.

We might have made a success of our marriage. We certainly tried for nearly 20 years. But several things happened within weeks of the ceremony. The first was unexpected and very unwelcome news delivered by my new husband one Saturday afternoon. He had just returned to our little rented bungalow high on a hill overlooking the Ohio River in Golconda from a short visit with his parents. (They lived on the other side of Golconda, less than ten minutes away.) He had to tell me, he said, that a letter had been delivered to his parents' home, addressed to him, from a woman who had seen our wedding picture in the local paper and wanted him to know that he was the father of her child.

I never saw the letter, and to this day I cannot remember her name. I have an amazing ability to block out unwelcome or unpleasant memories. Furthermore, I can't remember if I ever knew what Jay did with the news or if he took any action at all. Even after 70 years, I cannot be certain if I was "in denial," too afraid it might be true, and even more afraid of the consequences if it were. Or perhaps I was just incredibly naïve. Nor do I know if there was really a child or if she was simply looking for someone to be the father of a male child she had borne. But he did admit that there was a possibility it could be true, notwithstanding the fact that he had told me he could not father a child. That, at least, I would soon learn was quite simply NOT true. We were married on July 9, and our first child was born the following May 9, on Mother's Day. (That's ten months to the day, if anyone's counting.)

It was not an easy pregnancy. At first there had been morning sickness, so constant that I had to quit my job in October, long before I had intended. It had also become apparent that my new husband seemed to be unnaturally suspicious of any time I spent away from him. A trip to the grocery store, a visit to my parents, even a drive to the post office could become the subject of a lengthy inquiry into exactly where I had been, who I had seen, who had seen me, the content of any conversations that might have taken place. I told myself it was a sign of love.

When I showed physical signs that I might lose the baby, I was sent to bed for most of the last four months of the pregnancy. I spent what seemed that entire time in the front bedroom of my in-laws' home in Golconda, scared to death, with nightmares at night and a husband who worked during the weekdays and seemed (at least to my frightened and needy 19-year-old self) to spend all his spare time on weekends fishing and hunting with his father and brother. I came to know my mother-in-law very well during that time and to recognize what a wonderful and caring woman she was. And during the time we spent together, I also learned a great deal about the Crabb family and her own, about her children's younger years, their trials and tribulations, and her own triumphs and losses as the years passed. She seemed to have an endless capacity for love. So did my mother.

The pregnancy was probably difficult because of what was later described as a congenital disability (discovered only when I went into labor) which made one side of my pelvis nearly immobile. My body apparently knew more about that than the doctor had, so there was a difficult and lengthy labor. But I had also begun the marriage with hopes and dreams that were proving illusory, dissolving too soon into reality amid a maelstrom of distrust, as well as physical and, quite soon, financial problems. And of course I've written a poem about all that:

Of Disbelief

Is there a lie that I, love-blind, could not believe,

Pledges or praise a self-struck fool would not believe?

The very young, and very old, are drunk with dreams:

Youth of the future, age the past, all make-believe.

Man is adrift, alone, sinking in hostile seas,

With no rescue in sight in which he can believe.

Faith is blind as a wheelhouse mule, bereft of dignity,

Forever yoked to promises one did believe.

Doubt has a subtle strength faith lacks: uncertainty.

For doubt whispers to me what I should not believe.

When we married, we had rented a little one-almost-two-bedroom house in Golconda, high on a hill overlooking the Ohio River, with a single tiny bathroom and a screened-in porch off the kitchen. My grandparents visited for dinner one Saturday, and Pa told Danty (I learned later) that he was afraid I'd starve Jay to death. My 4-H culinary talents had extended barely beyond snickerdoodles and Swedish tea rings, and if my recollections are accurate, even the thought of food made me want to throw up as soon as my pregnancy began. Financial worries didn't help matters.

By the time our daughter Rebecca Rae was born (named after my mother-in-law's long-deceased sister but always called "Becky") Jay's job with M. W. Kellogg had ended when the job at Kevil was completed. He soon found a job in Tuscola, Illinois, again with Kellogg, and found a very tiny camper, barely 12' long (which may have included the tongue) and maybe 6' wide. We bought it on payments. The plan was to move on with Kellogg when the Tuscola job was finished. We sold all our furniture to Ethel's parents (Jay's brother Joe's in-laws), packed up all our wedding gifts, and got ready to move north. (All this before our first anniversary and the birth of our first child.)

.Jay commuted back and forth to his new job, and I stayed with my parents waiting for birthing pains to begin. Both my doctor and the hospital where he practiced were in Rosiclare, north of Golconda. Fortunately, Jay was home for the weekend when Becky was born. We were playing canasta with Joe and Ethel (their little girl Karen peeking at our cards) at their home near Dixon Springs when the labor pains started. We timed the pains while Ethel cooked breakfast (pork brains and scrambled eggs) and then headed for the hospital in Rosiclare. It was Mother's Day 1954l.

It was a long and difficult labor, and I was told later that I had "nearly died" during the delivery. But I already knew that something strange had happened, for at one point I heard a "buzzing" noise, and then felt my *self* rising up and out of my body, floating up to the ceiling and looking down at the doctor and nurses and what was surely *me*. But then I saw a bright light up ahead somewhere and began moving toward it and into the light where there seemed to be people waiting for me, and on ahead such promise of peace and joy that I did not want to "come back." Until, as I remember it, a voice said, "Lona, wake up. You're killing your baby." And I woke up. Or did I come back?

Although I did not forget, have never forgotten, where I had almost been, or at least seem to have been, I didn't talk about it either. Not to anyone. Not for a long, long time. I have since learned that most people who have life-after-death, or near-death experiences are also usually close-mouthed, perhaps because we are uncertain how we will be understood. The philosopher Wittgenstein wrote extensively about our inability to express the inexpressible. I've read Wittgenstein, and I am barely able to understand *him*.

After Becky and I left the hospital in Rosiclare, I stayed with my parents for two weeks. Then, I joined Jay in Tuscola, where, during that long, long summer, the three of us lived in a tiny camper. Within the first week I "came down" with mumps contracted from my preschool brother during the postpartum interlude I had spent with Mom learning how to care for an infant. For two or three days I ran a very high fever and crawled out of bed just long enough to feed Becky and change her diaper. She was a good baby and didn't seem to mind my rather inept mothering. But I was terrified.

I don't believe I had ever even held a baby before my own was born. There was no tub, no shower, no air-conditioning in the little trailer, and it was a l-o-n-g (I know I've already said that, but it bears repeating) and also very hot summer. I bathed my daughter in the tiny kitchen sink, and when dark sweat "beads" appeared in the crease of her chubby neck, I was terrified that if I bent her head back far enough to scrub them away I would break her neck. However, Mother Nature proved a far wiser mother than I, and both Becky and I survived.

The Tuscola job ended in late July, but Jay did not have enough seniority to go with the company to Portsmouth where the company was building another facility. The trailer disappeared behind us (truth: we left it in Tuscola and it was repossessed), and our little family moved back home and into the old house where I was raised. Once again, I had only the clawfoot tub, a relic of my childhood, draining under the house. There was no "commode" and only a cold water tap in the kitchen. History does repeat itself if you're not very *very* careful.

The outhouse just off the path between the house and barn was still functional, although now modernized with actual "toilet paper" instead of newspaper and/or the pages of the Sears Roebuck catalog I remembered from childhood. The old Warm Morning coal stove still stood stoically in the living room, ready to supply heat for all four rooms. But it was summer, so we didn't need the stove, although it had remained behind when the previous tenants left and consequently took up more than its share of the living room. It seemed almost to loom there, as though threatening to remain through fall and haunt our winter. We did have one of those box fans that sat inside a raised window. However, since there were no screens, the fan seemed to be good for little more than drawing flies into the house, but not all the way through it. I became adept at "shooing" them out of the house using two dishtowels, one in each hand. I would flap the towels up and down, ushering small swarms of flies up to and out of the front door.

The mulberry tree in the back yard still stained the ground with maroon-and-black berries that summer, as it had for all my life, and the row of catalpa trees on the west side of the house still shaded the front porch with their wide leaves on hot afternoons and would, I was sure, shed their long green-bean shaped pods in fall. I took my laundry to my parents' house to wash and line dry.

The furniture we had bought when we were married was, of course, long gone, so my husband and I slept in my parents' castoff double bed in the front bedroom. It was as though nothing had changed except the names on the marriage certificate pinned to the wall above the bed. I painted the framework of an old wicker set black, and wrapped wedding-gift towels around its worn seat cushions. I built a bookcase out of planks (painted black) and brick (left natural) and filled it with some of my wedding presents: the crystal goblets and Fostoria pieces. I don't remember if I owned any books then, but I had a bookcase. (If you build it, they *will* come!)

Somewhere we found, or perhaps were given, an old-fashioned kitchen cabinet for staples, the kind that included a built-in flour sifter. I cooked (when I cooked) on a two-burner coal-oil stove. We did have a refrigerator, bought on time payments from a furniture store in Metropolis, and for my birthday that year Pa and Danty bought me a portable electric sewing machine at English Sewing Center in Metropolis. It was a White, and they paid $8.00 for it; Mom's present was a buttonhole attachment. I used those two pieces of equipment to make nearly everything the kids and I wore for the next nine years until we moved to Lemont in about 1963, when I bought a Pfaff (also from English). It recently occurred to me that I may still owe Mr. English's son—or grandson--a payment or two on the Pfaff. The family is still in the sewing machine business, though now in Paducah. One of my daughters still has the old Pfaff. I have a newer one, fully paid for but seldom used nowadays.

Sometime that early fall I discovered (actually, Jay discovered) a lump in my left breast, which was surgically removed, dissected, and proclaimed benign to everyone's relief. But something, perhaps a bit of damaged nerve tissue, still lingers and comes back to haunt me now and then. Old wounds will do that, you know.

The only work Jay had that fall was painting my parents' house. His father, who had also worked on the Martin-Marietta job, had migrated back to Chicago after the work ended (they'd lived there years before) and so we, too, soon moved to Chicago where there was work. We were going to need it. By early spring I was already pregnant with our second child, born 18 months after the first.

Jay found a job at Chicago Towel as a maintenance engineer and a tiny two-room furnished apartment on the second floor of an old brownstone where we lived for the first couple of months. We shared a bathroom with two other families, and I'm quite certain I did not take an actual bath the entire time. I may have closed my eyes when I had to use the commode, which no one ever cleaned. It wasn't laziness on my part; I was just scared to touch it, and there were no latex gloves around in those days. The steam heat from the ancient radiators was inadequate and unreliable, and I remember turning on the gas oven when the chill became unbearable, so we must have lived there through at least the early part of winter.

But before Christmas we found a furnished studio apartment in a building at 25th and Stewart, next door to a Catholic school, which was next door to a Catholic church. (My minister back home would have considered it nearly the same as living next door to a "house of ill-repute.") We packed up our clothes and our few household goods–the crystal sherbets and water glasses had never come out of their boxes this time--and moved quickly and gratefully. Our building was only five blocks or so from the apartment building Jay's parents had owned during the war years, and near where Jay's sister Rosetta had once gone to school.

There was also a huge library just a few blocks away and a Sears store on nearby Halsted Street. It was at the Sears store that I bought my first vacuum cleaner and, of course, on the installment plan. We had our own bathroom, a table with four chairs, a rather dingy-looking couch, and a Murphy bed (which, for the uninitiated, pulls down from the wall every night and is neatly concealed during the day). There was a minuscule kitchen with an 18-inch wide gas stove and a cube-sized counter-high refrigerator. Across from the wall with the appliances there was a long shelf on hinges that could be raised or lowered for extra workspace. As my pregnancy advanced it stayed up most of the time. The doctor I consulted to deliver our second child found that I was anemic and prescribed a glass of Mogen David wine before dinner every evening. I have no idea if the doctor was Jewish (considering the brand of wine he prescribed), but I certainly enjoyed the wine. Johnny seems not to have been mentally affected by being introduced to alcohol *in utero*, except perhaps developing a taste for it.

When Johnny (John David Jr., named for his father) was born in November of 1955 (he was 67 yesterday as I write this), we moved to yet another furnished apartment in the same building which had a real bedroom. However, it was quite crowded, with a chest of drawers, a double bed, and two cribs. Nevertheless, it was convenient because when a child woke up in the night, you didn't have to go far to pick him or her up.

Work was scarce in southern Illinois after the construction work ended in western Kentucky, so within a very short time Jay's brother Joe and wife Ethel, together with their 5-year-old daughter Karen, also moved north and found an apartment in our building, although on another floor. I met a distant relative in the basement laundry room one morning when we discovered we shared great-aunts in

Southern Illinois. Wilma was the granddaughter of one of Pa's many sisters, Sarah Jennings Murrah, who lived just outside Vienna (a 20-minute drive from my family) on the Murrah family farm. Wilma had an 8-year-old daughter and a husband who worked nights. The first months in Chicago had been lonely, but having the company of the other two women, Ethel and Wilma, who quickly became friends, was a very real comfort. They were both mothers who had successfully steered a child through infancy, the "terrible twos" and onward. On Becky's second birthday they surprised her with a new dress (red, with ruffles) they'd completed together.

Jay was working the second shift as a maintenance engineer for F. W. Means and Company, a commercial laundry. Joe was a baggage handler for American Airlines, working split shifts. Jay's parents lived in a small English basement apartment on Lowe Avenue. Garvon was a building engineer for one of the banks downtown and Elsie worked in the silver department at Mandel's Department Store in the loop. I took care of two children, which was a full-time job with both in diapers, and made only three trips outside the house every week, one of which was to that very large library where I allotted myself as many books as I could carry stacked from my extended hands to my chin. The second was the family outing to buy groceries. If it was payday and we were "flush," we had dinner out once a month at the China Clipper. Sometimes we'd have drinks before dinner. Jay always had a beer. My whiskey sours came with little paper umbrellas and a maraschino cherry. The third trip was to Jay's parents, every Sunday. Sometimes Jay would come home at midnight with fried shrimp and donut holes from a takeout place near his work. Best shrimp I ever ate. (And it may have been the *first* shrimp I ever ate.)

Since every doctor in Chicago seemed to be Catholic and unwilling to prescribe birth control devices, and Jay was averse to more prosaic over-the-counter equipment, inevitably I became pregnant with our third child, born 15 months after the second. At Thanksgiving dinner at Aunt Maxie's, who lived with her husband and two boys in Riverdale, I broke the news to my family, and when Danty began to launch into a tirade against my husband, I remember saying, "Danty, I was there too."

I am not sure if she was intimidated by my "talking back" (her calls for her nitroglycerin tablets seemed defensive rather than panicked) or if she was frightened that I might continue to explain where I had been and what I had been doing while I was there. She had, it is true, been the one to explain the "facts of life" to me: things like menstruation and "where babies come from." But she had successfully avoided having to explain exactly how they got *to* where they came *from*. (I had finally obtained that information at Dixon Springs 4-H and church camps years before. I remember that one girl had been so disturbed by the unbelievable insinuation that her own parents had done and might even now be doing "it" that she threw what was described in those days as a "conniption fit" and had to be taken home.)

Late in 1956, Dad bought half of the family farm in the Big Bay bottoms. His brother bought the other half, and his sister took her one-third share in cash. My father needed help on the farm, and it was becoming obvious that we needed to get out of the city, so when Dad invited Jay and me to come home, we went. I was already pregnant again and not always feeling well, so Becky had stayed with Jay's parents, Garvon and Elsie, quite a lot on weekends that winter. She slept with her grandparents (there wasn't a "spare room" in their tiny apartment). Garvon loved to tell of the night when he and Becky were talking and talking and wouldn't go to sleep. Elsie finally told them they had to be quiet, to which Becky responded, "Hush, Elsie." (I've always thought she had a coach for those lines.) They were devastated when we left Chicago with the children. I've written a poem about our migration, of course:

Country

We fled Chicago late one night
as though escaping from a glittering cage
some careless trainer had left unlocked,
all we owned packed in the trunk
of an old Chevrolet,
a rented trailer tacked onto its bumper
like an ungainly caboose,
babies asleep on folded quilts stacked tight
on the back seat, the youngest caught
inside me, not yet free,
as people are sometimes trapped
in places where the sky is pale and bare
at night, bleached by neon –
nothing to tell time by, or show the way home.

We'd reached the prairies south of Kankakee
when our little girl woke up surrounded by
a million lights shining as though
a midnight sun had leaked through holes
punched by a carpenter's sharp awl in the night sky.

And she whispered, "Mommy, what's that?"

And I whispered back:

"Stars."

Our third child, Mary Elizabeth, named for her great-grandmother Mary Elizabeth "Molly" Kent Martin Sexton, and also the little girl my in-laws had lost to scarlet fever, was born back in southern Illinois in March of 1957 at Massac Memorial Hospital. Regrettably, I don't have any pictures of Mary Beth's first days because money was tight, and every penny went toward necessities. Even if I had film for our Brownie camera, I wouldn't have had the money to develop it.

Jay wasn't present for the birth this time; he was still working in Chicago until spring planting began on the farm. Mom had been ill with the flu for two days before Mary Beth was born, and someone had to stay with the children, so I had labor pains one whole night before Mom felt well enough to get out of bed. It was Dad who took me to the hospital, saw me inside, and then left to go back home to help Mom with Johnny and Becky, two very active toddlers. Becky was not yet three and Johnny was only 15 months old. After a brief postpartum stay with my parents, we brought our family home to the big old two-story farmhouse on the Korte family farm that my grandfather Charlie Korte built in 1913, just before my father's younger brother Ernest was born.

We'd had no furniture of our own in the apartment in Chicago, except for two cribs and two highchairs (Johnny's survived and is now in his possession), and a little red leather rocking chair Becky's paternal grandparents bought her for her first birthday. (I don't remember what happened to it.) We furnished the house with castoffs. My parents' old bedroom furniture was brought up out of their basement, where it had been stored when we returned it to them before our move to Chicago. There were also bits and pieces they had bought at estate auctions in preparation for our arrival: a table and chairs from the 1940s and a Kroehler hideabed sofa that I must have reupholstered or slip-covered four times over the next few years. It weighed a ton, but Jay and I moved it five times at least. We had the cribs we had brought with us and an antique youth bed Dad or Mom found somewhere, probably at an auction. (Becky would not be three years old until May.) At some point Mom bought a new spinet piano, and the old Jennings family upright was moved down the New Columbia Bluff and into our bedroom. (I gave music lessons on it to four local kids one year and bought a playset for our yard with my earnings.)

The Korte Family Homeplace, built in 1913

When we moved to the farm in April 1957, we had no tub, no shower, no hot water, and only one tap for running water in the kitchen. For two years, I heated water for baths and laundry in a copper wash boiler (the big old-fashioned kind, oblong, 18" deep, 30" long, and 12" wide, with handles on the short sides) on top of a small wood/coal burning stove in the kitchen. Baths were administered in a round galvanized tub near the stove on the kitchen floor. I also had a Maytag wringer washer on the back porch (brought inside during the winter) and a single square tub on legs for rinse water. During that first winter, Jay built a folding rack so I could dry diapers inside. He also strung lines in one of the two upstairs bedrooms, the same room where Mom and Dad had spent their "honeymoon" three years after I was born. But I hung the heavier things on the outside lines to freeze-dry in cold weather.

We planted our (at least *my*) first garden that spring, out back of the house where Grandma Korte had always planted hers. It was a nice, level place, and Dad plowed and disced the ground with the tractor. But when it came time to lay out the rows, I cajoled Jay into pulling a "one-horse plow" I found in the machine shed. It took some persuading, but he finally consented to be the "horse" if I would promise to never *ever* tell anyone. I kept that promise until after he died. I actually thought it was rather sweet that he was willing to do it.

The old house had not been occupied in a while and it was infested with mice. A cat solved that problem, although it took a while, and was obviously a big job for a small cat because, on more than one occasion, I found partially digested remains of kitty's lunch on the stairs going up to the second floor. One early summer morning, after sweet corn was "in," I had left the remnants of supper on the table, too tired to clear leftovers and wash dishes. It was so warm that we had also left the side door open onto the screened-in side porch overnight. The concrete floor of the porch had a rather long and deep crack running down the middle of it. And there, that summer morning, alongside the crack, was a large ear of our leftover sweet corn. No mouse could possibly have climbed up on the table, carried the ear of corn to the front porch, and left it behind when the corn proved too big to force down into the hole and on to wherever the culprit had intended to take it. We had either been visited by a very large rat or by a rather small possum or raccoon. The crack had to be filled in, of course, but until it was, we kept the front door closed at night.

That first fall, my sister Kay was married to Donald Rottmann. Mother made Kay's wedding dress and, for my dress, she cut down my own wedding dress and made a russet-colored lace overdress for the autumn wedding. She made the wedding cake, too. She was getting really good at wedding cakes. I was the matron of honor for my sister, as she had been the maid of honor for me just four years before. And one of Don's brothers was Don's best man. Kay and Don have had three children. Mark and his wife Debbie presently live in Pennsylvania with their two sons, although they have traveled widely; Lisa and her husband Jeff Bremer (both teachers) live on a farm in Massac County and have three children: Caroline, Laura (both married) and John, who just graduated from Murray State. Darian and his wife Heather have three children: Elizabeth (recently married), Natalie (in college), and Gabe (high school). Jeff and Darian are both ordained ministers, although both have other professions as well.

For the first two years on the farm, once more I had only an outhouse and a chamber pot on the (thankfully screened-in) back porch – with two small children still to be potty trained. I had three children in three years, no phone, only one car, and a very limited income (dispensed at the discretion of my father, a practicing alcoholic). I learned to garden, can food, milk cows, churn butter, raise chickens (including the process of killing, dressing, and freezing them, sometimes ten at a time), and bake my own bread. I once tried to make cottage cheese, hanging a cloth bag of clabbered milk on the clothesline. The experiment was not successful. I cut up my old dresses to make clothes for the children. I carried in buckets of coal for the stove, lining them up on the front porch so I wouldn't have to leave the children alone. I'm not sure why that job fell to me, but I had three children to keep warm and Jay always seemed to be working somewhere else when I needed more. If Dad didn't pay us promptly on the first of the month, I was the one who asked for the money. If I sound resentful, I was. But also afraid. So very often afraid.

I believe now that I had postpartum depression for a year or so after Mary was born, but since I had never heard of postpartum depression, I ignored the nightmares and the daymares too. I sometimes thought there was someone else, or something else, with me in the house when I was alone with the children, as though someone or something was just behind me and, if I turned quickly enough, I would see who or what it was. I was alone a lot, with no one to talk to except the children, so sometimes I talked to myself. Sometimes I answered myself back. I had many long conversations "in my head," most of them arguments with whoever or whatever had seemingly trapped me in a place and a circumstance that I had certainly never imagined for myself.

But it was the fear that brought me to a new place. And one night I told Jay about it, in one of those quiet and intimate in-the-dark moments when we can speak aloud to someone else those things we have told only to ourselves. And he said, "Well, I don't know what you can do except pray about it." And after he had gone to sleep and I still lay awake, staring up into the darkness, I closed my eyes and (in my head, of course, because I didn't want to wake him) said simply but fervently: "God, if you're there, please make this fear go away." And there, in the darkness, I saw a somehow-familiar light above me, and felt a slow, sure peace somewhere inside me, and when I woke the next morning I was no longer afraid.

In the winter of 1958, when Mary was not yet two years old, the chimney in the living room overheated from the coal-burning fire in our Warm Morning stove. The chimney had been built 40 years before for wood-burning stoves, and the studs against which the chimney was braced in the attic caught fire. I was banking the stove for the night when I "just happened" to look up and see a little lick of flame right where the wall behind the stove met the ceiling. (That is synchronicity!) I woke Jay and we formed a two-man (actually a one-man, one-woman) bucket brigade of water, which I carried up the stairs to where Jay was stationed on the inside of the attic and could carry the buckets across to the flue and pour the water on the flames. (We did have an electric pump on the well by then and running water in the kitchen.)

Although Jay and I were able to extinguish the fire before it spread and brought burning debris crashing down over the heads of our sleeping children, there was considerable smoke and water damage to the walls and ceilings. The good news: my father discovered that he had insurance to cover the damage, and we used the money that summer to install a septic tank (a very large metal oil or gasoline drum, as I recall). We built a bathroom by boxing off one corner of the large bedroom where the three children slept and also bought a hot water heater and a semi-automatic washing machine, both of which we installed in the kitchen. I was 25 years old, with a husband and three children, and I finally had my very own indoor plumbing!

Years later, I wrote a story about that fire: "What Happened to Mary." (It was actually about Margaret, my father's first wife, who had died either in that house or at her grandmother's in Metropolis. It's a mostly true story, ghost--or whatever--and all.) I suspect the story will one day appear in a collection of my short stories, if I ever find the time and inclination (and don't die before I have accomplished everything on my personal bucket list).

If my account of those years sounds terribly grim on reflection, I do remember that we were not always unhappy. And our lives were no different than those of many of the young couples we knew. We occasionally had friends over to play cards, but there was little or no money for movies or other entertainment. We acquired our first television set, although our access to stations and reception was limited to Paducah, Harrisburg, and occasionally Carbondale. Our recreation and other activities were things we seemed to do separately. I read (books were free--I've had a library card at every town I've ever lived in for longer than a week), played the piano, sewed, did laundry, decorated the house, and took care of the children.

Everybody I knew went to church, twice on Sundays and again for Wednesday night prayer meetings, and so did we. If Jay wasn't in the fields, he went fishing and hunting with his dad and brothers. I learned to dress and cook squirrel and rabbit, ducks and quail. I was performing the duties of "Adam's rib," as the religion of my childhood had preached to me, the role my mother had taught me by her example, a role that Jay expected from his own parental model. Was it fair? I was beginning to wonder. I had certainly never planned to be the wife of a farmer. Nor, I believe, had Jay planned to be a farmer. I blame no one. Once more fate had proved to be a matter of time and circumstances. And perhaps I was beginning to grow up.

There were problems that would prove longstanding. I had realized almost from the beginning that Jay's suspicions seemed to be aroused whenever I was out of sight. They were perhaps leftover feelings from the infidelities that had destroyed his two previous marriages, and he seemed riven with distrust that sometimes boiled over into accusations. My life was circumscribed by that jealousy and by the rather isolated nature of our lives, first in that apartment in Chicago where I saw no one except members of his family, and then in the old two-story farmhouse (my father's ancestral home) in the middle of 400+ acres of corn and soybeans with children for company and an occasional spectral (or more likely a postpartum-evoked) visit from the specter of my father's first wife, who Jay insisted he had seen dancing in the flames of our attic fire. (Yes, he Really *Really* said that!)

Our social life, what there was of it, revolved around the New Hope Baptist Church. We both taught Sunday School, though I had long since begun to wonder if I was rendering only lip service to the lessons, and we sometimes gathered around the piano to sing (always a pleasure). For a while we (the children, Jay and I) sang as a group, going to the regular Sunday afternoon gatherings that met in those days at different churches to provide an occasion for groups and individuals who liked to perform. Jay had a big Wollensack tape recorder which he had bought during his quartet-singing days, and for a long time I held on to brittle tapes of the songs our little family sang, but they've disappeared somewhere along the way.

And I had started to write. I still had the old portable Royal typewriter my Korte grandparents had given me as a high school graduation present, and at first I was just practicing my typing, thinking (hoping) that perhaps when the children were a little older I might get a secretarial job, because it was almost desperately evident that I was going to have to find some way to supplement our income. The $125 a month my father paid Jay was barely enough to cover a car payment, groceries (bought once a month in Metropolis), electricity and, in winter, coal for our Warm Morning heater.

But then I began wondering if perhaps I might actually be able to write something that could be published in a magazine. I don't know where the idea came from. It was more like an urgent demand from somewhere deep inside that could not be denied. We had partially furnished the two upstairs bedrooms, in one of which I had first learned one of our family's many secrets when, as a little girl, I discovered an abandoned scarf in the drawer of a dresser, and my grandmother confided in a near-whisper that it had belonged to my father's first wife. (Have you ever noticed that people often leave belongings behind to mark their territory or leave a breadcrumb trail for their return? Or a dog deposits urine on his spot to warn others away?)

In one of the bedrooms, where we had put an iron bed frame and a tufted cotton mattress on naked springs (for occasional overnight visits from Jay's parents), I also installed a table and chair in front of the east-facing window and, when I had a free moment, often late at night when the children were in bed and Jay was asleep, I would go upstairs and write. When I read Virginia Woolf's essay, "A Room of Her Own," I empathized with all my heart. That bare room with the iron bedstead and table at the window was my first. I vowed it would not be my last.

In the beginning, I wrote mainly poetry. My first published writing was a poem accepted by the Baptist magazine, *Home Life*.

Love

>Love is a mother cradling a child,
>An infant's fingers on a father's face,

A friend with helpful hand outstretched,
A kiss that touches gently, to embrace.

Love is a whisper in the stillness of the night,
A sigh that moves with sweetness to the lips;
Love is the flame that warms the wintry night,
To dry the tears that wet a wrinkled face.

Love is the steady sunshine on the summer grass,
Deep and dependent as the roots of growing corn,
As changeless as the elements of earth,
A solace for the ever-searching soul.

Love is a quiet that becalms the heart,
The ecstasy in every song of praise.
And love is hope with head bowed low,
Ever the humble supplicant.

Love is the offering of humankind,
For tenderness we feel, but do not see.
Love is a moment in the majesty of time,
That moves to leave its imprint on eternity.

I still like that poem. It speaks to me of what I must have felt and believed then and what I believe now. I did not know when I wrote it that there would come a time when I would doubt absolutely everything.

Family Reunion: June 7, 1958. Back row, our children's great-grandparents: John Thomas Crabb, "Molly" Sexton, Mary Quint Korte, LeMaude (Stokes) and Miles Marion Jennings; middle row, Garvon and Elsie Crabb, Raymond and Evelyn Korte; Front Row, John David Crabb Sr. and Lona Rae Korte Crabb; with our children Rebecca Rae, John David Jr. and Mary Elizabeth. *(Note that my Grandmother Jennings was wearing a hat. It was Sunday.)*

In May of 1961, Johnny was burned badly in a trash fire. He had been "helping" Jay work on an engine and had gotten oil on his flannel shirt. Either Jay or I had set the household trash on fire across the lane from the house, and while Jay was busy with something and I was in the house, the three children decided it would be fun to get sticks and "poke" the fire. Johnny apparently flipped a spark or an ember onto his shirt, and the oily shirt caught fire. He came running into the house, screaming, his shirt in flames, his two sisters close behind him.

I remember grabbing an afghan off the back of a chair by the front door and wrapping it around him to smother the flames, and then we were all in the car heading for the hospital ten miles away. I held him and sang to him all the way there, a nonsense song I had made up for the children about a little squirrel "with no tail to keep him warm," and so had to go to all the other animals begging to borrow their tails. If I stopped for even a moment, Johnny would beg, "Squirrel, mommy. Squirrel again." And I would sing. It may have been then that I learned how to be strong enough to stifle my own tears. I have often thought that if I ever allowed myself to really cry again, I might not be able to stop, and so I cannot remember the last time I cried—at least not that sobbing, gut-wrenching, heart-breaking cry of absolute powerlessness.

There were long days and longer nights in Massac Memorial Hospital as Johnny underwent extensive medical treatment for burns to his chest and arms, and I stayed with him around the clock. We caught a beetle climbing the window screen in the hospital room, and I tied a string around its leg so Johnny could walk it up and down. When I think of that beetle now, I also remember the "scarab" beetle that Carl Jung found at his window and showed to a patient. It enabled her to "break through" her denial and recover. Johnny's beetle helped the two of us through the days and the even longer nights.

I was able to control my feelings--I'm sure I was still in shock--until one night, long after midnight, the hospital was suddenly disturbed by the cries of children in the hallway. There had been an accident on Deadman's Curve outside Metropolis and both parents had been badly injured. Their children, asleep in the back seat (as mine had been so often on long trips to Chicago and back) were unhurt but terrified. I could hear them crying in the hallway, begging for their parents, who were both going into surgery. And suddenly I started shaking so hard, and for so long, I thought I might never stop. But I didn't cry. We were sharing the room with a little girl, in for an overnight stay for a medical procedure, and her father, who was also keeping watch over *his* child. We talked, and after a while the shaking calmed and I was able to curl up on the foot of Johnny's bed and go to sleep. I think of Blanche, in the play *Streetcar Named Desire*, who says, "I have often had to depend on the kindness of strangers."

Such deep burns cause nausea, and it was several days before Johnny could finally eat a hamburger and malt from "Charlie's Drive-in" that he had always considered a special treat. But when he was finally released there were still bandage changes, a procedure that had to be done every week, and so without anesthetic to avoid causing damage to his lungs. I held him as he cried (and often more than cried). Jay said he couldn't bear to watch.

We had no health insurance. Few farm folks did in those days. I have no remembrance of how we paid the hospital and doctor bills, or if we even did. As the weeks passed with little improvement, I had to visit our family doctor due to an extreme bout of pleurisy. Dr. Hard, not the emergency room doctor who seemed unable to think of alternate solutions, suggested that Johnny would recover faster if he had skin grafts. He offered to arrange for Johnny to go to Shriner's Hospital in St. Louis, where he would undergo a series of grafts. This treatment allowed him to begin to actually heal. He started first grade that fall with bandages still on his chest. He was six years old that November.

I went to work. For a year or so I had been writing a column for *The Metropolis News*, a kind of exchange I had arranged with the editor, Sam Smith. I would write columns for the paper and he would give me paper and stamps for the articles I was submitting to magazines (and sometimes having those articles accepted and published). When Sam's full-time assistant, Chuck Baccus, decided to quit and go to college that summer, Sam offered me the job. Mom offered to take care of Becky and Johnny when they weren't in school, and Mary Beth until she was old enough to go. I took the job, and I've never regretted it. It changed my life.

The *News* was the only newspaper in Massac County, published once weekly on Wednesday and usually containing three sections. My new job offered me what amounted to an apprenticeship in many aspects of the newspaper business. There was an actual printing press in the pressroom; two linotype operators set most of the type for the news columns, classifieds, and legal advertisements. There were two other men who handset the more complicated ads (grocery and furniture stores, for instance) and ran the press on publication day. In addition to editorial duties, I also operated a teletype machine, which produced a tape that could then be fed into the linotype machines. (I was paid far less per hour than the male linotype operators. Of course I was.)

There were three other women in the front office: a bookkeeper and two others who answered the phone and handled proofreading, intake of classifieds, subscriptions, and circulation. One of those women was "Miss Hattie" Mann, who had been with the paper for years and was kind of an *ex officio* boss of the front office. During the 1940s and World War II, when many jobs usually held by men were handed over to women, Miss Hattie had been the temporary editor of the News. And she reminded the rest of us frequently of just how it could and should be done and *would* be done if she was still the boss.

As time passed, I began to handle some of the actual newswriting in addition to just obituaries, weddings, and social events. I did a series on all of the schools in the County, and when the new baby of a local woman was kidnapped by a woman from Chicago, I was allowed to handle the news story from start to finish. (The baby was rescued.) During the first few weeks at work, a train wreck between Reevesville and Round Knob sent me on assignment with Chuck, the young man I was replacing. He was teaching me to use the paper's big Roloflex camera. He was, as I recall, 19 or 20, barely out of high school, and I was a married woman with three children, but the aftermath of that assignment made me realize just how possessive (at least in my view) Jay could be.

It was a hot summer day, and when we finished collecting facts and photographs at the site of the accident, Chuck and I stopped at my home to get some ice water. Our house happened to be close by the scene of the accident and on the way back to work. It never occurred to me that anyone would consider that brief visit scandalous. It seemed just common courtesy to a young co-worker, and we were both thirsty. (There were no McDonalds handy in those days.) But when I mentioned it to Jay that evening as I was telling him about my exciting day on the job, he was furious. "What do you think you're doing, running around all over the country with some guy and even bringing him to *my* house?" was the general tenor of the accusations. It was the first time the questions about "Where have you been and what have you been doing?" had taken an angry turn. It would not be the last.

Sometime in 1963 we both realized that the arrangement (you could not call it a "partnership") between my father and my husband was not working out for a number of reasons, including bad crops for three years in a row and my father's drinking, which was his response to a worrisome situation. It was not an easy parting. My uncle Ernest and his son Bill came and helped us move to Metropolis. We left the piano, the Warm Morning heater, and all the appliances at the farm, but we took the Kroehler couch and the rest of the furniture. It all fit into the back of Uncle Ernest's farm truck (with the stock racks up, as I recall). I was still working, Jay's objections to my job duties notwithstanding, and from that fall of 1963 until I retired in the fall of 2004, just before Mom died, I don't believe I ever stopped working except to exchange one job for another. And often I worked two jobs to keep ends meeting, or at least not stretching too far apart.

We had rented a small two-bedroom brick house on Butler Street in Metropolis, just two blocks up from the Ohio River. The house had been built for a brother and sister who had shared it for many years. Neither of them had ever married. She was apparently of a somewhat "nervous disposition," and I believe she may have been in a mental hospital during the time we lived there; the brother had died. But they had left behind an old upright piano and a bookcase full of Nero Wolfe and Earl Stanley Gardner mysteries. I played the piano and read all the books. There was a nice range and refrigerator and an automatic washer and dryer in the laundry room. I enjoyed those too.

The nervous lady's brother had built their house on the lot next door to a tall old Victorian occupied by a middle-aged spinster lady. Both he and the spinster lady had worked at the Metropolis Post Office, and she still lived in the house next door. There was tall and concealing shrubbery between the two houses and, I believe, a fence. There *must* have been a fence, because there was most certainly a gate. I will leave to the imagination any speculations about the reasons for the shrubs, the fence, or the gate.

I wrote a book based on my suspicions of that situation, "Something Still Alive." A little bit of it was true. It was never published. I never even submitted it anywhere for publication. It's still in my box of might-have-beens that never were. I'm not sure if it was life or lack of courage that got in my way. I've sometimes remembered my hesitancy this way:

Specters

My dreams are memories of my tomorrows,

Collections of half-wishes that come true,

Peopled with delusions, capitations,

The disembodied that elude, pursue.

With smoky elfin hands they pull me closer,

With chilly whispered breaths, they warn.

Dead to the present, their decay surrounds me

Until, repelled, I finally live them on.

(P.S. I'm not dead yet.)

The original owners of the house on Butler Street had apparently required a rather unusual bathroom arrangement: it was located between two equal-sized bedrooms, and each bedroom had its own door to the bathroom. I am quite sure that the brother and sister had some means of announcing who was currently occupying the bathroom since neither of the doors had locks. (Perhaps the mentally challenged sister had a habit of locking herself inside?) Our three children (then aged 5, 6, and 7—Mary Beth was in kindergarten) took advantage of the situation. I was then writing a column, "At Our House," for the *News*, and I quote from my February 6, 1964 column titled, "A Word or Two about Sex."

> *"A mother first discovers togetherness when her children are old enough to walk, and mother tries to take a bath in complete privacy--in a bathroom that has two doors and no locks. Remember that song about the 'train that goes through the middle of the house?' Well, at our house the "train" goes through the bathroom.*
>
> *"She also learns other things about bathrooms. One bathtub plus three children plus bedtime equals a riot! Children refute the law of gravity. Put three children, a bathtub and water together and what do you get? A flood . . . and most of it on the ceiling. I don't know how they get water on the ceiling. I have never been able to explain it to my husband, and the children only offer vague excuses. But the water is still on the ceiling. I'm not sure what this has to do with sex, except that I'm hoping the children will grow up soon, at least enough to make one-at-a-time baths essential."*

In the interests of full disclosure, I admit that my three children were, of course, taking separate baths by this time, but I recalled earlier years when that had NOT been the case, and I can only plead "poetic license" for my somewhat exaggerated description of events. I do distinctly recall my three children plus one young stranger entering that bathroom when I was reclining (sans clothing) in the tub and being asked if they could all have cookies. The answer, of course, was "yes." I was very *very* sorry that it was not a bubble bath. (NOTE: For Christmas a few years ago, I gave Becky, Mary, and Johnny copies of all the "At Our House" articles I wrote for the *News*, almost all of which are my reflections on their childhoods.)

I also wrote a weekly column, "Looking at the Files," for which I researched old issues of the *Metropolis News* and its earliest predecessor, *The Promulgator*, which triggered a fascination for the early history of the Ohio Valley. Fort Massac State Park is the site of one of the earliest forts in southern Illinois, its blockhouse overlooking the Ohio. It was one of George Rogers Clark's stopping places when he went on his long expedition to explore the West. That research would eventually result in an historical novel, *Down River*, which I began on my old portable typewriter on a rickety and somewhat rusty metal typing table tucked in beside the washer and dryer in the laundry room of the little brick house. The surface of the washer and dryer made an excellent desk for research materials and manuscript pages. I wrote when the children slept. Jay was gone most of the time.

When we left the farm, he had worked a while for an old friend of his who owned a service station just out of town where Route 45 intersected with what is now I-24. He even sold cemetery lots in Massac Memorial Gardens. But he eventually got a job as a guard at Joliet prison in northern Illinois and was gone for six months, coming home on occasional weekends while I worked and took care of house and kids. That winter, all three came down with measles at the same time. Alone, even with help from the neighbor across the street when I had to work, I often felt overwhelmed, but the experience did result in future empathy for single mothers who find themselves in the same position.

Jay had tried but simply could not find a job locally, and we needed to be together as a family, so we got ready to move, once again, "up north." He made a deposit and took measurements on a rental house about five miles north of Joliet and the prison. The owners were an Oriental couple with an export-import business somewhere in the area. I spent most of one month making new slipcovers for the Kroehler hideabed, and new curtains for windows

I had never seen. (Jay's measurements were accurate. The curtains fit.)

In August of 1963, just after my 29th birthday, we rented a small moving van and moved from the two-door bathroom house in Metropolis to a two-bathroom, three-bedroom house in a suburb (actually just a relatively new housing development in the middle of a cornfield) north of Joliet, Illinois. The address was 152 Delmar Drive, though the post office was actually Lemont. We did have running water, but we were short on cash as always, so it was two weeks before I drew my first paycheck and we were able to turn on the gas and the electricity, just in time for school to start. Until then it was cereal for breakfast, sandwiches for dinner (by candlelight), and cold showers or none at all. Johnny did have his own room, finally. But I'm not sure he liked it.

The year we lived there, the kids struggled with a new school and I struggled with babysitters, commutes, and the demands of learning a new community, a new publication, and a new way of life. Jay struggled with near paranoia at the prison. On his first day on the job, he learned that one of the prisoners was a man (Dr. Goodpasture) convicted of murder and serving life. Jay had sat on the jury at the man's trial while we were living on the farm. Although they moved the man to another state facility, Jay continued to look over his shoulder. Life as a prison guard is one of constant vigilance, and it does not end inside the prison walls, instead fostering suspicion of everyone on the "outside," even children and spouses. At least, that has been my personal experience.

We had a next-door neighbor who also had children and an enormous boxer dog, and she baby-sat for the kids after school. That winter there was a snowstorm that brought drifts as high as three feet against the back of the house. I do not miss northern Illinois winters, and this would not be the last one.

There are times in our lives when the choices we make result in both opportunities and consequences we could never have anticipated. When I sent out resumes exploring job opportunities in northern Illinois, I was offered two jobs: one as a typesetter for the *Joliet Herald News*, a large daily paper that served the area. It was a job for which I was technically qualified and would have been steady but also boring. The other job was editor of the *Downers Grove Graphic*, a suburban weekly that was an affiliate of the *Herald*. There I would be given creative freedom, a staff that included a photographer and a society editor, and an office in Downers Grove where I would also create re-makes of the *Graphic* which, with the addition of supplemental news, would be used as separate editions for both Naperville and Westmont. The choice between the back shop and the front desk offered a temptation I simply could not resist, so naturally I became the editor of the *Graphic*. I suspect (correction: I KNOW) that being the boss for the first time and the completely new lifestyle that went along with it went directly to my head. I felt a bit like a bird let out of its cage. I did a lot of wing-flapping even when I wasn't sure where I was going or if I would even know how to land.

The year we lived in Lemont, the car I was driving was rear-ended and I sustained a relatively minor "whiplash." Thankfully, the children weren't injured, and I'd almost forgotten about it until Johnny recently recalled it to mind. And "whiplash" seems an appropriate analogy for what happened to my marriage as a result of my decision. Fate: time and circumstances.

"When women take on a career, they don't discard their female values, but add them onto the traditional values of work achievement and career success. As they struggle to fulfill the demands of both roles, women can't understand why men don't share this dual value system."

-- *Seasons of the Spirit*

"Follow your bliss."   -- Joseph Campbell

The Newspaper Years

I remember my first week at the Graphic so distinctly, even though I took the job without a personal interview, or if there was one, I don't remember it. I had requested that I be sent back issues for the last year so I could familiarize myself with current stories, the layout of the publication, and its editorial stance. It was quite different from what I was accustomed to at the *Metropolis News*. (**Note**: That paper later became the *Metropolis Planet* when an enterprising promoter decided the town should capitalize on the association of the town's name with Superman. Once in a while I dream that I have returned to Metropolis; I am much younger in the dream, and am offered a job as editor of the *Planet*. I have no idea why I have that dream. I should know by now that you can't go home again. But for the years I was there, I was *the* Lois Lane of the *Metropolis News*!)

There was also competition in Downers Grove. A local daily newspaper that had been in business far longer had first chance at all the local stories on weddings, obituaries, and the breaking news: accidents, fires, police reports. The Graphic proposed to fill the gap with a number of columns devoted to personal interest subjects: golf, bridge, travel, etc. Some were syndicated, but many were locally written. There were no columns that described children's birthday parties or family events that ended "and a good time was had by all," as there had been at the *News*.

It was also a tabloid-sized paper; that is, rather than a full-size newssheet as the *Chicago Tribune* or the *Wall Street Journal* (and the *Metropolis News*) were, the *Graphic*'s front page was just one-fourth that size, perhaps better described as "magazine-sized," and it was more magazine than newspaper. Every week its front page was a full-size photograph, sometimes seasonal and sometimes related to a feature story, and its inside content was heavy on features rather than actual news.

The *Graphic* office was in a storefront located on a side street in Downers Grove, just one long room with desks lined along one wall, the editor's desk first, then the society editor's, then the photographer's, and two desks for the advertising staff behind that. And there was no printing press in the "back room" as there had been in Metropolis. There was, in fact, no back room at all unless you counted the restrooms, because this was a "cold-type" operation. All the news was written (typed) in the *Graphic* office, that copy was sent to a central office for typesetting and proofreading, and once a week the editor (yes, now *me*) went to the central location where the individual columns of type were waxed and affixed to layout sheets and then printed by offset press. I had absolutely no experience with the process, but I was "baptized by fire" the first week, and I recall telling someone a long time later that it was like having sex for the first time: I was scared to death when I started, but then I fell in love. It was also, I think now, a bit like playing paper-dolls with photographs and words instead of dolls and clothes.

I soon realized I had a natural aptitude for feature writing. The stories I had written for *Home Life* magazine when I first began to write had been word glimpses of family life. The first of those accepted for publication was probably "How We Have Peace in Harmony," which described our family's enjoyment in gathering around the piano for a group singalong. Features for the *Graphic* were just expansions of that genre, human interest stories primarily, but also in-depth stories about subjects of current interest.

One of those stories, for instance, was about hypnosis. The *Graphic* was carrying an advertisement by a local practitioner of hypnosis, who emphasized its medical usefulness for suppression of pain and cessation of smoking. It piqued my interest, and after a little investigation I submitted myself as a subject for a first-hand account, with photographs (and my new photographer as a witness) of what it was like to be hypnotized, pricked with pins, and experience no pain at all. As a sidebar (accompanying story) we also visited a local dentist who described having a patient undergo dental surgery without anesthetics but with the assistance of the hypnotist. When she began to hemorrhage, the hypnotist was able to help her stop the bleeding with his suggestions. Fascinating stuff.

But one incident that first week presaged a gradual change in my life which boded ill for both my marriage and my entire life. That Friday night the photographer, who was a tall and very good-looking man (once in a while he, too, appears in my dreams), and both the society editor and ad director suggested that we all meet for drinks in the bar of the local Howard Johnson's. Naturally, I accepted. It seemed rude to refuse, and I could not think of any reason why I should. I went with the group; the society editor was also a woman about my age who also had children and a husband at home baby-sitting, so I felt well-chaperoned. I ordered a whiskey sour, which seemed suitably sophisticated and not at all dangerously wicked. I may have had two. Neither had either maraschino cherries or little parasols. And it was certainly a bit more sophisticated than Mogen David wine.

I was late getting home, and Jay wanted to know why. I was honest and told him that I had gone for a drink after work with my new staff. I don't remember suffering any twinges of conscience. After all, when he had first gone north alone to work at the prison, he had spent many evenings out drinking with the guys, even going to strip clubs on occasion, all excursions which he seemed to find totally innocent. But my explanation met with an angry objection, the exact words of which now seem engraved on my brain: "No wife of mine is going to drink in bars." I believe I agreed my conduct was inappropriate. Or I hope I did. But I also recall my own (inner) retort: "Like hell she won't." But I didn't say that right out loud.

And so began another of what I have come to call the "reinventions of myself." The first was when I married and quite unexpectedly became a mother, and then the mother of three within three years. I had lived in furnished apartments in Chicago and fled back to the shelter and safety of family, church, and rural community, with their accompanying boundaries, values, and expectations. When I began work at the *Metropolis News*, the boundaries had begun to stretch just a bit, and I had gotten on-the-job training in what could and did become a career. I had gained confidence in my writing skills and learned something about working with others. But now the country girl had come to the city, and the wife and mother was becoming a woman who actually had a career and at least a degree of independence. There was also the fact that I was earning a good salary, we finally had health insurance, and I was contributing an almost equal share of the family income.

Life would never be quite the same. Not the least of the perks was the fact that there is considerable prestige in being the editor of a newspaper in any town, but especially in a small town. And I was a woman. Miss Hattie would have been so proud!

The lifestyles of most of the families of my generation and the culture in which I was raised assumed that a *good man* went to work, worked hard all day, earned a paycheck, and brought it home. Evenings and weekends were the man's reward, except perhaps for yardwork and household repairs. There his responsibility ended. A *good woman* had 24-hour responsibility for the house, the yard, managing the finances, managing a social life, childcare, cooking, shopping, and pleasing her husband in all ways. Also, when a man came home from work he expected to be waited on. I am virtually certain that Jay never changed a diaper, never washed a dish, never cooked a meal. But when there wasn't enough money for the necessities, and I took a job, I soon learned that I would still have to maintain all my "housewifely" duties. (Accent on *all*, please.) I had spent the past ten years determined to be a *good woman*, even if it killed me. But past rewards were beginning to look more like "inadequate compensation."

Looking back, I can see that the transformation from girl to woman began when my children were born, and I had to grow up in order to take care of them. I'd learned to put my needs aside in order to respond to theirs. And then, even before Johnny was burned in the trash fire, it had become imperative that I find a job to supplement Jay's income from the farm. It was then I made the first tentative steps into the world outside home and family.

Still, marriages have responsibilities, and the pattern of a marriage is at least partially formed from the way those responsibilities are divided. As I assumed more of those duties customarily performed by the man of the house, Jay did not assume any share of mine (and somewhat less of his). I had simply added bread-winning to bread-making. At least, that's how it seemed to me. (I may have been viewing the changing pattern of rocks through the wrong end of a kaleidoscope, but it was *my* kaleidoscope and *my* rocks.)

If Jay remained a bachelor both at heart and in practice in some respects, so did a lot of men in those days. Some still do. He hunted and fished when we lived in the country, continued in the city, and also added nights out bowling and days off playing golf. My entertainment was an occasional dinner out and perhaps, on very rare occasions, an evening of dancing. But it wasn't the life I thought I had bargained for, and I resented it. I learned to keep my mouth shut about what I didn't like because there was nothing I could do to change it. But gradually I found myself married to a man I didn't respect, a man I didn't trust, and a man I could not depend on either financially or emotionally. The only thing I could depend on was that he desired me physically, and that seemed to be the cement that bound the marriage together. So, of course, that was the last thing to go.

My new job was demanding, but it was also exciting and challenging on many different levels. Almost within the first month, I received an invitation to attend a press conference at the offices of U. S. Sen. John Erlenborn, whose headquarters were in Chicago at the Marina Towers, those twin circular structures that would look suspiciously like grain silos if they didn't have those little patios sticking out around them all the way to the top. I had butterflies in my stomach when I drove down the expressway into the city alone, located the Towers and the appropriate underground parking garage. (Remember, please, this was at least two decades before the days of cell phones and three or more decades before GPS.) I took the elevator up to Erlenborn's office and, pad in hand, attended my first-ever press conference with a political dignitary. It would not be my last. I had walked--well, actually I had driven--through my fear and arrived exactly where I was certain I was always meant to be.

My new job also allowed me to explore the creative world of the feature story and to combine the stories with photographs (conveniently provided by the handsome photographer). Within a year or so, the stories caught the attention of the management at the *DuPage County Times*, whose publisher offered me a job as editor. The *Times* was a 100,000 circulation weekly, usually containing 48 pages, which covered nine suburbs west of Chicago (including Wheaton, Glen Ellyn, West Chicago, Carol Stream, and Winfield). It was a subsidiary of the *Chicago Law Bulletin*, and financially its sole reason for existence was to provide a venue for DuPage County legal advertising, which was quite lucrative. With the recent dissolution of so many small-town newspapers, I sometimes wonder where legal advertisements are being printed these days.

At about the same time I was offered the job and accepted, Jay resigned from the prison and went back to the job he had left when we moved to Southern Illinois just before Mary was born: maintenance engineer at F. W. Means and Company/Chicago Towel. It had been difficult to combine our children's school attendance with both Jay's and my commutes to work, and the job at the *Times* was both an increase in convenience and a real step up in salary and opportunity for me.

The *Times* was headquartered in Wheaton, the county seat of DuPage, the largest county in Illinois. We moved to a two-story, three-bedroom Cape Cod house at 1408 Manchester Road, which had two bathrooms, one upstairs and one downstairs. I never grew fond of that house, mainly because the laundry was located in the basement. Jay and I managed to move the recently acquired washer and dryer down the basement stairs by ourselves. The kids slept in the two upstairs bedrooms, and it seemed as though they were living on another planet. We found, or were found by, a cat that insisted on urinating on the bed in the master bedroom. (Was that some kind of omen? Perhaps so. But we did get rid of the cat.) Once I fell down the stairs between the first and second floors, thankfully not the whole way. No bones were broken. Laundry had to be carried up and down the basement stairs and then to the upstairs bedrooms where the kids slept. They confessed, years later, that they once tied up the babysitter while we lived in that house. And I only recently learned that they also "pranked" her by putting a container of water on top of a door minutes before she walked through. (The babysitter quit. I don't remember being told the reason, either by the babysitter or the children.)

Jay went back to Technical School to get his Chicago engineering license. Nobody wanted to mow the lawn. The car was repossessed once; I can't remember if we were short of money or if I had simply forgotten to send in the car payment. I went to our doctor for tension headaches, and he sent me to a psychiatrist in the city, a visit prompting endless questioning from Jay, who wanted to know exactly what I had told the psychiatrist. I may have lied; I'd learned to lie rather than argue. I started a novel, "The Secret Self," to tell the truth at least to myself, the things I couldn't seem to tell the psychiatrist and was totally incapable of even hinting at to my husband. My life seemed divided between working dinners at Pheasant Run with the current candidate for President (Barry Goldwater) and trying to keep the kids fed and clothed and the bills paid. I learned later that a man had died upstairs in that house. I wasn't surprised. It wasn't the first time I had lived in a house where someone had died.

After only a year, we moved into a townhouse apartment at 708B Childs Street, where the logistics were somewhat better. We toted the washer and dryer up the basement stairs at the Manchester Road address and down the basement stairs at the townhouse on Childs. The Kroehler sofa, recently slipcovered again, came long. In the new residence, the heating and cooling systems both functioned properly. There was a large kitchen-dining room combination, which allowed us to have family visits from out of town. The house had a powder room downstairs, along with three bedrooms and a full bathroom, complete with a tub and shower on the second floor. Becky, Johnny, and Mary quickly settled into their new school, which was conveniently located within easy walking distance. Additionally, they found plenty of other children in the neighborhood to play with. To top it off, the landlord diligently maintained the lawn, ensuring it was always in pristine condition.

We were living in the townhouse when I dreamed one night that Danty had come to say goodbye: she was riding in their old black Pontiac, wearing her hat as she always did when she was "going somewhere." Danty had considerable self-assurance, and more than a touch of vanity. Her hair had turned snow-white while she was still in her thirties, and in later years she had her hair done weekly. But when she went anywhere, she always wore a hat. It was a touch of elegance certainly, but this was in the days when women still wore hats, especially to church or on any important occasion. My mother, too, wore a hat when she went anywhere of any consequence, and especially to church. One Sunday, after a trip to visit her sisters up North, she wore a new hat to church that she'd bought on her vacation. She very nearly blushed when the minister commented, "I see Evelyn is wearing a new hat."

When the phone rang in the middle of my dream, it was my sister Kay calling to tell me that Danty had died very early that morning. It was May 4, 1964.

We went home for Danty's funeral with the children, and I was asked to write the obituary and read one of her poems at the service. I remember people asking me afterward how I could have been so calm as I read, and dry-eyed. But I had shed all my tears in the car, alone with Jay, on the way to the service. I have never, not *ever*, wanted anyone to see me cry. Jay was driving, so I don't think he even noticed. They were very quiet tears.

Miles Marion Jennings (27 Mar 1884 – 10 Apr 1969)

LeMaude Stokes Jennings (05 Feb 1881 – 04 May 1964)

But, like her three daughters, I am often reminded of the impact Danty made upon my life. I remember one time, quite late in her life, when she went to some social affair she had not really wanted to attend. But when she got back, she said, "I'm so glad I went; everybody was so glad to see me." I've often thought she was more than a bit self-centered. I've heard that "Selfishness is always thinking of oneself, and self-centeredness is believing that everyone else should think of you." I would eventually recognize those same traits in myself. I've sometimes suspected that the reason she disliked having sons-in-law so much was because (1) they weren't women and (2) they took the time and attention of her "girls" away from her.

But I am also aware that her expectations for me have also influenced my expectations for myself. Three or four years before she died, while she was in a nursing home near Vienna and I was working for the *Metropolis News*, I got a call from Danty. Despite her fragile memory at that time due to Alzheimer's, a condition that Aunt Mary and my mother would also experience in later years, she still had enough memory to recall where I worked and the persistence to persuade the nursing home attendants to make the call for her. She had, she told me, been thinking about my future. And she had decided that I should run for the Illinois House of Representatives! I believe that, although her short-term memory was very fragile, her long-term memory was still intact. And she had probably been thinking with pride about her grandfather, Matthew Stokes, who had actually *been* a member of the Illinois House of Representatives. I told her I'd think about it. Maybe I even did.

I've inherited quite a bit from my grandmother, and I'm afraid that includes her vanity, her stubbornness, and even her looks. Yes, I also inherited that haughty "just try to prove me wrong" pride. In a way, Danty was my alter ego, and Pa was my rock. My third and last husband, Bill Babbington, always reminded me of Pa. Come to think of it (and I often have) Bill even looked a great deal like my grandfather Miles Jennings.

As our three children grew older, there was no longer a need for a babysitter, and Jay and I could resume some semblance of a social life. We developed friendships with one or two other couples. Sylvia and Bob Beamer (she worked in my office and he was a Wheaton police officer) became especially close. They lived in an old two-story house near downtown. The former owner had died on the second-floor landing and lay there for some time before he was found, so long in fact that some of him was left behind: the outlines of his position in death were clearly evident to anyone going upstairs to use the only bathroom. Fortunately, Sylvia's life-long dream was to become an undertaker, so the "Body on the Floor" was merely a conversation piece. I was rather glad when they added a bathroom in the basement for the convenience of guests who were a bit more squeamish.

I also began having serious dental problems, which had begun years before when I was 15 and had to have a root canal in one of my upper front teeth. Two of my cousins had dentures before they were in their mid-20s. So I had an upper denture and a lower partial in my mid-30s. Danty's soda-and-salt mixture had obviously not worked for me as well as it did for her. But I am almost certain that the number of people who have seen me without dentures (doctors and medical technicians excepted) could be counted on the fingers of one hand. And that includes husbands as well as both significant and insignificant "others." I'm still rather careful about looking at myself in the mirror when I take my dentures out to brush them. I have many character defects, most of them acknowledged and perhaps a few I have not yet uncovered, but I am sure vanity will be the last to go.

In some ways those were, as the opening lines of an old movie go, "the best of years and the worst of years." Work, for me, was engrossing, and I'm sure it often caused me to neglect both my children and my husband, sometimes from necessity and sometimes by choice. DuPage County was considered not just the largest but also the most Republican county in the state of Illinois, and it was inevitable that I become involved in its political life. My job required me to attend Wheaton council meetings and, although I had part-time reporters for some of the other cities in our circulation area, I often attended Glen Ellyn meetings as well. (Thank you again, Mom, for insisting that I practice my shorthand.)

And there were news stories that were exciting and sometimes intriguing: a young girl walking home from school who disappeared and then was found dead in a ditch by a man mowing the County right-of-way. The man who found her was, coincidentally (I'm almost sure), a former priest, and he and his wife, a former nun, had occasionally befriended the child. I'm not certain if they ever discovered who killed the little girl. The case was still open when I left the *Times*. One story was almost too close to home: a young boy who was playing "dare" with a locomotive on the tracks just outside of town did not leap aside quite fast enough. My own children were close to his age.

But not all the news was tragic. People offered their own interesting stories: one man came into the office touting a story about his "flying saucer" which was fueled by water, miraculously transformed with the aid of a secret ingredient for which only he had the recipe. I do remember the chemical formula for water from college chemistry classes, but I never learned the formula for his "secret ingredient." He offered me a planetary excursion in this exotic vehicle (what a story *that* would have made). The invitation was complicated by the present location of the saucer: somewhere in a Brazilian rainforest. He was trying to secure financing to make a secret ingredient for transforming water into fuel and suggested that any surplus funds obtained could be used to fly us both down there. I declined the invitation but doctored a paper plate to create a faux image and published it to poke a bit of fun at the idea. (Besides, I was quite certain Jay would object to my going all the way to Brazil with a strange man. It was already difficult enough to go alone on an occasional night assignment to the next town over.)

There were interviews with celebrities who appeared at the Pheasant Run playhouse, tracking ballgames of all the local teams, going to important social events to take photographs with – oh, yes, I *almost* forgot – the photographer I had persuaded away from the *Graphic*.

The *Times* had several people on staff full-time: we had our own backroom where the *Times* and two other subsidiaries of the *Law Bulletin* were "made up;" two ad salesmen and a classified clerk, the photographer, a society editor, and several part-timers. One of the part-time reporters was an elderly man, Norman Clegg, who drove a Nash Rambler (their interiors were Volkswagen snug) and was an avid environmentalist. His favorite topic was a version of "soapsuds on the river," and he knew absolutely everyone in DuPage County of any social or political consequence. He was also an excellent writer and contributed free-lance articles from time to time. He took me under his wing, introduced me to the local politicians, and escorted me to all his favorite haunts. Some of them, admittedly, were very nearly "dives," but he was always the perfect gentleman.

On the home front, I spent one winter making crewel embroidered drapes for the living room and dining room. They were beautiful: a red and green design in wool on linen. Jay and I went scavenging at a huge flea market (in Lombard, as I recall) and found a Duncan Phyfe mahogany dining room set, complete with 6 chairs, a china cabinet, and a five-foot buffet. I recovered the chair seats in a damask that matched the colors and design in the draperies. We converted one-half of the basement into a recreation room complete with a bar made from walnut paneling Jay's father had salvaged from the renovation of the bank where he worked. I also set up a sewing center there. I had continued (how, I do not know) to make most of all three children's clothes, including Johnny's jeans (he was rail-thin and it was impossible to find jeans that fit), until they were well into their teens. Since the sewing machine was in the basement, I spent a lot of evenings and weekends there. I especially remember making patchwork skirts for the girls one year. They were in fashion. And I began haunting the local resale shops and flea markets, an activity that quickly became an addiction.

One year, I can't remember which, we moved the old Kroehler sofa to the basement and bought the first *new* couch we had ever owned (actually the first piece of *new* furniture of any kind): a green and white striped loveseat, the upholstery specially ordered to match the linen draperies. It was delivered just a day or so before Christmas. And I found two old swivel rockers at our favorite flea market and upholstered them in a green damask. That may have been the same year (1969) that Johnny got hockey states for Christmas; on his first time out, the day after Christmas, he broke his wrist.

We also learned at some point that Becky had sustained an injury to her back (she refers to it now as an "old football injury") and she had to spend nearly six months in a full-body cast. Johnny and Becky moved up into high school, and I recall a slumber party where the girls were sequestered in the bedrooms upstairs, the boys confined to the basement (except for brief supervised visits to the main floor powder room.) Jay and I spent the night on the main floor, dispensing occasional treats and sleeping in shifts to make sure everyone stayed in their assigned spaces.

I learned to refinish furniture and found a library table that I moved into the big master bedroom and, at one end, created an area "all my own" (ala Virginia Wolff), including my old typing stand. I had, however, replaced my portable typewriter with a "correcting" Selectric. I had finished the historical novel *Down River* before we left Metropolis, the book inspired by the columns I had written every week for the *News* based on old issues of *The Promulgator*, but of course there was a love story too. Though I began writing short stories and started another novel, Jay begged me not to try to publish anything. "You'll get something published and be famous, and then you'll leave me." It would be another twelve years before *Down River* saw print.

I also built some bookcases at the end of the bedroom, alongside my writing table. I began to fill the shelves with the books in which I was exploring the world of the past: the very distant past of ancient history, and also the world of the mind and of the spirit: the investigations of science and psychology and unexplained mysteries. I read about the statues on Easter Island, which seemed to be the lonely and perhaps futile attempts of a forgotten people to contact something or someone "out there." I was fascinated for months by Erick von Daniken's rather far-fetched ideas regarding ancient aliens in his *Chariot of the Gods* and subsequent books. And it was about this time that I discovered there were other people – quite a few other people -- who had experienced life-after-death events.

Somewhere I learned about Edgar Cayce, the "sleeping prophet," and collected his writings, drawn to them perhaps in remembering Danty's stories of speaking to her deceased mother, and recalling those strange, infrequent occasions when I had personally experienced a fleeting and somewhat disconcerting knowledge of something happening "at a distance." The concept of reincarnation was new to me, although there were many places in the Bible that, on reflection, seemed to refer to strongly held beliefs of the people of Jesus' time regarding reincarnations of Hebrew holy men of the past. Why had the ministers at the New Hope Baptist Church never spoken of them? Could it be possible, I wondered, that there was more than one way of being "raised from the dead," of "living again," of being "reborn"?

And I soon learned there were books filled with writings that had not made it into the Bible, which had for many years been my only spiritual primer. Now I bought and read *The Apocrypha* (the Lost Books of the Bible). Through the years, of course, there would be others discovered and/or unearthed by desert Bedouins and a bevy of archeologists: *The Dead Sea Scrolls*, *The Nag Hammadi Library*. So those too were added to my growing collection. I would discover the book Evelyn Underhill (a woman!) had written years before titled quite simply *Mysticism*. What a fascinating word! And there were other books on esoteric (and occasionally occultic) subjects that were opening my mind to a world of ideas I had always suspected but had never had the opportunity to explore.

I was also discovering all of this, it seems now almost synchronistically, in Wheaton, Illinois, a quiet suburb west of Chicago, which also just happened to be the home of one of the great colleges of fundamentalism, Wheaton Bible College (the evangelist Billy Graham's alma mater), as well as the home of The

Theosophical Society of America (founded by Annie Besant, a very interesting woman who seemed part conjurer-of-spirits and just possibly part "con"). Was there something in the air? Wheaton College was actually only two or three blocks from the home on Blanchard Street we bought in about 1968. And, of course, I would eventually learn that a one-time spiritual leader of the Theosophical Society, J. Krishnamurti, would disavow both the leadership and the tenets of the Society and (even later) become a close friend and "fellow traveler" in the bewildering quantum world explained by physicist David Bohm in his book *Wholeness and the Implicate Order*. The books of their dialogues are interesting attempts to explain the unexplainable.

In those years I suspect I lived in two worlds: one in my head, the other in real life. I tried not to separate them, but of course I did. At the office, I wrote editorials and weekly columns, which sometimes created more controversy than they solved. I thus became embroiled in a city council dispute at the insistence of the *Times* publisher. The accompanying furor resulted in Jay's getting a multitude of parking tickets and, at one point, actually arrested for failure to pay them. Most of them seemed to have been issued in front of the *Times* office, where he had a habit of parking for an inordinate length of time on the nights when I had to work late. He was protecting me, he said.

There were difficulties and triumphs as I learned to live in this new milieu. One morning I came in to work and, when I walked into my upstairs office, there was a bulky middle-aged man sitting behind *my* desk as though he belonged there. It was the editor of one of the other newspapers in our chain, also owned by the *Chicago Law Bulletin*. I knew Ben (I'll call him) because his paper was "made up" in our production department. But when I said, "Why are you sitting at my desk?" I was more than surprised when he said, "Well, I guess Ernie (our mutual publisher) didn't tell you. You and I are going to be co-editing the Times." I can't remember what I responded. It might have been, "Over my dead body." I prefer to believe it was, "We'll have to see about that." Then I turned, went out the door, and down the stairs to Ernie's office.

I do remember what I said to Ernie: "I understand that you have decided to give Ben one-half of my job. I'll tell you what *I'm* going to do. I'm going to walk up to the restaurant on the corner and have a cup of coffee. That should take me about 30 minutes, and when I come back, I expect Ben to be gone. If he isn't, you'd better have my paycheck ready, because this will be my last day here." I came back half an hour later, walked up the steps to my office with my heart racing, and opened the door. Ben was gone, perhaps (remembering my one-room school days when the boys always got to pound the erasers) to go and find his own erasers to pound!

The growing self-confidence I was discovering (which might also be called false bravado or even, possibly, "Dutch courage") also propelled me into running for, and winning, election to the presidency of the DuPage County Press Association. I'm surprised that the final vote didn't kill me – I drove home that night from the Country Club in Naperville where the election was held to our home in Wheaton through a blinding blizzard, triumphant but scared to death I'd die before I had a chance to celebrate. I had not yet learned the limits of my own ego. And I am the first to confess that I'm also still working on lingering vestiges of pride and self-will. Those darned things stick like glue.

Alcohol, which seemed to be a constant part of this new social milieu, had given me the Dutch courage to venture far beyond my old boundaries. Jay was always upset because he could no longer control where I was or who I was with when I got there. And my work became my reason, or perhaps my excuse, for more and more freedom. I had been a child when Jay and I met. Now, I was a woman, and I felt attractive and interesting, seeking not only acceptance but, most importantly, recognition of my own identity – my separate self. And yes, much of this journey is documented in the appropriately titled book I wrote, *The Secret Self.* While it's been written and re-written half a dozen times, I'm pretty sure I'll destroy all the pages sometime before I die, unless I can muster far more courage than I presently have to actually finish the darned thing. (And no, this is not IT. But it might be just a little *bit* of *it*.)

As I have often thought and sometimes said, Jay believed the two of us should be one, and the one should be *him*. When he wanted accountability for everything I did, everything I said (including a word-for-word account of everything I told the psychiatrist), and finally, everything I *thought*, I knew that the time was coming when I would have to leave. But it was still incredibly difficult to extricate myself from our marriage.

I did make one final effort to save what was left: I quit my job at the *Times* and found a new position as assistant to the editors of *Office Appliance* and *Office Design* magazines, headquartered in Elmhurst. The job of creating product columns for the two magazines consisted primarily of sizing photographs and reducing press releases for office products to a comprehensive cutline. It was well paid, the benefits were ample, and the hours were 9-5 with an hour for lunch. But the work itself was incredibly boring. I was definitely overqualified, the fact that I had only a high-school education and barely one year of completed college courses notwithstanding. And my resentment at having to find such a self-defeating "solution" to our marriage woes had simply created another problem. Even more degrading: I didn't even have my own office!

Somehow we held everything together until the kids were all in high school, and we had bought a three-bedroom home at 123 Blanchard, two blocks or so south of Wheaton College. But as the marriage crumbled, so did I. While I recall distinctly all three bedrooms, the living room with its dining "L", the kitchen (complete with furnishings including avocado refrigerator and stove) and even the basement, which flooded the first year we lived there, I simply cannot remember where the bathroom was in that house. I do remember there was only one.

And I remember the basement quite well. The "room of my own" on Blanchard Street was *in* the basement, which also housed the washer and dryer, the old Kroehler sofa, and bookshelves. There was no sewing machine here. My children had outgrown my homemade garments (or perhaps outgrown my fashion designs), and I had become an avid shopper at the local K-Mart and several community resale shops. But there were lots of bookshelves. And more books.

Although we legally divorced in 1972, managing to stay married just shy of what would have been our 20th anniversary, separation (both physical and emotional) was a long and slow process. Living in a marriage is like weaving a piece of cloth until it becomes the fabric of our existence; male and female are the warp and woof, but the pattern is a complex matrix of differing backgrounds and ideas, desires and needs, personalities and characters, gender and age, intellect and experience. And the more tightly the marriage is woven, the more difficult and painful tearing it apart becomes.

In retrospect, I realize that we had married in that awkward decade after the end of World War II when the social and economic codes of the past were being rewritten. Women's lives had been changed irrevocably by a new economic and personal independence enforced by work outside the home and numerous and prolonged separations from "other halves."

I have also learned over the years that much of my attitude toward men and my ideas of what a family was (rather than what it "should be") were, of course, shaped by my relationship with my father and my grandfathers, my mother, and my grandmothers. Since my parents did not actually live together until I was three years old, my "first father" had been my mother's father, with whom we lived until I was nearly three. In fact, as I have noted in earlier sections, I called him "Daddypa" when I was first learning to talk, shortening that to "Pa" as I grew older.

As I also mentioned sometime before, Pa had served as a medic with Teddy Roosevelt's Rough Riders during the Cuban Pacification and, perhaps as a consequence, was always intensely interested in all things political. Yet strangely, and for reasons which I could never quite fathom, two of his daughters (my aunts) did not want a flag put on his casket when he died on April 18, 1969. They also refused him the gun salute he would have been entitled to. Sadly, he passed away five lonely years after my grandmother's death. In the end, he was all alone, except for the other lonely men in narrow, single beds in the ward of a nursing home in Johnson City. My memories of him now are shadowed by regret that the efforts of his life were so easily dismissed by those he loved and worked so hard to care for. But it was he, most of all, who taught me by his example what unconditional love was. It wasn't about telling someone you loved them. It was by *showing* them how much. And it is often, as I believe I quoted earlier, much less a feeling that it is an act of will.

Quite naturally, I wrote the obituary for his funeral service, held at the New Hope Baptist Church (this one in Lick Creek, founded in part by the Stokes Family after their Quakerism died of isolation), just down the road from where he and my grandmother had lived when they were first married, and within easy walking distance of the homes where my mother's Stokes cousins still lived. There is a lingering bitterness in the "remains of the day," as one of my cousins left the service to pick up a rented trailer so he could go to the house in Fudgetown and empty the garage of Pa's carpentry tools. As the oldest grandson, child of Aunt Mary, the oldest daughter, I'm sure he was entitled. My grandmother's writing desk went first to Aunt Mary and, eventually, to her daughter. Years later, I saw it sitting in the entrance hall of her home when we visited for her mother's 85th birthday. I felt a brief flair of resentment and even entitlement. There is a part of me that has always considered myself a kind of "fourth daughter."

But then I remember that I have the only things that Danty truly treasured: her poems, those bits and pieces of *her*self, her thoughts, her inner musings, scrawled across scraps of paper in her own handwriting. At some time I also acquired an unframed hexagon-shaped mirror from her living room and, when Mom no longer wanted it, Pa and Danty's ceramic Christmas tree with its tiny colored glass birds perched on its blunt clay branches. There's a light bulb inside that makes the little birds shine. I gave it to Mary this year for her new tiny-house. It seems to fit there. I have my own bird collection: ceramic figurines that perch on the long sill below my front windows. A red ceramic "calico cat," an antique doorstop, watches over them. An iron "pointer" bird dog seems poised to attack them all. The tableau is a bit bizarre, but visitors never seem to notice.

Danty had not married until she was 29; her first child was born when she was 31. If a woman can become a "bluestocking" while the wife of a coal miner in a southern Illinois coal mining town, she was one. Both my maternal grandparents were great readers and curious to learn more about the world. Conversely, my paternal grandmother was a painfully shy woman, and my paternal grandfather had been virtually paralyzed by Parkinson's disease for most of my memories of him.

And while my own parents' marriage may have appeared to be a traditional one, it was not really. My father's alcoholism and the initial strained circumstances of their marriage had required my mother to compromise over and over again in order to maintain that appearance. I have learned the hard way that we often behave not in obedience to what our parents tell us to do but rather by imitating their behavior, including their mistakes.

My parents' religious beliefs were different, as well. Although my father was raised in the Lutheran Church, my mother was Baptist and attended a Baptist Church all the years of their marriage. Dad went once a year, on "Homecoming Sunday," which was always on the Sunday closest to Memorial Day. There was always special musical entertainment from both local talent and an invited gospel quartet, and a potluck dinner on tables set up under the shade trees on the church's front lawn. There were prizes for people who had come the farthest distance to attend and for the couple married the longest, and the oldest church member.

When the minister asked for contributions to the Cemetery Fund, Dad always raised his hand and made a substantial contribution. (My baby sister, Molly Lou, was buried in the church cemetery.) I do not know to this day what other attraction Homecoming Sunday had for him. (I would like to think he also came to listen to the solo that I usually sang, but if so, he never even acknowledged he had heard it.) I also have no idea what his religious beliefs were, or if he had any at all. Religion was practiced (by my mother) but never discussed, and appeared to be virtually ignored by my father. But from the moment I discovered that many ancient Eastern religions believed in their leader's virgin birth, I wanted to learn more about how and what other people believed. I still do.

Jay seemed to pay lip service to the Baptist religion in which we had both been raised, but I don't recall ever hearing him speak of his own beliefs. And he had no interest at all in talking about anything except hunting, fishing, baseball, basketball, and football. He was also seven years my senior and had served in the Navy during the War. While his mother had been a schoolteacher, three years older than his father, who was barely 17 when they married, their marriage had been traditional. She had been content to follow her husband's lead in everything.

In contrast, I have never been a follower, yet I don't consider myself a "leader." I'm not affiliated with the Democrats, the Republicans, or even the Libertarians. I think I may be a Contrarian. If there's no party for that persuasion, perhaps we should form one.

Jay had been married twice before, and both women had been unfaithful. He simply could not trust that I would not also betray him, and any effort on my part toward independence of thought or action was regarded as an act of infidelity. (So was my buying strawberry ice cream when he preferred chocolate, but that's a separate matter. Maybe.) And I was a woman whose every instinct was to strain at any leash with which anyone attempted to control me. If it is true that marriage should strive toward becoming a "true partnership between two human beings," then our marriage was a failed attempt to meld two very different people.

In the last year or so of marriage, we had a consultation with our family doctor about the strain our marriage was undergoing. I recall Dr. Sanchez telling Jay, "If you don't allow Lona to be her own person, you will lose her." And Jay's response was, "You don't understand. She can't be her own person. She's my wife." I have come to believe that such a simple exchange, never forgotten, describes completely the underlying conflict that resulted in the failure of our marriage.

Often, when the accusations and arguments and demands had made communication impossible, I had told Jay, "You say you love me, but your definition of love is different than mine. You may love me, but you don't really *like* me." It was after the marriage ended that, in a rare burst of confidence, perhaps even apology, Jay told me, "You know, we were never friends, we were never lovers, we were never really *married*." He, too, was recognizing the truth I had felt in my heart, in my very bones, for a long time. We had never been able to be emotionally honest with each other, perhaps both of us too damaged by the past to trust. He also confessed that his jealousy had always been a projection (although he didn't use that term) of his own suppressed thoughts and desires.

I recently read in one of my morning meditations an apt and more objective description of what happened to our marriage:

> *"Our individual redefinition is a task that often involves role reversals for men and women. We women find ourselves becoming more assertive and independent as we men become more responsive to our emotions. Redefinition and change is a balancing act that challenges couples in new and compelling ways. Those of us who manage to ride out the storms of each other's changes and passages are in a unique position to negotiate and renew our commitments. When the*

dust settles, it is possible to view marriage from a more honest vantage point. Who are we now? What are our values and goals? How are we willing to negotiate and adjust to make our new pieces fit? When we engage in the process of finding these answers together, we are already enjoying the rewards of our new maturity." (From Seasons of the Spirit.)

But Jay and I failed in that process and, to quote the old Humpty Dumpty rhyme, the truth is that all our efforts to "put ourselves back together again" proved to be in vain.

During that difficult time, our oldest daughter, Rebecca Rae, or "Becky" as we have always called her, and Dennis Allen were married in the backyard of the house on Blanchard Street, and the couple settled into a new apartment a few blocks away. All the family was there for the wedding. Mom brought the cake, and Becky was married in her cousin Karen's wedding dress. The pictures were lovely, and we looked like a very happy family. Looks are deceiving.

Jay's and my divorce became final in June of 1973, our marriage ending just days short of 20 years. I lived in the house on Blanchard Street in Wheaton for a year or so with Johnny and Mary. But in the months that followed we all tried numerous living arrangements, a bit like musical chairs. Becky was pregnant and became unable to work and even had to have daily injections for severe nausea for a while, so she and Dennis moved in with me, and Jay moved from a furnished room to their abandoned apartment. I once thought of writing a novel about that period of my life. I would call it, I thought, "The Year of 40." However, in retrospect, I eventually summed the ending up this way:

On Married Bliss

Now that I'm past the middle years of life,

no longer daughter, mother, or a wife

to any man who can demand my time

for making dinner, making love (whose crime

was stealing little pieces of my self

and hoarding them, wasted, upon a shelf

he'd built for trophies of the heart),

now there seems nothing left to do but start

to be all that I might have been, pretend

I am not speeding toward a dismal end

but digging in my heels and screeching

to a metaphoric halt; stop preaching

freedom and start living as a being

whole, entire—one hearing, feeling, seeing,

answ'ring only to the sound of my own name

(not "mom" or "hon" or "babe"—those tame

endearments that once called me out

from all my hiding places, found my doubt

and used it as a weapon to control me,

kissed and caressed my body to console me).

Those who believe that "two become as one"

in marriage bliss have surely missed the fun

of overdrafts on joint accounts and grim

re-reckoning to find, in sum, the one was him.

One of my favorite spiritual writers, Richard Rohr, has another phrase for such midlife transitions and wrote a book about it, *Falling Upward*. But mine felt like a hard descent in the opposite direction. This is, at least in part, my book about *that*.

One day as I walked down the road that led to future plans and dreams,
I noticed that ahead of me the one road -- there-- turned into three.

One road said "Death" and I, dismayed, looked quickly at the other two.
One seemed so quiet, peaceful, calm, that first I chose its restful hue.

But then I glanced at what, it seemed, was the far brighter, gayer path.
And Fame and Fortune beckoned me; it seemed that everyone there laughed.

I stood, my thoughts in turmoil now, simply unable to decide.
Until Pride whispered in my ear, "Try the fun one, just for the ride."

Lona Rae

My Very Own Midlife Crisis

As I begin the story of this chapter of my life, it seems less the confession it will probably appear to others than the catharsis it is for me. One quote with which I began this Memoir declared an intention to "tell the stories of the unique epiphanies that have informed (my) lives." And as I have repeated, perhaps *ad nauseum*, my life has seemed to unfold in a series of "reinventions" of myself. The first nearly nineteen years were those of childhood and adolescence, the second twenty were of love, marriage, parenting, and a gradual disclosure of my "true self," or perhaps just of who I wanted to be when I grew up. The midlife years from 39 to 43 were chaotic and painful for me, and perhaps even more for those who were forced to either observe or participate.

There *are* epiphanies, or "awakenings," that are so slow to disclose themselves that they are only realized in retrospect, until (at least for me) the words of the first step in the program of Alcoholics Anonymous would one day make sense of my own unreason. It was the admission of powerlessness, that "our lives have become unmanageable." There is also a legal definition of sanity (a term used in AA's second step) that I have come to believe applies: "the ability to manage one's own affairs in a reasonable and responsible manner."

There was anger, too. Eliana Gil (I have no idea who she is or was, but I like this thought) says, "Anger is usually the flipside of helplessness." And, of course, sustained anger can erode our insides and keep us trapped in pain and frustration. I suspect that my own life was a mirror of the lives of many women in the 1970s, a period which historians have increasingly portrayed as a "pivot of change" in world history. I claim that as a *reason*, not an *excuse*, for what my life had become.

Social progressive values that began in the 1960s, such as increasing political awareness and economic liberty of women, were coming into focus in the '70s. Those were the years of the Women's Liberation Movement, demands for passage of the ERA (Equal Rights Amendment), women's marches for "equal pay for equal work," with signs that proclaimed "Sexism Kills—Stop Wife Abuse," and "Judge Women as People, Not as Wives." And even "Free Contraceptives; Free Abortions." The latter sign gave a shout-out to a new and very radical sexual freedom for women.

The lack of trustworthy contraception has kept many women trapped in situations beyond their control. (Thumbs up emoji, *please!*) Though birth control pills were actually created in the 1950s, they didn't become widely available until the 1960s and, in fact, it took a Supreme Court Case (Griswold v. Connecticut) to overturn the ban on contraceptives for married couples. It was not until 1972 that the right to contraceptives was extended to *unmarried* couples. The country singer Loretta Lynn wrote and sang a song about that, "The Pill." She also grew up without "running water," an indoor bathtub, or an indoor toilet and, just like me, in a place where the only "running water" flowed down the creek out back of the house. She died last month, just two years older than me. Today's Supreme Court battles over abortion rights, almost entirely efforts to overturn or contain laws enacted by men--with both pastoral and financial support from some religions--to control the rights of women, indicate that the war is not over. The days when men joked about keeping a woman home by keeping her "barefoot and pregnant" (imprisoned?) were slip-sliding away in 1972 and are not yet completely gone.

The writer Anne Valley-Fox, in her 1989 preface to a new version of *Your Mythic Journey*, a book she wrote jointly in 1973 with one of my favorite authors, Sam Keen, speaks of Keen introducing her to Joseph Campbell in 1972. He spoke with them of the "danger and bliss of the hero's journey." It was a subject Campbell had spent his life exploring in books, classrooms, and even a television series with Bill Moyer, which I recall watching with something akin to awe at his erudition. "So," she said, "I asked Campbell how it was that the hero was so often cast in the masculine form. Surely women are heroic, too?" And what he answered, she said, "caused everything else we spoke of that day to fall out of my memory. He said that he and his wife, Jean, had chosen not to have children because their life's work was already cut out for them. But most women are set inexorably on the heroic path through childbirth and the challenge of maternity." As I recently read her vignette (accidentally or synchronistically?), I didn't know whether to respond with pride or fury at having been set upon the hero's (heroine's?) path either inadvertently or inexorably. But then I remembered the plaque over my dresser, the gift from my granddaughter, "Great Women Raise Great Women Raise Great Women." Maybe that wasn't about ego after all. The title of the poem that began this section is and has been for 25 years (cross my heart): my own: *The Journey Toward Love*.

Yet Betty Freidan's book "The Feminine Mystique" explored the notion (she called it "false") that a woman's role in society was to be a wife, mother, and housewife – and nothing else. That mystique, Freidan said, was an "artificial idea of femininity," pronouncing that having a career and/or fulfilling one's individual potential somehow went against women's pre-ordained role. And Freidan and another prominent leader of the Women's Rights movement, Gloria Steinem, were simply telling me what I felt in my heart was true. I suspect Anne Valley-Fox would have agreed. She wanted to be a storyteller, but the stories she told "would not finally shape my life." And 20 years after that visit with Campbell, she said, "I feel I am washed of my gypsy, my poet, my fury which set me apart, and I am, as Joseph Campbell prescribed it, a woman among women, surrounded by mate, children, friends, and world peoples journeying together some distance down a road." And I'll bet she stumbled on that road more than once!

I yearned with all my heart to live my truth, whatever it might be. The desire to become a "conventional non-conformist," which I had once claimed in a high school essay, had indeed been prophetic. But it takes a great deal of courage (some would call it foolhardiness) to begin to live your dreams, to travel between two worlds, struggling against and through thousands of years of cultural conditioning and religious propaganda. Including, of course, the idea that when Eve ate the apple, she tempted Adam to sin, and "in Adam's fall, we sinned all." That's a bit of religious doggerel I thoroughly despise! While it has been said that "the hand that rocks the cradles rules the world," there was also a subliminal message that, if the world doesn't turn out right, it's somehow a woman's fault for upsetting the cradle. Even in solving crime, there is still a kind of rule that states, "Cherchez la femme," i.e., "look for the woman." Scapegoating—foisting one's mistakes on someone else—did not end with the death of Jesus on a martyr's cross. In my own family, too many women have raised their daughters to be martyrs. (There, I've said it, and I'm not sorry!) A copy of a poster from that era perhaps says it all:

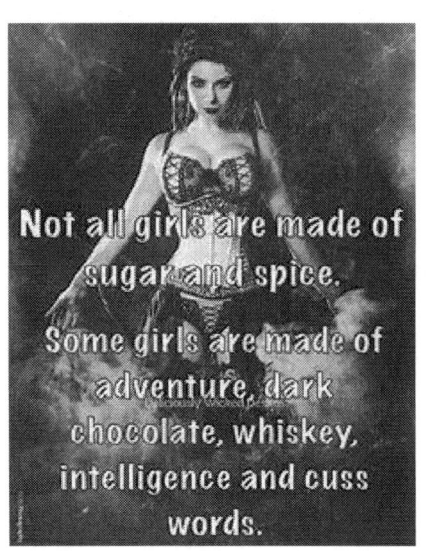

> Not all girls are made of sugar and spice.
> Some girls are made of adventure, dark chocolate, whiskey, intelligence and cuss words.

My husband should have been warned, when I went to the Halloween party at the Winfield Fire Department as an Arabian dancing girl in a long black wig, a huge fake diamond held fast in my navel with eyelash glue. A couple of years before I'd been "Little

Red Riding Hood," and he'd been "The Big Bad Wolf." Later, after the divorce, I owned and actually wore in public, not infrequently, a blonde wig and pink velvet hot pants. They were in style that year, but I wore them more as a declaration of independence (or a subtle disguise) than a bow to fashion. "Finding myself" as I turned forty was a wild ride down a rough and often lonely road. And, of course, I found companionship along the way.

> *There were knights in clumsy armor with their visors closed and rusted,*
>
> *for they did not even see me (or they looked, but glanced away).*
>
> *There were kings who sat on thrones, so lonely, gazing down upon me,*
>
> *and although I bowed before them, they did not ask me to stay.*
>
>
> *There were poets, too, who wooed me, with their words so neatly chosen;*
>
> *and I listened to their verse, but I could never hear a rhyme.*
>
> *There were soothsayers who told me they could see they were my future,*
>
> *but their crystal balls all darkened when the next tomorrow dawned.*
>
>
> *I met actors garbed in costume who could make themselves familiar;*
>
> *one or two who played the role I cast them in, almost too well.*
>
> *And, of course, the politicians, always running for election;*

their campaigns did not persuade me; they were finally sent to hell.

And occasionally, in wandering, I would meet the hollow horsemen,

brandishing their blunted sabers as they tried to cut me down.

Often wounded, blinded, bleeding, I thought often of retreating.

But I could not, for who knew what waited for me, round the bend.

(Yes, I wrote that!)

After my newspaper career had become collateral damage to numerous attempts to resolve Jay's and my differences and perhaps save our marriage, I went through a series of jobs and other changes so quickly that it's difficult to remember in what order things occurred. I was, not necessarily in that order: assistant to the editors of two magazines in Elmhurst, *Office Appliances* and *Office Design*; secretary to the partner of an insurance consulting firm in Wheaton; legal secretary to the partner of a Chicago law firm with offices that looked out over the plaza where the infamous Picasso statue was displayed; secretary at a Wheaton law firm, secretary to the manager of a computer firm in Oakbrook (ITEL, I think it was called), and secretary to the partner of an engineering consulting firm in Chicago.

When Tracie was born in February 1973, Jay moved into Becky and her husband's apartment, and the new parents and baby moved in with me. The house on Blanchard Street became too crowded, with Mary and Johnny still living there. So, I decided to move in with Jay temporarily. It didn't take long for me to remember why we had divorced, and I ultimately returned to the house. (I had taken only a few clothes with me.) The kids moved back into the apartment, Jay found other accommodations, and I finally sold the house in order, I suspect, to finally dissolve whatever financial ties remained of the marriage.

When I sold the house, I rented an apartment in a new apartment complex, Briarcliffe Village, south of Wheaton; Jay rented an apartment in the same complex (or maybe he moved in first). Again, I can't remember where the bathroom was, although I'm sure there were actually two.

I met Mike S. during that confused post-marriage time, a man I thought I loved. I had not yet learned to distinguish between love and infatuation. He was already married, with three (maybe four?) children, and a wife who was in a nursing home in the final stages of multiple sclerosis, a debilitating and degenerating disease. Mike was educated, European in both his birth and his views, an alcoholic (I later realized) and a womanizer (which I figured out right away). He was very attractive, with lots of charisma. But he was domineering in a different way, and I eventually realized that he considered himself socially superior to me. Born in Poland, he had spent his early childhood in Nazi Germany, his father (now deceased) had been a doctor conscripted into the German Army. His mother was a practicing psychiatrist. He didn't seem to like her very much.

He admired my intelligence and independence (I think), but also found it threatening. (I may have reminded him of his mother.) He was challenging and exciting to be with, but I couldn't trust him as far as the next date. He was always asking more than he was willing to give, and since I was accustomed to giving more than I got and asking for nothing—at least that's *my* perspective---it wasn't difficult to comply with his expectations. In fact, I probably offered as a gift more than he ever actually requested or even wanted. For a while, he was the center of my emotional life. None of my children liked him. I never met a single one of his.

Mike was already married and neither emotionally nor legally available, so I married John Cunningham, and I'll probably never know the reason why. Mom baked the cake and brought it to the wedding (and probably cried all the way home). It was a beautiful cake.

Marriage to John Cunningham - November 1, 1975

John and I were married after a very brief courtship and for an even briefer two months. I may have married him in order to escape from the possibility that I would completely lose myself in Mike S. Still, it is also true (as my daughter Mary Beth told me quite frankly) that John reminded me of her father, both in appearance and personality: he was blond, blue-eyed, about the same height and weight. He was also emotionally unavailable. I soon learned that he had lied to me about two things that were very important, though I'm also not certain which was crucial: his alcoholism and his financial status. He owed thousands of dollars to a former girlfriend. He even had to borrow money from his stepfather to pay the judge who married us and who just happened to be one of my former bosses (and perhaps even, at some point, just a teeny bit more).

John had, I believe, married me in the hope of marrying a meal ticket for himself and his two children. I'd have been deaf, dumb, and blind not to realize I had been trapped by a duplicitous man whose motives were questionable, whose values and ethics were totally different from mine (at least mine when I wasn't drinking), and who could not keep a job.

We were married on November 1, 1975, and almost immediately the marriage began to deteriorate. At Thanksgiving, he slapped me in the back of the head as I stood at the kitchen stove making dinner. I had challenged him on something. Actually, in the interests of at least partial disclosure, it wasn't just "something." He had gone to the grocery store and brought back a case of beer, but no Scotch. He knew I liked Scotch and despised beer, and I knew then I would have to leave; we were obviously incompatible! I could also not imagine staying in a marriage with someone who would hit a woman unless, and then only *perhaps*, she had hit him first. I had forgiven that once, and on exactly those grounds, but only once, and that had been a long, *long* time ago. Any intimacy, even conversation, soon became almost non-existent.

Sometime in early December, I met a woman on the commuter train I was taking into Chicago every morning to my job at the engineering consulting firm, and when I confided in her, daily and at great length, my growing disenchantment with my new husband, she confided in return that she was a member of Alcoholics Anonymous. The meetings were held in the building right next to the train station in Westmont where we were living, and I began to attend Alanon (only once) and then AA meetings, and to learn something about alcoholism. There was a blessing in that painful period of my life: I finally realized that I had also developed a problem with alcohol and even made a rather half-hearted attempt to deal with it.

Which also meant that my new husband and I had found even more grounds for incompatibility. In the years since I have learned that is usually the case when one of a pair decides to stop drinking and the other does not wish to participate or even cooperate in the effort. As noted above, I sometimes try to make a joke of that brief liaison by claiming that our major difference was that he preferred beer, and I drank only Scotch. Somewhere along life's journey I have learned that laughter, even at oneself, is better than crying. Laughter may not solve anything, but at least it gets you through the problem in a better mood. The alternative is self-pity, which kills you slowly and painfully. And is also extremely unattractive.

I stayed with John until after the New Year for the sake of Christmas and John's two small children, Crystal and John Paul, and then Mary and I moved in with Jay (yes, we did!) who had moved into my old apartment when I married John. Jay thought my return was a good idea, making no secret of envisioning this as the beginning of a permanent reconciliation. Our son Johnny had come home briefly while I was married to John and then left when (as I recall) things became too difficult with his stepfather. And Becky was beginning to see an end to her marriage to Tracie's father.

My "visit" with Jay only lasted about six weeks, and then I asked him to get a different apartment since, I reasoned, the one we were living in still had my name on the lease, and so was actually still mine. Was that extremely selfish and self-centered of me? Certainly it was, but I had begun drinking again, though even completely sober I knew I should not resume the relationship with Jay. It would not have been fair to either of us. There was entirely too much water under the bridge. But the ties of family and parenting were too strong to ever be completely severed.

It is very difficult even now, with so many years intervening, to look back on that chaotic time without feeling an almost overwhelming sense of helplessness and remorse. I will probably never know how much pain and heartbreak the disruption and dissolution of the family Jay and I had tried to create caused our children, nor how the long-term consequences of that damage have affected their decisions and their own lives. I have learned that I cannot change the past; I can only change my present, one day-- sometimes only one moment--at a time, in the hope that perhaps, in so doing, some of the old wounds will finally heal. Always realizing that, like the scar under my left breast, they will sometimes ache a bit.

I continued working for a while at the engineering consulting firm in Chicago, commuting this time from Wheaton, and then got a job with yet another law firm in Chicago. My office overlooked the Chicago River. Sometimes, the local newspapers said, bodies were spotted floating down the river, desperate souls who had stumbled and fallen accidentally, or found in its chill waters their only escape from a life no longer worth living. I knew that feeling but had never figured out a way to voluntarily stop living without causing a great deal of trouble for everyone else. I had thought very seriously about it on one occasion while I was living with Mary in the apartment Jay had vacated at my request. I actually announced my plans to God and said, as I remember it, "If I'm supposed to go on living, you're going to have to stop me."

And as grace (another name for synchronicity?) would have it, my telephone rang, and a little-old-lady voice asked softly, "Has anyone talked to you about God lately?"

To which I distinctly recall responding, "Lady, you've got to be kidding."

But she wasn't. Instead, she offered to come to my apartment with a friend (advising that she didn't see well enough to drive, and her friend didn't hear well enough, so they had to travel together). I agreed. It seemed impolite to say, "No," when she had gone to the trouble to call. I had at least enough sense left to realize that God--whoever or whatever God was--had responded to my challenge, was sending me a message, and I'd do well to listen. Actually, the two ladies listened while I talked (my customary way of communicating, unfortunately). But from that day to this I cannot recall having again had a compulsion to find a "final solution to a temporary problem."

It was about this time that Mary's high school boyfriend, Phillip Spencer "Phil" Culp, came home on leave from Germany, and they decided to marry. We had a simple ceremony in my apartment, and I recall letting them spend their wedding night alone in the apartment while I went to Jay's apartment (just a block away) for the night. But it was not an occasion for a reconciliation. I had too much wine at the reception and was sick all night. (I don't think I've had any wine since.) Shortly after the wedding (August of 1976) Phil returned to duty, and as soon as arrangements could be made, we put Mary on a plane for Germany, where he was stationed.

Since I had numerous contacts with the legal profession, I called one of the attorneys at the law firm I once worked for in Wheaton and, with astonishing ease and only the price of court costs (less than $100, if my memory is correct), I disentangled myself from John Cunningham, and was "Free at last, free at last, thank God almighty, I'm free at last." Well, I thought so at the time.

At least I was alone. But I began to think that a move completely away from all my problems would solve them. Or perhaps it was a hope that they would not follow me to the new location. When one of the other secretaries at the law firm where I was working mentioned an apartment available in her building, Jay helped me move to a little one-bedroom apartment at 215 E. Chestnut, an older building overshadowed by Watertower Place, kitty-corner from the John Hancock Building, and a short block and a half from Lake Shore Drive and Lake Michigan.

I had no way of knowing when Jay and I lugged what remained of my share of our "goods and chattels" up to the fourth floor on Chestnut Street (ever so grateful there was an elevator, and that we had sold the much-traveled washer and dryer with the house, and lost the huge cumbersome Kroehler hide-abed somewhere along the way) that I was about to begin another "reinvention" of myself.

Lest casual onlookers or those left behind think that I sailed through two divorces without regret or remorse, I wrote a poem years later about those experiences. Of course I did! For those unfamiliar with the term "Grass Widow," it describes a woman who is divorced, legally separated, or perhaps even spends a great deal of time alone without her husband.

Grass Widow

Though he's been gone a year

She still awakes to find
she has not crossed that line,
invisible, that in her mind
divides the bed into twin spaces:
"mine" and "his"; has not
in the unconsciousness of sleep
betrayed herself by laying where he might have been;
has not, even in darkest night and haunted dreams,
flung herself weeping into phantom arms.
She is consoled that,
though she finds the pillow wet with tears,
*it is **her** pillow – and not **his**.*

Death would be easier than this,
there'd be a corpse, a funeral, a grave,
headstone with fit and final epitaph.
Friends would bring flowers,
and send black-bordered cards
with kind solicitudes,
and sit with her and hold her hand.
Grief would not seem quite so unseemly then,
for she might dress in black
and even wear her wedding ring.
A grass widow must learn to sleep alone
in pride's boundaried bed . . .

                                        with her unburied dead.

Midway upon the journey of [my] life
I found myself within a forest dark,
For the straightforward pathway had been lost.

Ah me! How hard a thing it is to say
What was this forest save, rough, and stern,
Which in the very thought renews the fear.

So bitter is it, death is little more;
But of the good to treat, which there I found,
Speak will I of the other things I saw there.

I cannot well repeat how there I entered,
So full was I of slumber at the moment
In which I abandoned the true way.

    - From The Divine Comedy, by Dante Alighieri
    - (Translation by Henry Wadsworth Longfellow)

God forgive my little jokes on Thee,
And I'll forgive Thy great big joke on me.

                                Robert Frost

Falling Upward

The apartment on Chestnut Street was one-half of what had once been a much larger unit, so the bedroom was quite large, with its own small bath, and the living room and kitchen were also quite small – probably originally the kitchen and dining room. I'd learned of the apartment from the secretary of one of the other partners in the law firm where I was working, and the location was ideal – within a block of several neighborhood drinking establishments in which one could while away the evening hours and find pleasant male companionship, gentlemen who were more than willing to ply a nice-looking self-sufficient lady with drinks and flattery. The country girl was living "uptown" at last. And "uptown" proved to be my downfall. Thank God, I fell upward. (Yes, that is indeed possible.)

It was spring when I actually moved into the apartment, though I slept on a cot in the bedroom for a couple of weeks while I decorated. I am (a fact probably quite obvious to even a perfunctory reader by now), always very conscious of the layout, the furnishings, the colors, and the accessories of any place where I spend any considerable length of time. My home is my castle, no matter how humble the abode may appear to anyone else. And if anything in it doesn't move, I will eventually either paint it, wallpaper it, or wrap it in some kind of cloth. And there will be bookcases. With books. And more books. And then more bookcases. Eventually. Always.

The carpet was black. The previous tenant, my landlady said, had been a witch. (Truth!) Challenged, I decorated in red, black, and white, and on the living room wall hung a Joan Miro print as simply profound as a child's fingerpainting; in the print, a telephone with a black cord dangled, disconnected in midair. Was it symbolic? Maybe, although I didn't buy it for that reason. Its colors simply fit my color scheme. But yes, I seemed to have detached from everything. My husband of nearly twenty years, though also now disconnected, had been persuaded by some lingering loyalty to help me move. Our three children were gone: both daughters fleeing into marriage, our son hitch-hiking on some Pacific Northwest highway. The second husband was also gone. We had married in November and I had wished (or was it "witched") him and his two children away as soon as the Christmas tree was down. I don't like Christmas. But I've said that before, haven't I?

My mother, father, sister, brother–so far away they could be colored "gone" as well– were part of a shadowy chapter of my life in which I had milked cows and gathered eggs, raised gardens and baked bread, carried coal and hung white diapers on a winter line, cried dry soundless tears as I lay sleepless in the cold bed I'd made myself. Yellowing evidence of success from yet another chapter of the past was bound into scrapbooks piled in a corner of the tiny closet under a box of winter clothes. They kept company with books I'd kept from my brief sojourn in AA. I think I thought I might need them someday, or perhaps would give them to someone whose need was greater than mine. In one of them were scribbled phone numbers. I would need at least one of those numbers. I just didn't know it yet.

I slipcovered my green and white striped loveseat in a black and white floral design, made curtains in the same fabric for the double windows that looked out onto an alley, wallpapered the little vestibule with shiny black and white striped wallpaper, found a red coverlet for the queen-sized bed I'd bought new after Jay and I divorced. (I once had a friend—he was a man, but just a friend— who burned his bed after he and his wife divorced. Some things you have to live through to understand, if only in retrospect, why you must do them.) I even (eventually) crocheted an afghan in zigzags of red-black-white as a throw for the loveseat. My daughter Mary has it now, although her dog Finley thinks it's his.

My Wurlitzer organ and bench made the trip safely, and in the tiny kitchen there was a small round table with a red-checked tablecloth and matching cushions for the four antique walnut dining room chairs the kids had found at a yard sale while we all still lived in the townhouse in Wheaton. I'd sold the Duncan Phyfe dining room set when I sold the house on Blanchard. I was once again re-inventing myself, and the careful décor was a frame for the picture I envisioned of the new person I intended to become. Facades are vital when you're hollow inside.

Soon the tiny rooms of the apartment on Chestnut Street were crowded with the remnants of my past life, neatly arranged and color-matched. I barely noticed that it was always twilight, for the sun could never quite reach my fourth-floor (west) windows. My only view was of the brick walls of a narrow air shaft, just wide enough to be called an alley, towering 25 stories high. "Stone walls do not a prison make, nor iron bars a cage," the British poet Richard Lovelace wrote in 1642 "To Althea" from Stonegate Prison in London. I was about to test the truth of that poetic statement. . . in a prison of my own making, in Chicago. My letters home to my mother were carefully enthusiastic.

I was still working for the law firm overlooking the Chicago River when I moved, but when my boss left for Hawaii with his wife on their annual whale-watching vacation, I resigned while he was gone (for no good reason I can remember) and found, in rather rapid succession, a job with a property management firm (Lehndorff Properties) within walking distance of the apartment and—when that firm abruptly decided to relocate to Texas--a two-month placement with an attorney in the loop and then a job with a secretarial service owned by a woman named Joan Masters in the John Hancock building, almost across the street from my building. This re-inventing business is full of challenges, mistakes, loss of control, and necessary suffering. I've sometimes said that I was trying to figure out, "What am I going to be when I grow up?" Or even *who* was I going to be? My own identity seemed lost in the ongoing shuffle of my life.

William James, America's first psychologist, talked of the "persona," that image or personality that a person presents in public or in a specific setting, as opposed to their true self. I had been so many things to so many people: child, student, lover, wife, mother, editor, secretary – all those roles I had assumed to please someone else or to accommodate *their* choices--that I had somehow mistaken the image I saw, or at least tried to appear in *their* eyes, and had then mirrored that image and thus lost my *self*. And it was not in appearance only. I had somehow managed to allow even my goals and my values to be changed by others' visions of the person they wanted me to be. And when ideas, dreams, and even one's personal integrity are made the subject of ridicule, disapproval, and rejection (by our own self as well as the opinions of others), then it takes a great deal of courage to change.

Others may view it as abandonment when we move away from them or finally leave altogether. But when we reach a point where we look into a mirror and say to the image there: "I don't like you, I don't respect you, I can't stand to be *you* anymore, and I may die if I keep trying," then we are ready to change. I was about to reach that point, but I was not yet quite there.

Life on the near North side had begun with a series of brief relationships. But they were less "relationships" than "counting coups." Scalps that I could hang from my belt, that is. Women do that too, you know; we just don't usually talk about it. But I kept a little book that had a list of the men who might call me. The list had gotten rather lengthy as time passed. I can see in retrospect that many women in today's world go through the same period of trial and error as they commit to separation and divorce from a long-term marriage. But I've lived in, and through, and out on the other side of a day and time when it was not considered the "ladylike" thing to do. Still isn't in some places and in the minds of some people: the ones who've never been there. In the time and place where I grew up, you met a boy in high school and dated him until you either got bored or got pregnant, at which point (sometimes bored *and* pregnant) you married and stayed that way for the rest of your life. As a friend of mine's mother told her, "You've made your bed, now lie in it." No kidding, she said those exact words.

I was the first woman in my entire family, both maternal and paternal sides, to actually divorce. And I did it twice! But I was not the last. I was the first to go away to college and the first to come home in disgrace. But I was not the last. Some of those who went just came home as I had, but as time passed even more finished. I was the first to venture farther away from home than the Massac County line. But I was not the last. And some of those who have so ventured have gone farther than I even dreamed, much less dared. In days long gone by, they called people like that "pioneers." Society has often had less complimentary terms for women who conduct themselves in that fashion. Those terms are frequently epithets.

I've mentioned before my essay in high school, *The Conventional Nonconformist*, which is certainly a contradiction in terms. However, Pauline Artman, the English teacher who graded it, gave me an "A+" and, in so doing, may have given tacit consent to the course I was setting for my life. I've lost that old essay somewhere along the way, but I have a poem I wrote later about the consequences of following that course:

The Dance

The Dance I thought my life would be

became a March instead,

to cadence sung by cordoned Troops

who choreographed each single tread.

Clumsy, I could not step in time

nor keep my columned place;

I heard the Rhythm, felt the beat,

Yet always fell – *They* said, "from Grace."

I stumbled on against that League,

broke ranks with angry thrust.

And now the Regiment has passed

but I shall waltz on, in its dust.

    I felt as much a stranger in that black-carpeted apartment, which I have come to call "the witch's den" as I felt in the Chicago streets outside. Yet after work I went to the bar of the Drake or the Continental Plaza, wandered with bravado in and out of Rush Street bistros. Sometimes I wore a curled blonde wig and those pink hot pants, or a long black wig and a gypsy skirt, or simply changed my name, my past, my present. If I were remembered, it would be as someone else. But whoever I was or became, I was where I had wanted to be, or at least where I had willed myself to be.

At night, when I turned the lights off and pulled the blood-red coverlet up to my chin, if I was by myself – and I was not always by myself -- I sometimes felt tears gathering behind my closed lids. But I absolutely refused to allow myself to cry. I had wanted to be alone, yes. But I had never expected to be lonely.

A few drinks had always seemed to help me through the rougher passages of life. A few more made me cheerful, even exuberant (never silly, I hoped). With enough, I could forget the past, fake the present, fantasize a future, dance all night. But sometimes now there was not enough of anything. How had I let it all slip away – family, career, love, hope, joy? Was it taken from me? Had I discarded it, outgrown it? Had I traded it for a freedom that was simply a different kind of prison? Struck "fool's gold" instead of cherishing the "real thing"?

I could not remember, perhaps now would never know. I kept a pocket calendar in my purse and carefully recorded where I had been, who I had been with. I sat at my desk and made lists of things I could still recall, simple things like my children's birth dates, my sock size, my mother's phone number. I tried to call her at least once a month, and I wrote her occasionally. I read some of those letters when we cleaned out her house years later. They were filled with not-so-clever fiction, half-truths. Propaganda. Alternate facts. But I can still remember her long-since disconnected phone number. It's tucked away in a corner of my brain along with the chemical formula for water, the shortest verse in the Bible: "Jesus wept," the multiplication tables, the numbers for *pi* (at least to the fourth decimal place), my Social Security number, and the date of my birth.

My office windows overlooked the Chicago River. Every few weeks I would read in the *Tribune* that yet another corpse had been found along the riverbank or pulled from the water. And I couldn't swim; I had always been too afraid of water to learn. And when had I learned to be afraid of water? I had no idea. Maybe I wasn't afraid but had just refused to learn. When the window-cleaners came and opened the windows, I left my office until they were gone; the wind blowing off Lake Michigan and up the river seemed to breathe cold death. I no longer went to the 95th Floor of the Hancock Building for drinks or dinner, either on a date or alone. My presence seemed to make the building top-heavy, for it swayed until I was nearly seasick, the water sloshing back and forth in the commodes in the ladies' room.

When I couldn't sleep, I would sometimes remember that night over a year ago when I had decided to kill myself and had dared God to stop me, and that aging voice, far too trembly to be an angel's, asking, "Has anyone talked to you about God lately?" But I hadn't really wanted to be talked to about God. I had been "talked to" about God all my life, had even "talked God" to others, and it hadn't changed a thing. I had promised her and her friend that I wouldn't try to kill myself. (Perhaps whispered under my breath, "Not yet.") And I hadn't. Not yet. At least not quite.

I found a friend, a woman. Perhaps she found me, and at least she said she was my friend. We went to the Museum of Science and Industry to attend a concert on the south portico. My friend wore a wig all the time, with good reason: she had no hair. She had pulled it all out. I learned later that there's a name for that, trichotillomania. On the way to the Museum, she picked up bits and pieces of paper and metal, tabs off soft drink cans, cash register receipts, torn theatre tickets, and put them in her purse. It didn't seem polite to ask why. She told me that, as a child, she had buried her food in her family's back yard, but she told me proudly that she didn't do that anymore. Still, she was very thin. I wondered.

We looked at the Museum's Foucault Pendulum, and she told me its movements revealed the exact day, the hour, even the minute of her own death, but she was not at liberty to disclose the secret. When I mentioned the black carpet on the floor of my apartment and the supposed reason for it, she told me that she, too, was a witch and that she expected, any day now, to meet a warlock. I told her I was sure she would. I suspected I'd met some myself, men who seemed able to transform themselves into unfamiliar shapes, cast spells, appear and disappear at will.

We listened to a string quartet play Handel's Water Music. I'd never heard a string quartet before. I knew they were playing Handel because they passed out programs before the concert began. I had not lived a cultured life. Perhaps now I never would.

That spring and summer, drinking Black Label Scotch and chain-smoking Pall Mall cigarettes, I read the *Confessions of St. Augustine*. (He'd once been not-quite-saint material, you know.) Sometimes I looked into the Bible, not actually reading it, just opening the book at random as though seeking a message. There's a name for that, but I can never remember what it is. I know about "bibliophilia," but that's a different kind of mind-game, one with which I am *very* familiar.

I thought I might be dying. Surely no one could feel this sick, this tired, and still find the will to live. At least there was a name for my new friend's insanity. So I saw a doctor. For some reason he asked me how much I drank, and only after I had paid his receptionist and caught a bus for home did I wonder if he thought it unusual to count consumption in quarts and fifths instead of drinks.

The more I thought about it, the more I wondered if perhaps the drinking *was* a problem, even if I should do something about it. Late one night, after a particularly disconcerting evening, I decided I would. I stayed awake all that night so I would not forget my resolve, and next morning I called a number someone had given me a long time ago and was given an address just three or four blocks from my apartment.

I found the place. I even walked there. It was on a rather zigzagging course but not far, in fact just half a block from one of my favorite piano bars. It (not the piano bar) was called the Mustard Seed, on the ground floor of a crumbling old brownstone. The front two rooms (living room and dining room?) had streaked mustard-colored walls hung with slogans and hand-lettered plaques proclaiming "Live and Let Live," "Easy Does it," and "Think, Think, Think." The floors were covered in worn linoleum, and the rooms were furnished mostly with mismatched folding chairs. In the back room (formerly the kitchen?) a battered desk held a black telephone. Unlike the one in my Miro, this one was connected because it rang occasionally. An old card table in the front room, centered between two windows hung with torn plastic drapes, served as a podium for speakers. The cheap sound system spat and screeched like a scalded cat (well, at least a very angry one) every time it was turned on. The rooms smelled heavily of yesterday's smoke, occasionally of stale urine and sometimes even more putrid substances. No one seemed to be in charge. It was unlike any place I'd ever been or even seen in a movie; the people were all strangers, yet they seemed familiar. I was fascinated. I didn't really want to come back, but I couldn't seem to stay away.

I stopped in some mornings and had coffee before I caught the bus to work. I hurried there after work every night, then had a hamburger for dinner at the corner coffee shop so I could get back at eight. I listened to a black man with long dreadlocks braided into his graying beard who worked at the post office, a North Shore matron who was married to Chicago's garbage king, a six-foot tall Comanche who referred to himself as the "Indian princess," a scruffy little would-be pimp with dimestore rings on every finger who wore a broad-brimmed black fedora (they called him "Larry the Hat"), and others less colorful but just as interesting: secretaries, waitresses, socialites, bartenders, actors, doctors, gamblers, derelicts, housewives, lawyers, refugees from mental wards and parolees from prisons, defrocked ministers and disenchanted psychiatrists. There was even, occasionally, a recognizable celebrity. One and all, they greeted me as though I had been gone a long, long time. They said, quite simply, "Keep coming back." And one Sunday, two days after my 43rd birthday and my last drink--I'd had one to celebrate at the Drake Hotel dining room with women from my office--I heard one of them say, "Let Go and Let God," and realized it was not just a quote from a plaque on the wall. It was an order.

So I obeyed. Before I had a chance to change my mind, at about 2:00 in the afternoon on Sunday, July 23, 1977, down on my knees on the witch's black carpet, with my elbows on the bloodred coverlet, I gave as much of myself as I could to as much of God as I could understand. I understood very little, and there didn't seem much of me left to give. But apparently both the giving and the gift were enough.

I have never been able to explain what happened then. For a long time I could not even talk about it. Something I could not name filled the room: a vibrating soundless m-m-m-m like a tiny dynamo coming quietly alive and penetrating my very being. And there was peace that came in waves, flowing through my whole body in a river of content until that wondrous calm became at once luminous and personal, almost as though it was saying, "It's going to be all right." And somehow it was. And has been ever since.

Perhaps I exaggerate. Perhaps I romanticize. But even if I do, it doesn't matter. For though I still do not know what was in that room that day, now over 45 years ago, I have learned many names by which it *might* be called, or the names others call it: Tao, Atman, Jehovah, God, the Shekinah, the Christ, the Holy Spirit, Brahman, the Great Spirit, Ahura Mazda, even The Force. I know only that It was an Empowering Presence, and when It seemed no longer there, It left behind or perhaps had rekindled within me, an Indwelling Spirit; and whatever It was and whatever It left behind, It was enough to change my life. (If Gerald Schroeder, a Hebrew physicist/molecular biologist, whose most recent book was "God, According to God," can call God "It," capitalized, so shall I.)

For since that day I have sat in half a hundred places like that old brownstone building, shared my dark night of the soul and the change that penetrated every corner of my being and returned my life to me, transformed. I share the only Truth I know: what happened to me that day so long ago when I knelt on the witch's carpet and became subject to what was, I've come to believe, a kind of miracle. That feeling, that Memory, that Truth, is held safely in that same place where I keep close those memories of things I must never forget, nestled very near to my mother's old phone number, which has never--at least for me--been *Really* disconnected.

Carl Jung's prescription for recovery would describe my "miracle" as one of those "vital spiritual experience[s]…in the nature of huge emotional displacements and rearrangements" which could result in a "completely new set of conceptions and motives." He also mentions in other writings that, after the age of 30, most problems are spiritual rather than psychological. AA, and most religions, encourage personal inventories, beginning with one's past actions and relationships, and continuing that practice for a lifetime; I began. I continue.

In his book *Addiction and Grace*, one of the best descriptions of addiction I have ever read, Gerald May (doctor, minister, and psychiatrist) says: "Addiction is natural and pervasive in human life. . . We become addicted to our beliefs, our relationships, our understandings, and almost every other dimension of behavior and experience…It severely impedes human freedom…and makes us slaves to our compulsions. Grace, the freely flowing power of divine love in human life, is the only hope for true freedom from this enslavement."

When I knelt by my bed and spoke my prayer of capitulation to a power I did not understand, and experienced an Empowering Presence I have yet to more than barely comprehend, I have come to believe that grace had brought me "out of the pit," or, in my case "out of the witch's den." But I still had to somehow unlearn many of those intruding beliefs from my childhood that are always popping up unexpectedly.

I was in the ideal place to do it: in Chicago and in walking distance of that haven I had found (the Mustard Seed) where a tribe of recovering alcoholics was eager to assist me in my quest. They were reading the book sometimes known as the "Big Book", i.e., *Alcoholics Anonymous*, and the *Twelve Steps and Twelve Traditions*, which describes the AA program's practice and structure in greater detail. But they also suggested William James' *Varieties of Religious Experience*, Karen Horney's books on neurosis, Rollo May's *Courage to Be*, Bucke's *Cosmic Consciousness*, and anything by Carl Jung. One tall and emaciated man was working on his own translation of the New Testament because he didn't trust the original. I understood that so well. As a friend of mine often says of his own introduction to AA, "I had found my tribe."

They were indeed a bunch of people who would not ordinarily mix: the famous and the infamous, the very rich and the very poor, some who lived on "Park Avenue" and some who had spent the night on a park bench, the black man with the braided beard, doctors and lawyers, street punks, former (and current) panhandlers, the young Indian man who called himself the "Princess," all sitting with me in creaky folding chairs, alongside recently discharged patients from the local mental hospital (where alcoholics were often "treated" in those days) and recent parolees from the Cook County Jail. Jail, I learned, was the "winter resort" for street people.

My first sponsor was a young man who was spending his evenings having out-of-body experiences in which he visited the pyramids and other exotic points of interest. Or at least he said he did. He was "my kind of guy." His excursions were obviously free because he certainly didn't have money for more prosaic transportation. I remember vividly two things he told me. The first was, "You know everything you need to know; you just don't know you know it." And the morning I was writing this, one of my morning meditations ended, "Even if we have never done it, the knowledge of how to live our lives fully lies deep within us." Talk about synchronicity! That, my friends, is how *my* god talks to me.

The second thing my new friend told me was to "Expect the unexpected but expect that you won't expect it." For an egomaniac with an inferiority complex (which is a descriptive phrase sometimes used to describe self-centered tendencies) that was like being given a Buddhist koan, something like: "What is the sound of one hand clapping?" Still, my own experience in the years that followed has confirmed that the statement is true. All of which keeps me wondering if my sponsor really *did* visit the pyramids on those midnight trips. It was suggested that women should not have men as sponsors but, of course, I could not possibly comply with such a sensible suggestion. However, the one I chose seemed impervious to my feminine charms. In retrospect, I wonder if perhaps he had also taken a vow of celibacy.

I also lived just across the street from Water Tower Place, where there was a Kroch's and Brentano's bookstore to feed my hunger for understanding, and just a few blocks down the street was the main branch of the Chicago Public Library, where their stacks held translations of the writings of the early Church fathers, even the gnostics with their pneumas and pleromas. I spent the first year of my sobriety going to meetings and reading, and I've never stopped.

Mike S. reappeared on the scene briefly (his wife had died) and it was soon obvious that he was also an alcoholic. But he was not interested in sobriety. He made fun of my decorating taste, which he described as "middle-class bourgeoisie." His dismissal of my new life was disconcerting; his description of my decorating was insulting. There was obviously a reason he called himself the "Polish Prince." If, as Shakespeare said, "All the world's a stage and all the men and women merely players," at this point in my life I chose to pick up my red dancing shoes—the ones with rhinestone bows on the toes—(Really!) and walk through the nearest door marked, "Exit." I left no shoe behind for the "Polish Prince" (or any other prince) to find. But those red shoes remind me of the ones Dorothy wore on the way to see the *Wizard of Oz* in the movie of the same name. For I had been, like Dorothy and her friends, looking for someone or something to give me what I seemed to have been either born without or something I had once possessed but lost somewhere along the way: courage, a heart, and a brain (my sanity?). I had already learned that, like Dorothy, I couldn't seem to find my way back home again. Clicking my heels wouldn't do it, though. Steps might.

So I persisted, immersing myself in the books and meetings. First I decided I should avoid all members of the opposite sex until my head was more firmly screwed on. My little black book became slimmer until, finally, I put it away altogether. I also found a woman who proved the perfect combination to mentor my self-searching. She was a psychologist and a Presbyterian minister. For six months, I spent one evening every week talking to her about my past in what was probably a kind of extended confession. I do not remember her name, nor do I recall any advice she might have given me, but she listened as I began to shed my past like an outgrown garment and began the process of becoming someone entirely different. She helped me save my life.

As the weeks and months passed, I began to make friends with several women who were on the same journey. It had always been difficult for me to have real friends, male or female. Jay's and my friends tended to come in couples, perhaps because that was easiest, but also because Jay always seemed jealous of the time I spent with other people. And, outside of his father and brother, he didn't have many close male friends either I don't think we were unusual or that either of us was at fault. Marriage can do that.

There was also the "empty nest" syndrome to contend with. Most of my life outside work had involved our children and now they, too, were gone: Johnny had left on his own adventure, hitchhiking somewhere in the northwest; Mary was living in Germany with her soldier husband, and Becky was also living a single life now in the suburbs with her daughter Tracie. Letting go of our children, releasing them to make their own mistakes and learning from them is a wrenching, painful process. It may have looked, at least to them, as though I had abandoned them. But to me it seemed that there had been no other course. I was not strong enough (or perhaps not weak enough) to convince them, or even allow them, to stay. The only thing that seemed certain was that I had to learn to live this second half of my life on a new and different path.

As the months passed and I approached the end of a year of sobriety, I also realized that I was not a woman who wanted to live my life alone. I remember so clearly sitting down one day and compiling an inventory of all the things that would be important (and unimportant) in a relationship if I chose to have one and realizing that none of the men I had been either married to or involved with in the past fit the criteria on that list. I wanted someone who was intelligent, with a sense of humor, capable of tenderness and sensitivity, self-assured, with personal integrity. I was not at all interested in anyone with money, never had been and almost certainly never will be. Men with money thought they could control you. Still, it was important that he, whoever he might turn out to be, was at least "self-supporting from his own contributions." But most important of all was that any man who became a part of my future must first be my friend. Bill Babbington was a friend who became my husband.

Bill wasn't rich, important, or successful. He had once had money but hitting bottom with his own alcoholism had taken that away. His first wife had been killed in an automobile accident while pregnant with their first child. He spoke often of needing to go through a grieving process for her after he got sober, because he had used her memory as a reason not to commit to anyone else. He had no children (except, perhaps, a child with a woman in Texas that might or might not have been his).

He was alienated from his family by choice, partially because of his alcoholism but also, apparently, because he was afraid that their Irish-Catholic drama would destroy his sobriety. He asked me before he died not to get in touch with them. He said it was because he was afraid they would try to take away what we had accumulated monetarily (which, frankly, didn't seem enough for them to bother). Still, there had been a lot of bitterness over money in their family. It might possibly have been because he was concerned they would tell me things about his past that would turn me against him. I don't think they could have told me anything that would have done that.

Bill was an interesting man with a bucket load of confidence (call it arrogance and you might be more accurate). He was also a member of AA and dedicated to those principles. But most importantly, he treated me as though I was a person and not just a possession or his private cook, mistress, maid, and housekeeper. Both of his parents were dead--he took me one day to visit their graves--and it was apparent that he had respected his father, loved and liked his mother, and I have always believed that men who admire their mothers make good husbands. (Jay's mother loved him unreservedly, and his grandmother adored him, but I don't think that's the same thing.)

Perhaps most importantly, Bill valued in me all those qualities I valued in myself. I respected his opinions: he could advise me, and I would actually take his advice (after a suitable period of hesitation to prevent his possibly thinking he was the boss). We had similar interests, and he encouraged me to grow and develop as I needed to. We were both alcoholics, each of us devoted to recovery, we had both had life-after-death experiences, and we both loved to read. I may have been the one who proposed to him. I wanted marriage, perhaps so that he wouldn't go away. I remember asking once, in the beginning, if he would love me "forever." And he said, "I'll try, but there are no guarantees, and no one knows what will happen down the road." I didn't like the answer because I wanted absolutes. But I knew he was telling me the truth, and truth had become very important to me. I'd learned that it really *can* set you free.

We were married, on July 22 of 1978, just one day after my first "anniversary" and (not coincidentally) one day after my 44th birthday. Officially, we were married by a judge at the Cook County Clerk's office, with two friends as our witnesses. One was a young gay black man who had been a dancer on Broadway. He would later commit suicide. We have lost so many friends to death and self-destruction along this way.

The next day we had a reception at our apartment for 20 or so of our friends, and ALSO Johnny, Becky, and my first (and at that time my only) granddaughter Tracie. And there we said private vows that we had each written. We would remain married until Bill's death on February 28, 1995, nearly 17 years. And here we are:

A few weeks after our wedding Bill came home pulling a little wagon with the first batch of the 62 volumes of The Great Books of the Western World. Someone in the building where he was working was throwing them away, and he knew exactly where they belonged: on his new wife's bookshelves. I started to read my way through the Great Books– skipping, I'll admit, anything having to do with science or mathematics. (Science came later, but mathematics will still have to wait its turn.) And, of course, I read Emmet Fox, as I still do today, as well as Joel Goldsmith, a Christian Science healer whose books on meditation had become the foundation for a spiritual practice he called *The Infinite Way*.

During that first year, I had begun looking for answers to what made me tick. I read a lot of books, and one of them was Karen Horney's *Our Inner Conflicts*. It's still on my bookshelf, on the "psychology-philosophy-science-quantum physics" side of the room. There's even a bookmark at the chapter "The Basic Conflict," which says, in part (and I've changed only the gender words), "*As I see it, the source of the conflict revolves around the neurotic's loss of capacity to wish for anything wholeheartedly because her very wishes are divided, that is, go in opposite directions.*" Carl Jung (Horney also quotes him often) "*placed considerable emphasis on the opposing tendencies in human beings.*" But Jung believed that those opposing tendencies were complementary, not conflicting, and the solution was to bring them into harmony. And how do such tendencies develop? Horney believed that they went back to childhood when the child is raised in an environment that produces a feeling of being "*isolated and helpless in a potentially hostile world.*" She goes on to explain it far better than I ever could:

> "*A wide range of adverse factors in the environment can produce this insecurity in a child: direct or indirect domination, indifference, erratic behavior, lack of respect for the child's individual needs, lack of real guidance,*

disparaging attitudes, too much admiration or the absence of it, lack of reliable warmth, having to take sides in parental disagreements, too much or too little responsibility, overprotection, isolation from other children, injustice, discrimination, unkept promises, hostile atmosphere, and so on and so on.

"The only factor to which I should like to draw special attention in this context is the child's sense of lurking hypocrisy in the environment: her feeling that the parents' love, their Christian charity, honesty, generosity, and so on may be only pretense. Part of what the child feels on this score is really hypocrisy; but some of it may be just her reaction to all the contradictions she senses..."

And so the child gropes for ways to keep going, ways to cope with this menacing world. "Despite her own weakness and fears she unconsciously shapes her tactics to meet the particular forces operating in her environment. In doing so, she develops not only ad hoc strategies but lasting character trends which become part of her personality."

Eventually three main lines crystallize: the child moves *toward* people, *against* them, or *away* from them. If she moves *toward*, she tries to win people's affection and lean on them; only then can she feel safe. If she moves *against* people, she accepts and takes for granted their hostility and determines consciously or unconsciously to fight, to rebel in any way open to her. When she moves *away* from people *"she wants neither to belong nor to fight, but keeps apart. She feels she has not much in common with them, they do not understand her anyhow. <u>She builds up a world of her own—with nature, with her dolls, her books, her dreams</u>." (Emphasis added.)*

And that, for anyone who may be interested, is how I believe I became: "A Conventional Nonconformist." The next chapter in Horney's book is heavily underlined, although I do not ordinarily underline my books. But I wanted to remember the things she helped me to understand, and to forgive in myself and others. All my young life I had grown up in the midst of contradictions: two different households, two different worlds, four very different people and, quite simply, I tried to please them all. And so, today, I understand so much. But only in retrospect.

Residue

I raked the last of summer's leaves today. It's nearly spring,

But leaves of some trees—oak, especially—take all winter to fall.

People in China, I've heard, save tears of joy in tiny jars

To drink in times of grief. I wish I'd known…when I still cried.

But I didn't cry, either in joy or in grief. I always wrote instead, and my words fell on the page like tears, the tears I could not, or *would* not, cry.

When I was about two years sober I met a woman who became my mentor for a while. Barbara was interested in *A Course in Miracles*, which was being taught at Unity School of Christianity. We attended those classes together, and later my growing family went to occasional services on Sundays. I have "flirted" with the *Course* through the last 45 years, but I can never quite overcome my suspicions regarding anything "channeled" from Jesus to a psychiatrist, reportedly despite her objections to being singled out for the experience, as the course is reported (or purported?) to be.

There was also a *Science of Mind* service on Sunday mornings in Water Tower Place. Those were my sources and my influences in those early days of recovery, and I've had many more teachers, living and dead, in the last 45 years – now over half my lifetime. My husband Bill was one of them.

Perhaps Bill's and my marriage worked because I first asked myself, "Am I capable of being a good and faithful person, and really working on this marriage?" He certainly was. He really wanted what was best for both of us, and I believe I did too. He had a problem with anger, but he was aware of it and tried to handle it in such a way that it did not affect our marriage. He wasn't always successful, but only once or twice did his anger cause a problem in our marriage, and in neither instance was that anger directed toward me. I also realized at some point that his anger felt like safety to me once I realized it would never be directed against me but would be available should I, or anyone in our family, need protection. For the most part he was a patient, generous, and thoughtful man, but with an edge that made you realize he definitely had boundaries.

Even before we married, I had moved to a larger apartment in the same building, an apartment which was the other half of a unit similar to my first one. This new one had a non-functioning fireplace and built-in bookcases in the living room and a miniscule corridor kitchen that reminded me very much of the tiny kitchen in the Chicago apartment where Jay and I had lived after Johnny was born in 1955. It may have been built in the same era. The bathroom was not much larger.

We lived there for the next four years, and they were years of growth and change for me. I worked first for a secretarial service headquartered in the John Hancock Building, which was just kitty-corner across the street, and Bill worked as a security guard for an apartment building on Cedar Street, a four or five-block walk northwest of our apartment. But his strong independent streak soon made it imperative that he start his own business. He first began a window-washing service for downtown high rises with very little equipment: a moped for transportation and squeegees and sponges for the jobs. He would exchange that eventually for another startup: a bulk newspaper delivery service for suburban weekly newspapers, which required graduating from the moped to a pickup and then a box truck.

As things settled down, and I began to feel my feet on solid ground, I took a job at the American Institute of Steel Construction as secretary to their Director of Marketing. It would lead, over the next few years, to my appointment as Director of Public Relations.

My scrapbooks began filling up with pictures of a growing family. Mary Beth and her husband Phil returned from Germany in the spring of 1979, and their first child, Scott Spencer Culp was born at Fort Carson, Colorado, where Phil was stationed.

That fall, however, was a sad time for everyone. Dad had been having difficulty with COPD for some time, and in October he was hospitalized. Except for a brief attempt to bring him home, he remained hospitalized until his death on November 18, 1979. Bill and I went home by train for the last few days of Dad's life, and I stayed on through Thanksgiving to be with Mom as she took care of the necessary details and the aftermath of adjusting to life without Dad.

And while I couldn't be in Colorado when Scott was born, the summer after Dad died, Bill and I borrowed my brother Kent's Thunderbird and, along with Mom and her friend Frances Rice (widow of my eighth-grade teacher Jack Rice) went to Colorado Springs to visit Mary Beth and the newest addition to the family. It was a wonderful trip, and we got to do some sight-seeing at the Garden of the Gods and Cave of the Winds. Uncle Ernest had been a bit concerned about traveling arrangements. He asked Bill, "How are you going to take three women on a trip?" Well, Bill managed just fine, and Mom and Frances were good traveling companions. The following spring, Mary's second child, her daughter Terri Lynn Culp, was born in Colorado.

Bill worked the second shift most of the time, so in the evenings I had begun to write again, and when he insisted that writers try to get published, I gave it a shot, and my novel, *Down River,* was purchased and finally published in 1981. We went back home that fall for a book-signing party in Metropolis, which Mom happily arranged. And while we were there, we bought a pickup truck, our first vehicle as a married couple. Becky and Tracie were with us.

In June of 1982, Jay remarried, to LaVinia Garland. They came down to Pope County for the wedding. The same weekend, whether coincidentally or on purpose, Phil brought Mary, Scott, and Terri to Mom's house in Massac County and left them there to "go find himself," a journey of discovery which brought him back on only three or four occasions over the next thirty-five years.

Phil had been having his own difficulties with addiction and, as a consequence, had been discharged from service. Terri Lynn was just recovering from extensive cranial surgery. The sutures in her skull, which should remain open enough to "spread" and allow for brain growth, had closed prematurely. She was fortunate that one of only three hospitals in the country that performed that surgery was in Colorado, and the expense of surgery had been covered by the Army. As soon as we realized that Phil had no plans to return for his family, Bill and I knew that Mary and the children belonged with us. Sometime in late June or early July we loaded everybody up and brought them home to Chicago.

There were some hurdles to overcome, of course. The first was that the one-bedroom apartment where Bill and I had lived since we were married was far too small with the additions to our family, and we were also in the heart of the city. It was certainly no place to raise children. Mary was also expecting another child in January, so we found an apartment at 2809 West Logan Boulevard (I know that's the street; I'm pretty sure that's the number, but it might have been 2908).

We moved before Christmas, and Raymond was born in January of 1983. I doubt if Raymond realizes even now that he was born just two days after his "Grandpa Bill's" actual birthday (which Bill had changed to an earlier one so he could join the Army, serving in the 101st Airborne). I didn't know that myself until a few months before his death when he revealed the location of the birth certificate he had kept hidden all those years. I still have no idea why he had kept it secret, but he didn't tell me, and it never occurred to me to ask. Mother came to help with the new baby, and Bill and I picked her up in the pickup truck we had acquired that previous fall when we had gone back to Southern Illinois for the book signing party. (That was also the day I had my last cigarette!)

By this time Bill had started his new business venture, delivering bulk newspapers from Indiana, where they were printed, to their individual offices in various suburbs. I had pneumonia that fall and winter, and Bill, Mary and I decided that we would quit smoking a few days before Raymond was born. Mom was coming to visit to help with the baby, and when Bill picked me up at my office for the trip to pick her up at the train station, he said, "Lona, do you have any cigarettes left?" I had only one, and I gave it to him. He smoked my last cigarette, and that was 39 years ago this past January. I have never smoked another. Unfortunately, he was not so successful at quitting. Mary didn't stop until 2019, and then for reasons of her own.

The apartment on Logan Boulevard was on the ground floor of a well-built brick four-flat. There were three bedrooms (one had obviously been a maid's room, off the kitchen), a large living room with a pseudo-fireplace, and a glassed-in sun porch (which became "*my* room," a huge dining room with built-in oak bookcases, and a functional kitchen (but no upper cabinets). There were washers and dryers in the basement, but Mary spent more time doing laundry in the months that followed than I did. I don't recall all the other tenants in the building, but I do remember the couple across the hall in the other ground floor apartment were from Cuba, with two sons in their late teens or early 20s.

I also remember distinctly the day Bill and I unloaded the boxes of my books onto the back porch of the new apartment and carried them inside. "I hope you read these while we live here so I won't have to do this again," he said. I'm not sure if he was just joking, but I know I didn't tell him that I'd already read almost every one and was planning to buy a lot more, and carry them with me wherever I went. They were a whole lot more precious than that old Kroehler sofa Jay and I had lugged around for nearly 20 years.

At some point that late summer or early fall (my memory falters, but it was before Mary's pregnancy was too advanced), she and Bill made a trip back to Colorado Springs to pack up whatever belongings she could collect from her marriage to Phil. I do remember that one or both were sick with the flu even before they left, but they went anyway and returned with a full load in the pickup truck. We bought whatever furniture we needed to accommodate all the extra people, and I made frequent weekend forays to every resale shop on the North Side for clothes and other equipment necessary for a new infant and two growing children. We hung the quilts I had been making the last two or three years on the walls to brighten up the space. It soon felt like home.

The two years we lived on Logan Boulevard were busy. There was an AA Club, "Logan Square," that we attended frequently, and Mary joined the Alanon Group. Since there were three adults in the house, one could always stay home and babysit while the other two went to a meeting. And there was an occasional dance at Logan Square for entertainment. On holidays, especially Thanksgiving and Christmas, we hosted an open house that sometimes welcomed as many as 30 or 40 people for the day. (Becky was not quite sure what to make of all the strangers.) Johnny was still in Colorado Springs, where he had been living the last couple of years after joining Mary and Phil there.

When our family suddenly expanded, I had already been working for a year or two for the American Institute of Steel Construction as secretary to their Director of Marketing. After we moved to Logan Boulevard, Bill drove me to work every morning, often bringing either Scott or Terri, and sometimes both, with us. There was a ferry that docked on the Chicago River, right beside my office building on Michigan Avenue, which carried suburban commuters to and from the train station; it provided an inexpensive morning boat ride for Bill and the kids if the weather permitted. Some mornings they would stop on the way home at the Lincoln Park Zoo, where they would often be just in time to help feed the animals.

I remember when Mary found Bill giving the three children a bath. She was astonished. She had never seen a man give a child a bath before. When my mother came to visit early in our marriage, he had made dinner (rock cornish game hen and wild rice). She said it was the first meal a man had ever cooked for her. He enjoyed the children and was so unselfish where things for them were concerned, almost overly generous at times. He loved them. He loved me. I don't think I ever doubted that for even a day.

Soon after we were married, Bill acquired a camera, and he became a compulsive photographer. I have three scrapbooks full of pictures from the next ten years. One is of the years when we lived in the apartment just a block and a half from Lake Michigan, one is of the trip we took to Colorado, and one of the seven years we lived either in the apartment on Logan Square or the house we bought on North Oakley. They track the passage of the years of our marriage, the growing up years of my grandchildren—Becky and her daughter Tracie were frequent visitors--and the many occasions we all celebrated together.

Although our family required most of our time, Bill and I took a real estate course together, planning to look for and buy a property to either "rescue" or "flip." So when we had an unexpected windfall (a very *very* small inheritance from Bill's maiden aunt, who had probably forgotten he existed but nonetheless had left behind a savings bond in his name), we bought a three-flat at 2913 North Oakley which we rehabbed in the beginning solely with the help of a Reader's Digest Home Improvement Manual, and some expert advice from the employees of the local Ace Hardware Store.

This was an adventure of another kind. The house was built in 1903, and it was not in good condition. But Bill and I had taken that real estate course and convinced ourselves that investing in an older property, rehabbing it, and then flipping it for a huge profit would be the key to success. We had absolutely no idea what we were doing. But we did it anyway. Therein, of course, lies a story that demands to be told.

The building we bought had three apartments and also an English basement that had been rented as an apartment at one time; the entrance to the basement was underneath the front steps. The top floor had previously been an attic, but the roof had been "raised," and one side "bumped out" to allow for head room. The first and second floors had each been divided into two units, so the building actually had six kitchens, six bathrooms (and five bathtubs!). To someone like me who had been raised with none at all, we had what might be described as an "embarrassment of riches." It was actually an embarrassment on several scores, as we were to discover. (The previous transformations were from the World War II years when housing was at a premium in Chicago.)

It also had three tenants at the time we bought it, which meant that while we owned an apartment building, we couldn't move in right away. The people who lived on the second floor finally moved out--they may have been the previous owners--so we decided to occupy that floor, although we planned to eventually live on the first floor and put in a spiral stairway that would allow us to access the basement directly from the first-floor apartment.

But the first-floor occupants didn't want to move, insisting they didn't have to. They were Spanish-speaking, I believe from Puerto Rico, and attended the local Catholic church. There was a mother, a grandmother, and two or three children (no males present that I can recall), and the adults were convinced that they could not be removed because there were children in the household. We tried several ploys to convince them that moving would be a good idea, but all arguments failed until Bill said, "Let me talk to them." I have no idea what he said that changed their minds (although I have a slight suspicion that it might have had something to do with his (absolutely fictional) connection with someone in the Puerto Rican Mafia. I believe the Church rescued them when they decided that Bill was a man to be reckoned with, because they were gone by the end of the month. If I owe them any amends, they will have to be collected in my "afterlife."

So we moved downstairs, and while we were trying to exist on the first floor (storing our tableware in plastic bins between meals to protect it from the creepy-crawly critters that seemed to live everywhere, including the ceilings and light fixtures) we proceeded to repair and refurbish the second floor, which involved scraping off nearly 80 years of wallpaper (under which we found live roaches busily making babies) down to the Victorian-era green and gray painted walls. We tried everything to speed up the process until we were finally forced to rent wallpaper steamers. It was the middle of July with no air-conditioning! It gave new meaning to the phrase, "It works if you work it." We ripped up carpet and linoleum, put a dropped ceiling in the original kitchen, and ripped out the second kitchen that someone had installed in a too-narrow hallway. We painted and sometimes wallpapered, refinished woodwork, and scrubbed neglected appliances.

Meanwhile, we also had tenants on the third floor who seemed to think it unnecessary to pay rent. They also seemed to have rather interesting lives. Two young women and their two or three very small children lived there and had a constant stream of visitors, almost exclusively male, including an occasional police officer in full uniform, stomping up and down the stairway at all hours of the day and night. Since the police officers seemed to be arresting no one and merely stopping for a brief "visit," we came to possibly unfair (but more probably accurate) conclusions.

I do not remember why the young ladies (and I hesitate to describe them as "ladies") finally left, but I do remember that **when** they left, there were mattresses tied on the rooftops of cars with front ends that were absent working headlamps, and back ends that blew black smoke. They left behind three garbage cans full of dirty diapers and two more of trash, which had to be handled and disposed of wearing rubber gloves. We did not, unfortunately, have access to gas masks. Those books on flipping houses had not mentioned having to dispose of hazardous waste.

While all this was going on, Bill was trying to run a business. Mary was trying to raise three small children in a construction zone. I was going to work every morning in a business suit and high heels and coming home at night to chaos. When winter arrived, we realized the antiquated furnace in the basement which supplied steam heat to all three apartments was woefully inadequate, so we installed individual forced air heaters in all three apartments. I believe we at least hired professionals for that. But maybe not. We were not only ambitious, we were also quite possibly dangerous to ourselves and others.

Mary and I installed a closet in the third-floor apartment, boxing off a corner of one bedroom. It was our first carpentry job (but not our last). And when I had just finished wallpapering the living room there, Raymond (not quite three) climbed up the stairs on hands and knees, found a brush I had left unattended in the roller pan, and tried to "help" by painting the brand new, still damp from paste, wallpaper. It is, I believe, one of his earliest memories. He has become much more adept with a paintbrush since and has developed other rehabbing skills as well. Who knows, we may have inspired him!

There was a "synchronistic" moment when we decided to cut all the old radiators out of the first and second-floor apartments and realized that we would need a saws-all to cut through the old iron pipes. Short of cash as always, we were about to consider simply delaying the job to another time when Bill remembered a metal case of some sort which he had agreed to "hold" for a young man he had tried to sponsor. He had never looked inside the case, and the young man had disappeared and never reclaimed it. But, lo and behold, when he looked inside there was a nearly new saws-all. We were surprised, but Mom, who was visiting at the time, said simply, "God has a way of answering our needs even before we know what our needs are." What a beautiful description of grace!

We rented the attic apartment to one of Bill's sponsees, Dave McNair, and the (finally finished) second-floor apartment to two single women, and almost asphyxiated the women when the gas connection to the kitchen stove proved faulty. Bill's and my pipe-fitting skills left much to be desired. One of the few arguments of our marriage involved a dispute over whether one should screw clockwise or counterclockwise in order to "unscrew" a stubborn pipe connection. We were trying to install a new kitchen sink in our own apartment on the first floor. Bill ended the somewhat heated discussion by taking a deep breath and saying quietly, "Would you please go away for a little while and come back later?" I complied, quietly, I hope. (Maybe not *too* quietly.)

One Sunday morning I visited the local Ace Hardware Store with another serious plumbing problem and was introduced to compression fittings. Google them if you've never been introduced to the concept. Compression fittings may very well have saved our marriage. And I am absolutely convinced to this day that I was correct about which direction one should turn to *un*screw a pipe fitting!

One Easter weekend, we disconnected piping in the basement and then discovered, quite late in the evening, that we did not have the necessary supplies to reconnect it. We were left with no way to provide water for anyone in the building. Since the next day was Easter Sunday, all the hardware stores in the city were closed. I went to bed, pulled the quilts over my head, and cried in sheer frustration. It was not one of the best days of my life, but it wasn't the worst one either.

We installed all new fixtures in one bathroom, and I learned how to cut and install ceramic tile on the walls and floor. Hardest physical work I've ever done. I went to my company's annual convention one weekend during that particular remodeling job, spent four days in a luxury suite at the Arizona Biltmore in Phoenix, ate dinner at a 5-star restaurant in the desert, danced to the music of two bands (country-western in jeans and boots on Friday, swing-and-sway in a red ballgown on Saturday) and came home to bathroom walls so denuded of plaster that you could see daylight through the cracks when you took a bath. (The truth, I swear!) And that red dress was the most expensive one I've ever bought for myself. (It was NOT from a resale or consignment shop.) I have never told anyone how much it cost, including Bill. There are some things that should remain forever secret. I've worn it at least twice more (once for Halloween). But I will be prepared in the event a ballgown is again required.

The weekend of my Arizona excursion was also Thanksgiving weekend, and Bill had taken Mary and the kids to a Chinese restaurant for Thanksgiving dinner. "Those were the days, my friends; I thought they'd never end; oh yes, my friends, those were the days." That's an excerpt from a song about (I think) young life in Paris that bears repeating; I can't imagine why it fits middle-aged life in Chicago, but it does. I've heard that song in my head more than once in my life. Sometimes in good times, sometimes not-so-good.

But we proved unstoppable. We finally reached a stage where we could obtain a second mortgage and hire a construction company to finish the outside work: siding and roofing the house, bumping out the rear wall of the kitchen for a dining room, with a patio on two sides and sliding doors to the outside, and even replacing the broken sidewalks in front of the house.

Mary exercised her green thumb with planter boxes on the patio railings and the backyard. People drove down our back alley just to admire the display. She also got a part-time job at the greenhouse just a block down the street, and Bill marked the years with photographs of the children's birthdays, Christmas, and Halloween (always a very big holiday in our family, along with Thanksgiving, both bigger even than Christmas).

Phil came home just once, the first time Mary and the children had seen him since before Raymond was born. He'd asked to visit, and after some consideration Mary decided that the children needed to see their father in the flesh. For Raymond, it would be the first time ever. Scott could vaguely remember his father and had begun to develop outsized ideas of what their relationship had been and could be. But a single weekend, which provided a healthy dose of reality, was enough to convince the children (and Mary) that things were fine just as they were. Phil left once again, and I don't recall seeing him again until he came back for Terri's marriage nearly 15 years later. The kids have stayed in touch though, at least on occasion.

The years on Oakley passed so quickly. Bill's business increased and my career with AISC blossomed into a promotion to Director of Public Relations. I still did a great deal of writing, but it was almost all public relations and news of the industry, and most of my work after the promotion was managing the details of the conferences and trade shows, even one of which could involve 1,500 or more people in attendance.

That meant out-of-town travel at least twice a year, once for the Annual Convention-- always to a resort spot--and once for the Annual Conference and Trade Show for those in the steel construction industry: steel manufacturers, fabricators, and builders, engineering professionals, and those in engineering education. On those occasions, many of the attendees' wives came along. I got to spend time at places far out of my usual budget and social milieu: the Greenbriar in West Virginia, the Broadmoor in Colorado Springs (where I visited Johnny, who was still living there), the Arizona Biltmore, The Hilton in New Orleans, Boca Raton Hotel and Golf Resort in Florida. It was, in many ways, the "flip side" of newspaper work. One year, AISC held the annual trade show in Nashville, Tennessee at the Opryland Hotel, and the whole family spent the week there. While it was a working vacation for me, it was definitely a "playing vacation" for them, with daily visits to Opryland Theme Park (since turned into a shopping center), evening and afternoon swims in the hotel pool, and a show at the Grand Ole Opry theater. I'm pretty sure it's a week that none of them ever forgot.

In about 1987 or '88 we bought a camping trailer parked in a year-round camping village near Aurora. It was a carefully protected place with 24-hour security, two swimming pools, ponds for fishing, and other children to play with. Some of the occupants lived there year-round while other retirees stayed in summer and then left for

Florida or Texas in winter. I cannot recall how we discovered it, but it was a great getaway place for all of us. Mary and the children spent a couple of summer vacations there, and we bought a 9-passenger Ford van to haul us all around.

In October of 1988 Jay's father, Garvon Crabb, died in Southern Illinois, where Jay's mother, Elsie, had been living for a number of years. It would have been awkward for Bill and me to bring Mary and the children down for the service. Jay's wife did not particularly like me or any of Jay's and my children or grandchildren. School and work made it difficult for Mary to attend by herself. Johnny was still living in Colorado, and Becky and Tracie were living in the suburbs. Broken families seem to always reveal their brokenness in the most naked way when togetherness would bring the measure of comfort that is so sorely needed.

Bill and I, however, were in Southern Illinois in October of 1989 when my brother Kent and Donna Kay Cooper were married at her sister's home outside Paducah. Both Kent and Donna had been married before; both marriages had ended in divorce; Kent had no children, Donna has two: Charles and Jodi Price. Kent and Donna celebrated 34 years of marriage in 2023.

Following the timeline of these events, it occurs to me that being home for the weekend and attending a family occasion may have put the idea in my mind that it just might be time to go home for good. While Mom was still living at home and seemed in good health, she was getting older. We were also experiencing some problems with living and raising the children in Chicago. The friendly corner store was bought by a stranger who spoke only broken English; the students at the school Scott and Terri attended were of so many backgrounds that our three seemed lost in the shuffle. Scott's new bicycle was stolen – actually just taken – by three boys who simply demanded he give it up to them. We were also awakened in the middle of the night by a police officer who advised that he had just arrested a thief who had broken into our garage and was hauling away its contents in our own rolling garbage can. The officer's visit to the burglar's home revealed that he had made more than one trip.

And Bill's health was obviously deteriorating. An episode of "cat scratch fever" –acquired from the kittens of a stray cat who had delivered them under our back deck--had put him in the hospital for several days, and his respiratory problems seemed to worsen every winter. How much longer could he continue with his business? And was I really happy with my own job? No, not really. Having a great deal of responsibility with little or no power to manage it is one recipe for resentment.

We finally put the apartment building on the market, planning to move to the suburbs; it seemed the logical course of action. We even found a place (in Elmhurst, as I recall, a house with a swimming pool), and made an offer contingent on the sale of the apartment building on Oakley. Although the other two apartments were rented and the renovations all completed, it was becoming far too confining. We all lacked privacy, and although the Aurora vacation property offered temporary escape, it had merely whetted our appetite for a safe place with good schools, compatible lifestyles, and closer relationships with family.

We had at least one offer for the building, which would have cleared our mortgages and the other debts we had incurred for construction and also given us a comfortable profit, which would have allowed us to purchase the house in the suburbs. But it didn't "feel right," is the only way I can describe it. I had lived in the suburbs. It just wasn't enough. And while Bill and I were both making good money professionally (that last year in Chicago our combined incomes were well over $100,000), it wasn't buying us the life we wanted for ourselves or for Mary and her three children.

Mom was living alone on the farm, and the children had almost no contact with her or other members of our extended family. Becky (now disengaged from her long-time companion) and Tracie were frequent visitors, but they still lived in Wheaton. Nor did we have any close friends with children the ages of Scott, Terri, and Raymond. Mary was single and dated, but she had few opportunities to develop a long-term relationship with someone anxious to share responsibility for three small children.

Finally, Bill and I sat down and talked about the whole situation and he asked me a very simple question: "What do you *want* to do, Lona?" The emphasis on the "want" seemed to demand honesty. The answer came tumbling out with all the certainty of a "done deal."

"I want to go home." And so we did.

"There's a happy land somewhere,

And it's just a prayer away.

All my dreams and plans are there,

And it's just a prayer away.

Where the skies look down

On a friendly town

Filled with laughing children at play.

And my heart will sing

For it means one thing,

We'll be home at the close of each day.

There's a happy land somewhere,

And it's just a prayer away."

Song Lyrics from "Just a Prayer Away"

"It ain't what I don't know that hurts me. It's what I know for certain that just ain't so."

- Anonymous

Home Again, Home Again, Jiggety-Jig

We went home. Or perhaps that's a misstatement. Perhaps what we really did was to *make* another *new* home. But it took us a while, and there were more than a few doubts, debts, detours, and disappointments along the way. It was the spring of 1990 when we made our decision.

The apartment house was already on the market. But a move back to Southern Illinois, or at least in that general vicinity, would also necessitate Bill closing his business and my leaving the job at AISC. We were nearing the end of the school year, and it seemed advisable to relocate before the beginning of the next. Bill had no written contracts, only oral agreements with the several newspapers he served, so that presented no particular difficulties. But leaving AISC was a bit more complicated. I was 56, not yet old enough to retire, though we eventually learned I would be old enough to move my (not abundant) retirement funds without penalty. Still, neither of us was old enough, and we certainly didn't have nearly enough money to simply retire. We were hoping to realize quite a lot out of the sale of the building. But we would both have to find other employment wherever we lived. And Mary also wanted to work.

After considerable discussion, we decided that moving to Massac County, where all my family lived (mother, sister, brother, nieces, nephews, cousins, and uncles) was not a good idea. I had been gone a long time, and I had serious doubts about whether my city lifestyle would fit in with my hometown, or even with my family. There was also employment to be considered. Options in Metropolis, the only town in Massac County, were very limited. There were no positions available for public relations directors or newspaper editors and, even if available, that sort of work seemed a part of my past and not particularly attractive for my own future.

Paducah, just across the river from Metropolis, was a larger metropolitan area, though not quite large enough to be considered an actual city. But a few miles east of Paducah in Marshall County there was a large industrial complex that seemed to offer possibilities. The school system in Marshall County also seemed to be a good one, and the idea of being within thirty minutes driving distance of Murray State University was definitely an attraction. I had the idea that sometime in the not-too-distant future I might be able to finish my bachelor's degree. And if any of my grandchildren should want to go to college, it would be both close and economical for them as well.

Bill and I spent one or two long weekends driving around Western Kentucky with Mom for company, surveying the area. We began to zero in on Marshall County, and particularly Calvert City, found a real estate agent and began looking at houses. Bill thought a house out in the country would be great; he'd never really lived in the country, so the idea of privacy and solitude was very attractive to him. But I had my doubts. I knew how isolated the country can be, and I also realized, though we didn't talk about it, that Bill's health wasn't good and that the children and Mary might be happier at least somewhat close to a town and perhaps even within walking distance of a school.

In fairly short order we found a house that seemed ideal, a tri-level brick at 588 Oak Park Boulevard with four bedrooms and two baths on the third floor, a large living/dining room with fireplace and kitchen large enough for a breakfast table on the main floor, and a large family room with yet another fireplace, a laundry room and powder room AND two-car garage on the ground floor. The house was also just off the entrance to the Purchase Parkway and I-24. Driving time from our house to Mom's was only 45 minutes, so we'd be close enough to visit often. The price seemed quite reasonable and very affordable considering the amount we were expecting to realize from our three-flat apartment building. We made an offer contingent on the sale of the building, put down some earnest money, went back to Chicago and started figuring out what we were going to do to make a living in Kentucky.

Based on several stints of work as a legal secretary over the years (none recent), I sent resumes to all the law firms in Paducah. Bill contacted the Paducah Sun and soon arranged to work for them delivering bulk papers to their newsstands in the area. He would later begin night-time delivery to individual homes in Marshall County. I found a job with a fairly large law firm located in the Executive Inn. We turned over management of the apartment building to the real estate firm that had the for-sale listing and started packing.

By this time we had acquired three vehicles: a large box truck which Bill used solely for bulk newspaper delivery, a nine-passenger Ford van we used for family travel, and a little Ford Focus for those times when two of the three adults in our family had separate plans.

Over the last weekend in June, we loaded the box truck with as much as it would hold and Bill headed for Southern Illinois with me following a couple of hours later in the Focus. He arrived safely at Mom's house, but about 2 hours into my solo trip, I entered a single-lane construction zone, boxed between two semis traveling at high speed. I hit a huge pothole that bounced the little lightweight Focus into the adjoining lane, which was blocked by orange traffic cones. In my efforts to avoid the cones (and have them bounce up into my windshield), the right-side tires of the Focus slid off the roadway onto a grassy slope, and I began sliding first sideways and then, as the slope became steeper, slowly turning over until the Focus landed upside down in a rather deep depression formed by a curved exit ramp leading off the expressway at just that point.

Fortunately, my automatic seat belt held me in place, though leaving me dangling upside down, my head not quite touching the ceiling of the car. The engine was still running so I was able to lower the driver's side window, turn off the engine (which automatically released the seat belt) and crawl out onto the ground. My only injury was a slight scratch on one of my elbows. I did have to reach back in and retrieve my upper denture from the roof of the car. I had deposited it temporarily on the dashboard just before the accident, and gravity had done the rest!

An elderly couple who had witnessed the accident stopped and rescued me, drove me to a motel and restaurant rest-stop within sight of the accident, where we called the police and I called Bill at Mom's. (This was *still* before the days of cell phones.) The police officer took me back to the scene, agreed with my version of the accident (no sobriety test!) and then back to the motel where I took a shower--the accident was ***very*** stressful--and waited for Bill and Mom to arrive in her car six hours or so later.

Mom confided that Bill didn't say a word the whole trip. His first wife had been killed in an automobile accident several years before I met him, and he had seen it happen. He was following her in another vehicle when a drunk driver T-boned her car, killing her instantly, along with their unborn child. I am quite certain that he wasn't sure I was OK until he could see for himself. We retrieved the few belongings I had been transporting south—some luggage, my Pfaff sewing machine, and my computer--left the car to be towed to a repair shop in the town nearest the accident and headed south to unpack the box truck.

Fortunately, my brother Kent sent two of his employees to help us unload at the new house in Kentucky. When we were finished, we spent the night at Mom's and then headed back to Chicago to finish emptying the apartment and return to Calvert City with Bill driving the truck and Mary with the kids in the Ford passenger van. It was the 4th of July weekend, 1990.

It was not a promising beginning. But we were all in one place, and thankfully all in one piece, ready for whatever came next. My first AA sponsor had warned me a long time before to "expect the unexpected, but also realize that when it arrives, you won't have expected it." An enigmatic phrase if I had ever heard one. But it has proved to be absolutely true.

Our first year in Calvert City was a rapid series of learning experiences. First we learned that the real estate market in Chicago and various other places had just bottomed out. New offers on the Chicago building were far below what we had anticipated, and we finally accepted an offer simply because we couldn't afford not to. After paying off mortgages and some credit cards we had used to finance the last stage of construction, we were left with what I can only describe conservatively as "far less than we had expected." (The fact that the current tenants had used the basement as "dumping ground" for a year's worth of beer cans may have reduced the market value of the property. And Mary's lovely back deck had been transformed into an outdoor beer garden.)

Also, living expenses for the Calvert City house were literally "through the roof." Although all-electric, including both heat pump and air-conditioner, the house had been built with the apparent intention of actually heating the three floors with fireplace heat, circulated by built-in fans. The fireplaces required wood to operate, and we didn't have a local source of timber. There were a lot of trees behind Mom's house, but that was a 45-minute drive plus a long hike through the woods.

A new friend offered us the use of his chainsaw and whatever firewood we could cut and haul from the woods behind *his* house, but a single trip made it obvious that we were neither physically, technically, nor emotionally suited for lumberjacking. The only tree I had ever cut down was a Christmas tree, and it was a very small tree; I believe I used a hacksaw. I doubt if Bill had ever cut down a tree at all. He was a city boy who had been trained by the military when he was just 17 to use a gun or a knife, but not an axe. And the only chopping he knew anything about was a Judo chop, which was of no use at all in our situation. There was a fairly large wooded area between our new house and our next-door neighbor; however, when Bill cut down one of the trees, using the borrowed chainsaw and believing the tree was ours, the owner of the other house advised that Bill was mistaken. He was kind enough not to charge us for damaging his property. Maybe he also had a fireplace and appreciated the wood.

We thus found it necessary to use the house's electric heating system which, while it kept us warm, also drove us into near bankruptcy. Although we had done our due diligence and checked the past year's utility bills when we bought the house and believed they were well within our means, we now realized that the electric bills were based on a year's heat provided by the two fireplaces. And, to make matters worse, we were in the West Kentucky Rural Electric system rather than the Jackson Purchase Electric Cooperative (which began on the *west* side, not "*our* side," of Oak Park Boulevard). West Kentucky rates were reported to be more than twice as high as Jackson Purchase, and we were heating three floors of a 3,000 square-foot house. Our first month's electric bill was over $600, and it seldom got any cheaper than that and sometimes much higher.

We were able to manage with only two vehicles until the Ford Focus was repaired, and Bill and I could drive up to get it in the Ford van. The day I finally drove the Focus home, neither of us realized that when the accident happened, it was left upside down for some time (after dark on a Friday night) until the wrecker was able to retrieve it, and in the interim all the oil had drained out of the crankcase. Unfortunately, the garage that repaired the damage either neglected to--or did not realize they needed to--add several quarts of oil to replace the oil that had drained out. Blissfully unaware, I drove it the 250 miles home quite dry, and the engine couldn't take it. The garage refused to take any responsibility for the damage, which our insurance company also refused to cover, so we were left with a car that looked like new but wouldn't go anywhere. Scratch one car.

Bill soon realized he could probably make more money driving a delivery route to individual homes than delivering bulk newspapers, which had the additional advantage of being a night job, thus leaving him (and a vehicle) free during the day. But he would no longer need the box truck. So we sold it, after cleaning off all the Chicago-style graffiti that made it a traveling billboard for our former life, and bought a new Ford four-door sedan. I used it during the day, he used it at night. When school started in September, Mary got a job as a checker at a Paducah grocery store and drove the van back and forth to work.

However, even with three incomes we knew we couldn't afford the house we had originally purchased contingent on the expected windfall from profits on the Chicago building. We notified our real estate agent in Calvert that we would have to opt out of the contract, forfeit our security deposit, and look for a place to rent.

Once again we scouted the market in the Calvert City area, this time looking for a rental that was close to the Calvert City Elementary School, and actually landed in the place we should (perhaps) always have been. The house was at 555 Cherry Street, with four bedrooms (three bedrooms and a bath on one side of the house and a large bedroom, bath, and dining room addition on the other side). It was one block from Calvert City Elementary, had driveways on either side of the house, a smallish yard, a manageable rent and a nice landlord. It was also in the Jackson Purchase Electric system, so utilities were reasonable. I had no way of knowing when we scaled down from the big house to the little house that I would live there, on Cherry Street, for the next 28 years (1991-2019). There's an old song, "It looks like rain, on Cherry Blossom Lane," that could apply. But everything in life, I've discovered, is always a matter of perspective.

Deciding to buy the Oak Park house had been an exercise in ego, but I was learning an important lesson: God would not give me what I wanted but would always provide what I needed. And I believe, as my mother had told me long before, God (at least the God of my understanding) can "see around corners" and anticipate my needs even before I ask. In the years still ahead, with their many ups and downs, I would see evidence of that over and over again.

Tracie was the oldest, and the first married, of my four grandchildren. And, as the old nursery rhyme goes:

> First comes love,
>
> Then comes marriage.
>
> Then comes Tracie, pushing a baby carriage.
>
> Or two.

Tracie and Brad Reisinger's first child, Samantha, was born in October of 1991. And she was not yet a year old (Tracie was expecting her second) when Becky, Mom, and I traveled to Iowa for a visit and a photo of the five generations.

Then in the late spring of 1992, we learned that Terri Lynn had scoliosis, a curvature of the spine which, if left untreated, would inevitably result in a severe deformity. (Terri, you may recall, also had cranial surgery when she was barely a year old.) And while the children had all been covered by my insurance in Chicago, my new insurance carrier in Paducah did not consider my grandchildren to be my dependents for insurance purposes. Bill's work for the Paducah Sun was as an independent carrier. No help there.

Terri was getting ready to go into middle school that next fall, and she was reaching a point in her growth when she desperately needed surgery. Once again, help was provided when we learned that the local Shriner's organization would subsidize all necessary treatment at Shriner's Hospital in St. Louis. That summer she went there for surgery to insert a titanium rod in her back, straightening her spine and keeping it straight (and reminding me inevitably of the time so many years ago when Shriner's had helped our family when Johnny was burned).

Terry went through a very difficult time, but she was the tough little trooper she had always been. When she had first come to live with us, still in recovery from serious cranial surgery to repair closed sutures in her skull, she was wearing an infant-sized football helmet. Still, she had to be restrained from climbing the bookcases in the dining room of the apartment on Logan Boulevard, and she's not stopped testing her limits ever since. I suspect that going through life sandwiched between two brothers has been an advantage in some ways.

Although she could have had home-schooling for the first weeks of the fall term of middle school after her spinal surgery, and perhaps even longer, she was determined to go to *real* school and arranged with friends to carry her books and help her with other chores that she was forbidden to perform alone, and somehow managed to sail through the entire experience with flying colors.

In September of 1992, Tracie had an "Irish twin" of her daughter Samantha when Tyler Reisinger was born. (Irish twins are siblings born within a year of each other.)

Sometime in the fall of that year Mary began dating Russell Gordon, and in February 1993 they were married. They had planned for the marriage to be a family affair, but a sudden snowstorm made travel seem a bit dangerous for everyone, so they just went ahead, met with the minister, and got married anyway. For the next six months or so, the newly married couple lived with us so the kids could get used to a new stepfather (and so Bill could get used to having someone else fill the role he had long assumed as grandfather/substitute father). In early summer, the newlyweds bought a house in Gilbertsville and suddenly Bill and I were empty nesters.

But not for long. Becky decided to come "home," assuming, I think, that "home is where the heart is." If my memory is accurate, Mary and Russell packed all the belongings Becky wanted to keep from her apartment, piled everything that would fit into our van, and moved her into the back bedroom of the house on Cherry Street. She soon found a job in Paducah. In August of 1993, Mom's whole family and many of her friends gathered to celebrate her 80th birthday with a dinner at the New Hope Baptist Church.

It's difficult for me to recall the exact sequence of things as they unfolded over the next year and a half. We had managed to clear the financial wreckage of the past, but the emotional toll that accompanied it had affected my job performance. I found it hard to keep my mind on my job and inevitably my supervisor thought it best that I leave, although indicating that I could begin drawing unemployment compensation immediately. Although it was a blow to my ego, it was actually a timely development, because Bill's health was making it difficult for him to continue working for the newspaper. His breathing difficulties (always a problem) had accelerated, and he had begun to use oxygen. For six months or so, he had taken a job as a security guard at one of the Calvert City plants, watching the back gate where there was very little traffic. To prevent his employer's knowing how disabled he was, he kept his oxygen tank in the trunk of the car and only used it when he was locking up at night and opening in the morning.

In the spring and summer of 1994, before Bill became seriously ill, I put in applications at some of the employment services in Paducah and worked periodically at part-time jobs; however, I needed to return to full-time work. I recall distinctly driving down the road from Benton to Calvert City one day and having a conversation with God in which I said, "I've done everything I know how to do, and now I need your help. I NEED a job." There may have been a few tears trickling down my cheeks as I made my plea, but I put the request out there.

Two days later, on a Sunday afternoon, I got a call from the daughter of Jim Story, an attorney in Eddyville, Kentucky, who wondered if I would like to come to work for her father. It seems he had just discovered that his current secretary had been dipping into his bank account to finance her boyfriend's drug habit, and he planned to have her arrested Monday or Tuesday but really wanted to have a replacement on standby. I said I'd go talk to him, went that evening, and we agreed that we'd give it a try for a couple of months and, if we suited each other, we'd make it permanent. Jim and his wife Barbara were very kind to me during the months of Bill's illness, and I continued to work for him for nearly ten years, finally leaving a few months after my 70th birthday, and then only because Mom was critically ill.

On June 12, 1994, my children's other grandmother, Elsie Martin Crabb, died after a long illness. She had lived with her daughter Rosetta after Garvon's death, and I had visited her at Rosetta's with the children many times. However, once again, I chose not to personally attend the services. I was all too aware that my presence at a family gathering where Jay's wife was present would be awkward for everyone.

After Becky came home, her sister introduced her to Larry Brooks, and after a courtship that was sometimes complicated by the extended illness of her stepfather Bill, she and Larry were married in January of 1995 at the Methodist Church in Benton.

My attention had been distracted for some time before their marriage as I tried to balance my job in Eddyville with Bill's increasingly serious illness. His respiratory doctor prescribed cortisone to reduce the inflammation in his lungs, and there were side effects, the most apparent being weight gain. He hated gaining weight. He'd always been pretty trim, and he was determined to take the weight off, so he started eating popcorn, thinking it would fill him up, suppress his appetite, and bring his weight down. He didn't realize that he had diverticulosis and that the popcorn was about to kill him. And, in fact, the cortisone reduced pain symptoms emanating from the colon so that an infection had progressed to a critical stage before he even realized he was in trouble.

He did not want to go to the hospital, but when the pain became so severe that he could barely walk across the bedroom to the bathroom, I took him to the emergency room, where his problem was quickly diagnosed. But within 48 hours, and before anything could be done for what had become diverticulitis, he had also suffered double (both lungs) pulmonary embolisms, and while he was being treated for *that* his colon ruptured, and infection quickly spread. The next six months were spent in the hospital, with first a colostomy, then a rupture of the incision (he eviscerated himself struggling against the breathing apparatus) which required that he be placed in a medically induced coma.

It was touch-and-go for several days. They gave me a bed in one of the vacant wards, and one night the intensive care nurses woke me and told me that Bill's blood pressure was dropping, and they didn't think he was going to survive the night. I stayed with him until morning, watching the blood pressure gauge and, when it dropped below a certain level, talking to him through another crisis until his blood pressure slowly went up again. He did survive the night, and then two months more in the hospital waiting for his abdomen to shrink enough to allow the incision to be re-sutured, then a reversal of the colostomy, and finally the diagnosis of a staph infection, which proved to be antibiotic-resistant. But when the staph invaded his bone marrow, with accompanying pain and debility, he stopped fighting.

He had come home for a week, and the three grandkids came over to spend the night. They made spaghetti for supper, and Bill came to the table, but he ate very little. The next morning, after the children had gone back home, he told me that he didn't think he could go on in so much pain. We returned to the hospital with an unspoken feeling that it would be his last trip. And it was. He died on February 28, 1995, in the early morning. I've always wondered if perhaps he willed himself to die. He had worried that Medicaid, which had been paying his hospital bills (we had no insurance) would cease on March 1, leaving me with a huge debt. I was holding his hand as he slipped away. I'm glad he didn't know that, when he died, he left behind over $300,000 in medical bills. But perhaps he *did* know, because in the next six months, with a little help from the State of Kentucky and more than a little help from God-as-I-understand-Him/Her/It, I was able to dissolve all our indebtedness and have enough left over for a very small emergency fund.

Bill was 56 years old; I was almost 61. We'd been together for nearly 17 years. He had been ill for a long time, and the last six months of his life were, for both of us, a preparation for dying. I am quite certain, even to this day, that there are things I do not know, will never know, about Bill's life before I met him. But I always knew that I was the most important person in his life, and for the years that we were married, he was the most important person in mine. I have always been grateful we had those 17 years together and were given time before the end to say our goodbyes, and to make any amends that either of us felt necessary.

It was during those last six months that he told me that the financial reverses we suffered when we moved south had caused him a great deal of depression: "You talked about it, and dealt with it, but I felt like I had failed you," he said, "and now it's killing me." It was just that important to him that he take care of his family, and he felt he had not been adequate to the task.

I remember telling him, during those last weeks, that I would never marry again. I'm not sure if I believed it; perhaps it was simply a way of assuring him that I loved him. But he said, "Sure you will. You like being part of a couple. Men and women are supposed to be together. I hope you will grieve me for a while, but I also hope that you will find someone who loves you, and someone you can love." Bill knew me very well. But the simple fact is that, for whatever reason, over 27 years have gone by, and I have not married again.

Several pages back, I included the first part of a poem, "The Journey to Love." But there was more; the whole of it was what I asked the minister, Billy Hurt, to read instead of a sermon at Bill's funeral. I think it's time to continue it, with perhaps a few deletions.

Then one day I saw a man who was just sitting by the roadway.
I am sure I would have passed him if he had not raised his hand.
First I thought it was in greeting, just a simple salutation.
Then he crooked his finger, beckoned. Curious, I left the path.

"Come and sit down here beside me, you look tired out from walking."
That was what he said, at least that's what I thought I heard him say.
"Have you ever felt like that?" I asked him, "Tired, a little lonely?
Felt as though you were forever lost, could never find the way?"

"Yes," he said, "but sit and rest now, while I tell you all about it,
for I've only just arrived here, and I've nowhere else to be."
So I sat with him and listened as he told to me his story,
And it seemed the one I'd told myself, though in a different key.

"Once I was a knight in armor, slaying wicked dragons,"
he said, smiling, "But the dragons soon grew tired of the game."
"I became a king of hearts then, but there was no queen beside me,
so I stepped down, thinking that I'd find someone to share my throne."

"Can you tell me of the future?" I asked then, wanting to see it.
But he answered, "No, how can I? That is where I've never been."

"Well, what shall we do today then?" I asked, hoping now to linger,

for I liked sitting beside him; it was calm and pleasant there.

"Well," he said, "there is a spider, spinning. We could sit and watch it.

If you like, we'll sing some songs that I learned once, in other days."

So we sat and watched the spider, and we sang the songs he taught me,

and I cooked us both some dinner on a warm fire that he built.

And when suddenly the night fell, we lay down beside the roadway,

and we held each other tightly (just in case the dragons came).

I did most of my grieving during that last six months, as my mother had grieved for my father during his last long illness. But she had also shown me the path forward and taught me, in doing so, the truth of something I had realized long ago: "To live is to learn the art of dying and to die is to teach the art of living."

Not a day passes that I do not think of Bill. He had indeed been the "wind beneath my wings" for those 17 years. When Raymond's first son was born, he named him William.

. . . we cannot live in the afternoon of life according to the program of life's morning. For what in the morning was true, will at evening have become a lie.

C. G. Jung

In mid-life, one of our most important tasks may be the journey we make back to ourselves. Coming to know ourselves, we learn to listen to the messages sent by our minds, hearts, and bodies. We learn to give time and thought to our own needs. In this way we approach health and serenity.

Sally Coleman/Maria Porter

(From "Seasons of the Spirit"

And Then There Were More of Us

I'm not sure when and how I began again. But the *why* of it is not in question because, of course, there was nothing else to do. Bill's life was over, but mine was not. And it was not just mine that mattered; there was a whole family that would have to continue on without him. There was, as another of those old songs goes, still "a lot of living to do."

I was glad that there was also work to do, a job to get up for every weekday morning, a family still needing my love and attention, my mother still alive but living alone on the farm (at 85, she was just four years younger than I am now), a house to be kept, holidays to be celebrated, grandchildren growing up, some already teenagers. Tracie was already a parent with two children of her own.

I grieved in my own way, not in one great big chunk but in bits and pieces, a little at a time, and mostly when I was alone. And I made myself some promises. Even as I helped Mary choose clothing for her children to wear to the memorial service for Bill, I bought myself an outfit that was only appropriate for dancing. For as I sat in the waiting room of the intensive care ward those long months before Bill died, a trio of widows sometimes came and sat there too. I can't remember why they were there, and together, but they talked about what it was like to live alone. One of the women simply could not do it and spent every night with another of the trio. And they talked, all of them, about going dancing, and I told myself two things: "I will learn to live alone." And "I'm going to dance again."

When someone suggested that one of my grandchildren should plan to spend nights with me, I said, "No. I'll be all right." I'd learned long ago (after refusing to get back on that quarter horse) that postponing the "next right thing" sometimes meant it would never get done at all. So that next week I spent the nights alone, and the evenings emptying the second closet in the big master bedroom, the one that held Bill's clothes. I offered some to my grandsons, kept one sweater that I thought would be comfortable on cold winter mornings, carried some down to the men's halfway house in Paducah, took some to the Salvation Army, and stored a few things in a closet in one of the back bedrooms, things Raymond or Scott might "grow in to," or, perhaps, things I was not yet ready to part with.

One day as I was sitting at my desk in the law office in Eddyville, where I was still working for Jim Story, I started making a list of "things I want to do before I die." Some were silly, some were important; there must have been at least 20 items. Over the years that followed I have gradually, if only mentally, checked things off that list as they were completed: having something blooming in my yard all year around, building a garage, visiting all 50 states, going back to school and actually getting my bachelor's degree, letting my hair grow long again. There were books I wanted to read—a long list of those--maybe *writing* another book, buying a home of my own. (We were still just renting the house on Cherry Street when Bill died.)

I started in the simplest, and perhaps the healthiest, way possible: I got a spade out of the utility room (building the garage came later) and started digging up the ground between the front porch and the south end of the house–a plot about 5 by 24 feet. And I dug it 12 inches deep, taking out all of the old shrubbery and mixing the clay with good dirt and fertilizer. And I planted it with azalea bushes and perennials: hostas and clumps of lilies. At night my muscles were sore, and my body was tired, and I went to bed and slept the whole night through. Alone.

In late April, two months after Bill's death, I put on my new dancing clothes and went to the Spring Fling at the Brown Street AA Club. And I danced all night with anyone and everyone who asked. It's very hard to dance and cry at the same time, so I didn't do any crying that night. I just danced. I don't know if anyone else had a good time that night, but I did. I had no way of knowing it, but two of the men I danced with would become part of my life in the years that followed.

In early October, I took the kids to the AA campout at Energy Lake, a first for any of us. We had two tents: one for the kids and one for me, and--as the old newspaper cliché goes—"a good time was had by all." That campout became a family tradition for the next several years. The second year I graduated to a small camper that my brother Kent had used as an auction trailer. It wasn't plush by any means, but it worked for me--I had learned that first year that I wasn't fond of sleeping on the ground. I can't remember what I pulled the camper with—the van, I think--but that year I also went with four or five girls (women, actually, but they were still girls to me) to the Rough-it Roundup, a campout in Tennessee, held on an old Methodist Camp Meeting Ground. There was a big "brush arbor" with split logs for benches, ancient log cabins with lean-tos attached (for cooking spaces, I was told, and as shelter for horses in days long gone by). The cabins had no air-conditioning; their bunks were just one step up off the bare ground without mattresses. And no one brought any horses these days. We all loved it, and I went three years in a row. Can't think why I stopped.

That first Halloween I took Bill's dress suit out of the closet, a very proper suit with a vest, and I wore it for Halloween. It fit me perfectly, including the vest. I needed a little help from one of my grandsons, tying the necktie. Bill had always tied his own. I'm sure some people must have thought it was in poor taste, but I thought–still think--Bill would have been amused. He had told me he wanted me to be happy, and I was working on it.

I started going to meetings at the Brown Street Club, a lot of them. I was alone in a big house, and at Brown Street there were always people around. One of the guys thought it would be fun on Friday nights to get a bunch together and go bowling. I'd probably never gone bowling more than two or three times in my life. Jay had bowled often, played golf, gone fishing and hunting. I'd either stayed home with the kids in the early years or, when they were older, worked a second job or did laundry and housework. There was always something to do at home.

The guy who started the bowling nights was David "Dave/Cowboy" Kingsley, who was born and raised in Massac

County, home territory for me, although I had never known him or any of his family. And he played guitar, and he liked to dance. Since he'd learned in the same places where I'd grown up, we even danced the same style. He also owned two sets of encyclopedias (my kind of guy!). And he seemed to show up on a fairly regular basis wherever I was planning to be. We were friends before we started dating sometime in the late winter of 1995 or spring of 1996, a year after Bill died.

Dave was raised in the Brookport/Unionville area. The Kingsleys were long-time residents there; several of his uncles either owned taverns or played music in local drinking establishments. His father's band played for many years at the Twin Gables near Brookport. I'm sure I danced to his music in the "Atomic Years" after I came home from college. When Dave was old enough he had joined them—he might even have been in one of those bands I danced to! Dave had three sons: David (actually his ex-wife's child by her first husband), Darrin, and Damon. When he and the boys' mother were divorced, he traveled the country for a while, stringing TV cable, but ended up in California where he became a technician in one of the electronics factories. When his father Nick died, he came back to Southern Illinois to settle the estate and never left, Unionville until he joined me in Kentucky:

With Dave Kingsley

I'm not sure if it was 1996 or 1997 when Johnny came home from Colorado. I know he was here at Thanksgiving 1997 because I found a picture taken when Jay and his wife LaVinia stopped by for a brief visit, and the kids wanted a picture to be taken of the five of us (LaVinia not included). I think Dave probably took the picture. At least, I know *he* wasn't included in it either.

In September of 1998, my oldest grandson, Scott Culp, married Pam Filbeck. They simply went down to the Marshall County Courthouse and "tied the knot." A year and a half later their son, Dillon Jay Culp, was born in February 2000. Just four months later, Terri Lynn Culp married James Cowart. It was a June wedding, and Mom was able to help decorate the cake we made for the ceremony and reception at the park in Benton. A year later my son John and Martha "Rose" Jackson were married at the Courthouse in Lyon County. We had a reception on the front lawn for the immediate family, including John's Uncle Joe and Aunt Ethel Crabb. As I recall, this time I made the cake—and decorated it--all by myself. Mom supervised, of course.

While all this marrying and production of grandchildren was going on, I continued to work on that "bucket list" I had created after Bill died. In August of 1999, less than a month after my 65th birthday, I went down to the Paducah Community College and signed up for classes. I'd waited until I was 65 because, in the state of Kentucky, any resident 65 or older can take college classes at a state college or university almost for free. Tuition is waived, and the only cost to senior students is for books and miscellaneous fees (parking, sports activities, etc.). I was prepared: I'd already gone through the admission process at Murray State to begin work on a Bachelor of Independent Studies, which allowed me to gain some extra credit for work and other experience, and to transfer my year or so of credits from Southern Illinois University. I'd have had two years of credits if not for those many incompletes. I was also allowed to begin taking some Murray State off-campus and online classes that year and in the years that followed. I finished work on my Bachelor's Degree in 2002 (I was 68), almost precisely 50 years from the time I was scooted out the back door of Southern Illinois University. I was within sight of my Master's Degree in the Fall of 2004 when Mom became terminally ill. I dropped out of the Fall Semester to spend time with her.

It's just never seemed important to finish my Master's, although I did register to "begin again" in the fall of 2019 after I moved to Murray. However, I withdrew before I started going to classes. The piece of paper I would have earned didn't seem worth the time and effort, and the subjects I would have been required to take no longer held any interest for me. I'd been an English and Creative Writing major, but when I packed up the house in Calvert and moved to Benton in July of 2018, I put most of my books in storage—they were crowding shelves in two of the bedrooms and the big family room--and, shortly after I moved on to Murray in April of 2019 I donated all my fiction library to Hertown, a sober-living house for women. I did retrieve most of the non-fiction books that had been stacked in a storage shed at Neartown, a recovery center for men near Kirksey. I have probably not read more than two or three novels in the last two or three years, although I keep the mail carrier so busy delivering non-fiction books to my mailbox that I suspect he/she would like to throw them at my front door rather than try to overstuff another batch into my woefully undersized mailbox.

Being *un*married for the last 27 years has also given me the opportunity to develop close friendships with other women for the first time in my life. Marriage had always narrowed my social circle to occasional friendships with women I worked with, and since I was almost always the boss, it was difficult to get very close. I learned very early that it's hard to fire a friend, even if they're not doing their job. Jay and I were friends with several couples over the years, but what was a "good fit" for him was not necessarily the same for me. Most of our free time was spent with members of his family: his brother Joe and Joe's wife Ethel, and his parents. All the years of our marriage, if we lived within an hour's driving distance of his parents, we spent Sunday with them. It was traditional, conventional, even convenient. But it was also confining. I vowed then that when our children were grown, I would never demand the same kind of attention from them. So "Sunday dinner at grandma's house" has never been a tradition at *my* house, although the door has always been open to anyone who wants to come or needs to stay. Christmas, Thanksgiving – and especially Halloween – have been exceptions to the rule.

These days my friendships with women have become a mainstay of my life, most especially the women I've met in Alcoholics Anonymous. Although the relationships may start with sponsorship or a common interest in spiritual matters, some of them have become close friendships over the years. A difference in ages has never seemed to matter. Most of my friends are actually about the same age (or younger) than my daughters, but the relationships are based on our common interests and not a pseudo-maternal dependency. And this is, I think, a good description of what my life has been like for the last 20 years, written at the same time as a previous poem: "On Married Bliss." This one is:

On Unmarried Bliss:

I've found it's true, as I grow older,
Both my heart and feet grow colder –
sleeping alone in that broad bed at last,
(hiring someone to cut the grass).
Reading 'til two, I'm undisturbed,
there's no one there to be perturbed.
I can always go out for dinner,
and forget that I'm not thinner.
Do my housework bare-ass naked.
Let my hair grow long and wicked.
Curse all beautiful young bitches.
Scratch exactly where it itches.
Leave my teeth in cups 'til morning.
Ignore dust and weeds, while scorning
all those old gray-headed codgers
and their passions (for the Dodgers).
Watch tear-jerkers from the forties.
Spend my days in shopping sorties.
Snore and swear and eat raw onions.
Cut holes in my shoes for bunions.
Waste my money playing bingo,
living free and wild and single.
But should I miss the company of men
I shall learn bridge and chastity—or live in sin.

OK, that's not all strictly true. I stopped swearing long ago, don't have bunions, can't eat onions (at least not raw; they give me heartburn). I haven't played Bingo for at least ten years, and I've never learned to play bridge. And I don't miss the company of men; I've chosen to enjoy it, instead. (And I've been told, by those who profess to know, that I do not snore.)

While I have stayed unmarried, there has been a lot of marrying, and some un-marrying, going on in our family. Scott and Pam's marriage ended in divorce. They were both so very young, and I've learned in my own life that what I wanted when I was very young no longer seemed quite so desirable as the years passed. Dillon has always remained close to our family and is always included in family holidays. Scott remarried, this time to Jeneie West, and their first child, Devon, was born in January 2003.

The year 2004 was a difficult one. Jay, my children's father, died on October 4 after a long illness. He suffered from leukemia, as his grandfather had done. There were two services, one in Chicago, where he and his wife LaVinia had lived for many years, and one in Southern Illinois, where he is buried in the Crabb family plot at Harrisburg. I didn't attend the services out of consideration for his widoz. But our children, and all their families, were there.

Just a month later, on Thanksgiving Day, November 25, 2004, my mother, Maude Evelyn Jennings Korte, died after a ten-year battle with Alzheimer's Disease, the "self" we had always known slipping slowly away into a darkness of mind that only love could penetrate, and even then for only short periods of time. I have always been so very grateful that about three weeks before her death the fog lifted long enough for her to once more know each of us and call us by name, and that we could be by her side and hold her hand as her spirit left us softly and without a murmur of protest. One of the last things she said to me was, "I love you very, very . . ." She could not finish. But I had always known the rest.

And of course I wrote a poem about that; not about the end but about living toward the end, and living afterward. I almost hesitate to reproduce it here, but perhaps it will help someone else sometime, somewhere, to understand. Forgive the length, but it is what I wrote, and I can't find a thing I'm willing to delete. (Another fault I'll give up reluctantly.)

Evelyn Jennings Korte

(Aug. 8, 2013 – Nov. 25, 2004)

The Hex

Within me, buried deep in chromosomal time,

a coiled and doubled helix waits to kill my mind,

stalking its prey, a patient hunter in a hidden hole

watching doomed victims playing tag: the running, laughing dead.

I will play, too, at life's mischievous games, while in my soul

I am already IT, the "X" cut deep, bloody tattoo of fear.

I hold my mother's hands and feel her fear
trembling in mine as she thumbs through pages of time,
shrinks from the predator who haunts and taunts her soul,
until I tell her once again, "Oh, Mama, never mind,"
and watch sad eyes turn inward to the fleeing, fading dead
brought back to die again: crude phantoms, never really whole.

Scheming to foil genetic codes, I've found whole
tomes of scientific diagrams to still the haunting fear
which follows in the footsteps of the walking, talking dead.
My grandmother, my mother, stumble past; it is not yet my time
to fall in line, sink in their quicksand path and lose my mind--
a zombie yanked on voodoo strands encrypted on my soul.

Their epitaphs are prophecies, their legacy a sole
fault line in yesterday's hard crust, a widening abysmal hole.
Small freedoms slip away: all of the treasures we once mined;
names of sons, daughters, lovers, hopes, then dreams, are lost to fear.
We'll never find the way back home, for we've run out of time:
the creeping, crawling, sliding, falling not-yet-dead.

My mother hides in silent terror that she is already dead, except for days when a semblance of self escapes, a sly and sole

survivor creeping out of a dark distant place, a time

of lingering midnight. She talks of dreams then, life made whole

by some shadowy presence nearing and whisp'ring, "Never fear,"

its mystery a shout: "Come forth," that quakes and wakes her mind.

So I protest, resist, refuse to yield my sanity: this mind

that still remembers faces and loved places, names of dead

and living poets, passion and its throbbing sequel, and the fear

that haunts the hills and hollows of my shambling, trembling soul.

I will make tea and never drink it, losing my cup to find whole

hours untasted, minutes dissipated -- dreading that time

when, struggling through mind's labyrinth, I'll seek my own lost soul,

waste breath on the dead corpses of old thoughts, once live and whole,

to live a death which neither molecules nor miracles can resurrect in time.

And perhaps it will explain, too, both to myself and anyone else who may have wondered, why I could not properly grieve (how *does* one grieve properly?) when my sister Kay died in March of 2020, just before the world closed down against the pandemic. I had believed with growing certainty for a year or more that Kay, too, was being tugged slowly into that darkness, and I was grateful that she and her family were spared the last awful ten years our mother had known. I'm 89 years old this year. Have I escaped? I can't know. I hope so.

But whatever the future holds, we must live it on. When Mother's great-great-granddaughter was born in December of 2005, she was named for both her great-great-grandmother and her grandmother: Evelyn Elizabeth Cowart (for Evelyn Korte and Mary Elizabeth Crabb). And just a month after Christmas, in January 2006, Scott and Jeneie had their second child (Scott's third), Alexis Paige Culp.

It was in 2005, the year after mother died, the year after I "turned 70" and had retired from work and found time hanging very heavy on my hands, that I realized I was once again going to have to "reinvent myself," or perhaps just find a new purpose in life. I remember so clearly sitting on the couch in the living room one day, bored almost to tears, and trying to think of something—anything! —interesting to do. And it occurred to me that with the new arrivals in the family and two other great-grandchildren growing up in Iowa, perhaps I should update my family calendar and the family history I had started some time before.

I went directly to my computer and began searching for and then pulling together all the information I had collected, updating the dates of the births, the deaths, and the marriages that had occurred in the last few years. But when I came across some notes I had made long ago about Danty's family, I became curious about the parents of both sets of grandparents and started visiting the Metropolis Public Library, where the whole basement is devoted to county and family history. There were census reports, church and cemetery records, and materials gathered by members of the Massac County Genealogy Society. The library even had librarians who devoted all their time to helping people find information about their families.

My favorite high school teacher, Pauline Artman, had been very active in researching much of the material, and I soon learned that Chesalyne Krueger Quint, who was an old family friend and married to a distant Quint cousin, had been busy researching the Korte and Quint families (mostly Quint) as well as my brother-in-law Don Rottmann's ancestors for many years. I was off and running. (Did I mention that I have always loved libraries and been fascinated by cemeteries? You meet the most interesting people that way. Most of them don't talk much but they have incredible stories to tell.)

At some point I realized that just writing all that stuff down in a document was probably not the most efficient way to proceed and, remembering that there were computer programs for all sorts of things, I discovered that there was a program for this as well: The Family Tree Maker, created by the Church of Jesus Christ of Latter Day Saints (Mormons, for short). The Church also had a website, Ancestry.com, where one could find all kinds of documents their researchers had gathered in one place: census reports, marriage licenses, military histories. It is also a site where a lot of other families share the results of their own research.

The Mormon Church also takes very seriously the idea of a "Communion of Saints." In order to assure that none of their ancestors are left in "purgatory," or whatever they term their concept of a hereafter occupied by the "unsaved," their practice is to appoint a descendant of anyone who died unbaptized as a surrogate for the deceased, and to then baptize that descendant in place of the "lost one," who is then assured of entrance into paradise. I am inclined to question the practice—as I seem compelled to question a great many religious practices—because a rather substantial entry fee to *their* paradise seems to be involved, and that fee is paid to the church rather than to St. Peter, who I had been taught was the official gatekeeper in paradise, and therefore surely entitled to collect any "tolls" which might be assessed. I'm joking. I think.

Perhaps it is my father's Lutheran conscience (if he actually had one) that rebels: Martin Luther also objected to the collection of "indulgences" by the clergy. I have been at many funerals where the minister preached a soul into Heaven with a "thief on the cross" salvation sermon. However, being "saved" at the very last minutes of life is not quite the same as *posthumous* salvation. I am also disturbed by the fact that Mormon women are only allowed into Mormon paradise (my distinction, not theirs) if accompanied by a husband—a cunning ploy, it seems to me, which allows a man to collect a number of wives. In my view, women should be allowed the same opportunity. My own life has not been monogamous, as evidenced by three marriages, two long-time dalliances (I love that word; it's so Victorian), and my previous rather oblique references to a "little black book," and other perhaps less obvious attempts to be somewhat discreet.

But on to more serious matters of begetting, as in genealogy. I began sometime in 1970 and I have never really stopped. The first was the Korte-Quint Family History, then a History of the Struve, Moorman, and Gieseke Families (one great-grandmother was a Gieseke). Chesalyne also had material on the Struves and Moormans that could not be allowed to simply go to waste, so we did that. Then I did a history of my brother-in-law Don Rottmann's family (Rottmanns, Weavers, and Strohsicks), which was 600+ pages. I may not be perfect, but I am prolific!

When the Korte-Quint and the Rottmann-Weaver books were complete, we had big parties for each and distributed copies to descendants of their family's history. When the New Hope Baptist Church had its 150th Anniversary, and my brother Kent asked if I would be willing to help, I had plenty of material to produce a history of the church and most of the families and communities the church served.

I could certainly not neglect my mother's side of the family, especially when I was told I could probably find some Revolutionary War veterans in case I ever wanted to join the Daughters of the American Revolution. Again I encountered another family member, this time online (perhaps a 4th cousin twice removed), and ended up with more than one veteran and also three 2 1/2-inch binders of family history reaching back to the 1500s in some family lines. Combined with my brother-in-law Joe Crabb's genealogy work on his family roots, I now have more than 32,000 names on my database and a seemingly unquenchable thirst for more. Addictions, I have learned, come in all shapes and forms, and not all of them are destructive.

As I acquired the names and histories of my ancestors, I also began acquiring more descendants: Raymond's firstborn, William Steven Culp, born in August of 2006, was a redhead (since turned blond), named for my husband Bill, who was the only father Raymond really knew, although he has kept in touch with his birth father, Phil, over the years. (William recently spent a week in Europe with his high school class.) And in November of 2007, Scott and Jeneie had another daughter, Angel Marie.

Sometime in 2006-2007, I sold an old camper (my second) I had bought for $1,000 and used for a couple of years, mostly for AA campouts, and bought a brand new one. In the winters of 2007 and 2008, Dave and I went to Florida during January and February. The first year we saw the sights from St. Augustine where we drank from Ponce de Leon's fountain of youth (I think it's working for me), on to Cape Canaveral and the Daytona Speedway, then down to the

Everglades, where we took a boat trip and saw a lot of alligators. (I would have been pleased to skip the alligators. They have terrible body odor!)

In August of 2008 we made a trip to Marshalltown, Iowa, to visit my granddaughter Tracie (Becky's daughter) and her family. Raymond came along for the ride, appointing himself a one-man entertainment committee and helping with the driving. It was a wonderful trip and we enjoyed every minute of it.

The ice storm in November 2009 was traumatic: weeks of cleanup but, fortunately, no lasting damage. In December, Tracie and Samantha came from Iowa for Christmas, in time to be introduced to Raymond's early Christmas present: Jacob Edward Culp, who is now 15 and 6'1" tall according to recent family chats, a redhead like his father.

On March 10, 2010, my companion for the last 13 years, David "Cowboy" Kingsley, died after a lengthy battle with congestive heart failure. Although few people realized it, he had struggled with depression for most of his life, although his mother called it "the blues." It was his nature to refuse to yield to either depression or heart attack; he was always ready with a joke. I knew he was having a hard time coping when he went out to his truck to go bowling one afternoon and came back into the house to ask me if I would come and help him put his bowling bag in the back seat. (It held three balls and took up the whole seat, so this wasn't a puny little thing.) He even joked about what he seemed to feel was the end. When a friend, a woman who happened to be on the Paducah police force, came to the hospital and asked if there was anything she could get him, he said a pizza would be nice. When she brought the pizza back, he told her, "Well, I must be dying when the police deliver my pizza. *And pay for it.*"

He had gone to the hospital on his doctor's orders when he started experiencing severe dysrhythmia. There was some delay in arriving because he wanted to go home and get his nicotine patches and his robe, and also stop at the Dairy Queen to get a hamburger. I'm surprised he didn't want to take his Stratocaster guitar. When he went to treatment (for alcoholism) years before, he had taken his portable typewriter, thinking he might need it. For what reason I have never known. I hadn't even known he could type!

He absolutely refused to allow me to drive us to the hospital, so I rode beside him from Paducah to Calvert City and back, wondering the whole way if he might have a heart attack and kill us both. The heart doctors used every possible medication to persuade his heart to resume a normal rhythm, and after more than ten days it seemed their efforts were finally successful. I left him in the cardiac care ward and went home to get some sleep, thinking all was well, but when they called me four hours later, I could tell from the compassion in the nurse's voice that there was no need to break speed limits to get back to the hospital. He was already gone.

The nurses there told me he had slept for a while, then woke and said he was going to read his newspaper and would "sure like a fresh cup of coffee." The nurse left to make a pot, and when she came back with the coffee he was lying on the floor beside the bed. He'd always made a joke of getting up in the morning. Just "spring out of bed," he called it. I am convinced that he simply "sprang out of bed" and into eternity. And somewhere in Louisville, someone else is reading *their* newspaper out of Dave's eyes, which were donated to the Kentucky Eye Bank.

We held a memorial service for him in Paducah, and the chapel was filled: one-third with family, one-third with AA friends, and the other third with the women and men he had bowled with almost right up to the end.

There's a song that was popular about the time I met Dave, and it kind of expresses the quandary I faced when I decided that I wanted him in my life. The song's tagline was:

What are you going to do with that cowboy,
When he don't saddle up and ride away?

Well, I figured it out. You dance a lot, and you laugh a lot, and you share a lot, and you worry a lot, and you love more than you had ever intended, and when he's gone you shed a lot of tears every time you remember he's never coming back (but not where anyone might see you), and you treasure the good memories, and eventually you give away all the cowboy boots you bought when the two of you were together. Well, maybe you keep one pair: the pair that's soft and supple, with a smooth leather sole that's great for dancing. Just in case you ever dance again. And then you move on. You may not want to. You may think you can't. But you have to. So you do.

My women friends were a big help through all that. One of them, Nelda, was going through chemo for a kind of leukemia with an unpronounceable name. But when I told her that I was going to take one of those bus trips to New England that are popular in the fall for "leaf-peepers," she asked if she could go along and managed to schedule the trip in between chemo treatments. We traveled quite well together.

We did all the New England states in three weeks, with a very compatible busload of people. The scenery throughout was breathtaking. We visited the place where "the shot heard round the world" was fired, beginning the Revolutionary War. (I surprised myself by getting teary-eyed.) Sat in the church where Paul Revere hung the lantern in "the old North Steeple," stepped on Plymouth Rock where the first pilgrims landed, ate an Italian ice in the Boston Market (where I barely made it to the bathroom—*not* the fault of the Italian ice), chowed down on lobster in Kennebunkport, Maine, visited a lighthouse overlooking the Atlantic, toured the Hershey factory in Pennsylvania (bought and ate lots of chocolate), and I personally survived a headfirst plunge off a curb in one of the National Parks. First aid was in order and provided, and I thanked God my dentures weren't broken! (I'm quite certain I would have flown home alone rather than appear in public without them. I did not even consider Crazy Glue as an option.) And I checked off another ten states from the ones on my "things to do before I die" list.

I doubt if it was a surprise to anyone when, eighteen months or so after Dave's death, the *other* man I had met right after Bill died, Amos Wahl, began showing up wherever I happened to be. It was the second time since I'd known him that we'd both been single at the same time: once after Bill died and Amos was just ending a marriage. This time there'd been another death for me and another divorce for him. We'd known each other for 15 years by then, so when he invited me to go to Branson, along with his AA sponsor and wife, I went. It was actually the weekend of my 77th birthday and my 34th AA anniversary. I seem to have made a habit of doing memorable things on my birthday. Marriage, divorce, sobriety, friendships, accidents. If I die on some future birthday, don't say I didn't warn you! But hopefully that won't be for a while. I'm aiming for 100.

I *did* have an accident before we left when a speeding SUV in Paducah hit the left rear quarter panel of my car, totaling it. I went to the hospital for a checkup, and the ER doctor sent me for a stress test. I told the nurses in the heart lab that I just had to be OK because I was going to Branson for my birthday and I was going to go zip-lining. When the nurses passed the word on to the cardiologist, he proclaimed that my heart was in great shape, but, he said, "You're crazier than hell." That is an exact quote, and I may very well have been. But I did it anyway.

The Bronson trip went pretty well, chaperoned by his sponsor and wife, so a month later Amos and I decided to take a trip out west. Amos had been before, and I had already planned a trip to the western states with Dave before his health made it apparent that the trip was never going to happen. But Amos had a nice big toy hauler with plenty of room for his Harley, a Dodge Ram truck to pull it, time on his hands, and enough money in his pocket to assure that we wouldn't run out of gas somewhere in the back of nowhere. (Actually we went 50-50; I have never wanted to be known as a "kept woman." I've also observed that men with money often feel it gives them the right to tell the woman in their life what to do and how to do it.)

We took off in late August, beginning with a stop at the Sikeston rodeo--Mary and her husband Russell were there too--and then a visit to a Harley factory in Iowa. We were gone for over two months, but we packed them full: we visited every state west of the Mississippi River that I hadn't seen before except Utah (just a bit out of the way) and Montana (it was flooded). Did the Black Hills, both Dakotas, Idaho, Washington, and Oregon, and most of the national parks, saw the giant redwoods and sequoias, the mountains and the deserts. Drove the length of California, into a bit of Texas and then New Mexico, stopped at the Grand Canyon and again in Albuquerque to visit an AA meeting one of my sponsees had attended when she lived there, and several others along the way. And went to every Harley store between Kentucky and California in every town that had one. Cross my heart and hope I never have to do that again – the Harley stores, that is. The rest of the trip was close to perfect. (That means unforgettable, too.)

First Stop: The Harley Factory

And, of course, we learned a lot about each other, principally that we both expected to be the boss. Amos learned that I could cook dinner faster than he could set up the camper for the night. I learned that he was a very impatient man where small things were concerned but surprisingly calm and almost unflappable in a major crisis. He yelled a couple of times, and I cried (not out loud) a couple of times – but not during the same incident. We had a rather wonderful time learning how to survive each other's character defects and got back to Kentucky just in time for the Fall Campout at Energy Lake.

In January of 2012 Amos invited me to go to Florida with him for his annual three-month sojourn. He remembers it a bit differently, insisting that I wanted to go and he was a bit concerned about how happy I would be. We were both partly right. But when it was time for Amos to leave for Florida in January 2013, I told him that I was going to stay in Kentucky and look for a man who didn't like to fish but did like to dance. It is now 2022, and I still haven't found one, but I haven't been back to Florida either, although we still spend quite a lot of time together, especially when he stopped spending his winters in Florida. I did spend the early months of 2013-2015 entering the Kentucky Opry's annual singing competition. I won a little, finally lost, and thoroughly enjoyed every minute.

Tracie married Chris Anderson in September 2012. Becky and her husband Larry attended, and this year Tracie and Chris celebrated their 11th wedding anniversary. .

In July of 2014, a lot of us were together for my 80th birthday celebration, hosted by my three children and their children. I can duly report that, as the old *Metropolis News* would have reported, once again "A good time was had by all." Since it was also my AA sobriety anniversary, there were two cakes: chocolate (AA) and vanilla (birthday).

Amos and I went to AA's International Convention in Atlanta, Georgia, in 2015. It was exhausting but also exhilarating. (We didn't have to go fishing, and neither of us was up to dancing.) There were 50,000 happy (and sober) alcoholics from more countries than I could count. And that fall, in October, Raymond and Megan's third child was born: Scarlett Annalise Culp. She's also a redhead!

In the spring of 2016 Becky was ordained a Deacon in the Episcopal Church with all the pomp and ceremony attending the occasion at the Cathedral in Louisville and, in October, her granddaughter Samantha was married to Micah Engle in Des Moines, Iowa, at home plate on the Chicago Cubs farm club's ball diamond. My family does seem to find the most interesting venues for celebrations! Johnny drove me up to the wedding in his new pickup truck, and we had a wonderful trip going and coming. My grandson-in-law, Chris Anderson, who was DJ-ing the wedding (Samantha is his stepdaughter) was kind enough to ask me to dance. So I did. And discovered I hadn't forgotten how. And in September of 2017 my first (and at this time my only) great-great-grandchild, Calliope Rose Engle, was born to Samantha and Micah. For those who may have forgotten, calliopes were the musical instrument of choice at Wrigley Field in Chicago for all Cubs baseball games through the years. My great-great-granddaughter was named for *those* calliopes and not for Calliope, the goddess of poetry. Darn!

Time flies—and when it seems that all that's left of life are memories and an uncertain future, it's time for another reinvention of one's self, or at least one's situation. I had lived at 555 Cherry Street for over 25 years, and they had been good years despite life's necessary losses. It was, as I remember, in the summer of 2017--just before Calliope was born--that I realized it was time to move on, or at least OUT. For the last two years I had become more and more dependent on my children for help with lawn care and maintenance. My grandchildren were in their mid-30s, and I now had a great-great-grandchild. (How did I get so old so fast?) It was often difficult for everyone to come home for holidays at the same time, and while I loved having everyone together, there were days and weeks and months when I was alone in a big house with too many empty bedrooms and far too much yard. I had all those plants and bushes blooming, just as I had promised myself, but they required weeding, feeding, and much watering.

I remembered my mother saying, when she was about the same age and living by herself on the farm, "Lona Rae, I'm just lonelyen myself to death." I know that "lonelyen" is not a word, so I have no idea how it should be spelled, but it could be and maybe *should* be included in next year's dictionary, because I believe there are a lot of people dying of loneliness. And while I enjoy solitude, I am also convinced that, like candy, too much solitude can kill you. I am also convinced that it would be possible to live forever on ice cream. (My mother certainly tried. Her favorite flavor was butter pecan, but her last food on earth was a cone from Dairy Queen.)

I began the process of preparing the house and grounds for sale, starting in the back bedrooms: stripping woodwork, painting walls, making new curtains, changing and rearranging pictures, linens and accessories, removing old and faded carpets. I took my time. There was no hurry. Some days I did nothing at all except make a list of things to do, or just think about what I was going to do tomorrow, grateful that I was still able to climb ladders, paint ceilings, move furniture. It was good exercise, even if I was a bit slower and less agile than I had been in years past. (I was, after all, 83 years old!) As I cleaned and updated, I also packed and threw away. I had two or three yard sales. I made lists of things to keep, things to sell, and things to throw away. I made trips to the New-to-You shop, St. Vincent's and Goodwill with bags of things no one in my family wanted but someone else might like to have. (I have been known to go back to a place where I donated and actually buy something I'd previously given away!)

Through the fall and winter of 2017, I worked and planned, and when early spring came I called in reinforcements: Johnny and Mary joined me and, with the help of a man who often worked for Amos, we got the yard in order and spent a couple of weeks on repairs to drainage and other details. Becky and Larry helped with yard sales and, eventually, final packing. It was evident as things proceeded that my children were *also* no longer as young as they once were!

When my insurance company inspected the roof and advised they could not renew my policy unless the roof was replaced, it seemed a synchronistic omen that I was not planning this move a moment too soon. With the help of a friend of a friend, I found a roofing contractor who did a great job fast, and also reported to the insurance company that there was storm damage to the roof that required the company to pay for the work, with the exception of a deductible which, gratefully, I could afford.

Although everything may not have happened exactly in the order I've reported, it all *happened*. With everything ready, I called a real estate agent and put the house on the market in late February or early March of 2018. And about that same time, Mary came home. She had decided to end her marriage. Only a few weeks later, while she was still in the process of making plans for her future, almost simultaneously I received a bid on the house that I decided I could not reasonably refuse. I had accepted the offer just as she learned she had lung cancer and was going to have to have surgery and, quite possibly, chemotherapy and perhaps radiation.

It was an emotional time for all of us and sometimes seemed impossible. Mary crawled under the house one day (before her surgery) and came out to announce that there was a small lake in a rather large hole in the southeast corner. I'd always known about the hole, left by a previous owner who had apparently planned a bomb shelter in the 1950s when everyone was preparing for a possible atomic bomb attack by Russia. (Same threats this year. Last year too. History repeats itself.) Workmen had discovered the hole when they spread black plastic under the house to reduce moisture, a requirement of the Kentucky Housing Authority when I bought the house. But the lake was a new development, which proved to be the result of a drainage problem and not the sudden eruption of an underground spring. That black plastic had become the lining for my "underground pool."

I first proposed (jokingly, I swear!) that we hire the "Munchkins" from the day nursery on the corner of 5th and Cherry to come and bail out our new lake. I then promptly had an anxiety attack, which bore all the symptoms of a stroke, and was carted off to the hospital in an ambulance by my concerned children. After thorough testing and the determination that I was probably still sane, if not *fully* in my right mind, I was sent home. Once again, I didn't quite know how I was going to do it, but I did it anyway. We closed the sale of the house on July 9. It would have been Jay's and my 65th wedding anniversary. Talk about synchronicity!

Since we had no idea how long and how difficult Mary's treatment would be, I rented a house in Benton so we could all be close together for as long as necessary. She was only ten days out of surgery when Johnny and his foster son's brother, together with two carloads of guys from Neartown Recovery, along with Becky and Larry and some women friends from AA, picked up the (already neatly packed!) contents of 555 Cherry Street and moved Mary and me, together with all our bags and baggage, to 1307 Shelby McCallum Drive in Benton. As Mary made a slow and painful but also positive recovery, we spent Halloween absent the usual 200+ Calvert City trick-or-treaters. On Thanksgiving Day most of the family gathered in the large dining room for dinner, and the great-grandkids entertained themselves rolling up and down the yard in the huge windrows of leaves that Johnny had lined up along the driveway. Then it was a very quiet Christmas.

As spring approached and Mary continued to improve, I got restless. I do not do well with boredom! The house in Benton was OK to rent, but it wasn't available to buy--and it wasn't really amenable to a retirement lifestyle: a big yard, a carport but no garage, a cluttered basement apartment that would require expensive renovation if it was ever rented out. And I had zero desire to become a landlord again. So I began looking for houses in Murray, which I had long ago determined would be my eventual destination.

But buying a house seemed to be inviting back old trouble, and I eventually rented the south half of a duplex on Michelle Drive. A two-bedroom, two-bath with an attached garage and all appliances, it was convenient to everything, comfortable, and within my budget. I moved slowly (compliments of a very gracious landlord who was so happy to have a respectable widow with a stable income that he gave me a month's free rent), and with the help of Johnny and another crew of guys from Neartown, I was out of Benton and into Murray in one swift but sweaty afternoon. Once again I was home, while Mary transitioned through her own "reinvention" to live as a single woman in a home of her own near the Lake, a "tinyhouse" in Running Bear Subdivision.

But everyone was together again when Terri married Brett Vaughn in June of 2019, in the gazebo at Patti's Restaurant, where she has been co-manager for several years. And there was another, more private wedding in June of 2021 when Raymond and Jennifer Williamson combined their families.

That old warning of "expect the unexpected" came true again on March 6, 2019, when my sister Kay died, quite suddenly, just before the pandemic separated us all for a long, long time. Almost my entire family was there for the funeral service. They made quite a crowd, and they made me very proud. (Sorry, I accidentally made a rhyme of that.)

Someone once said that living life is like playing a violin solo in public and learning to play the instrument as we go along... Your life has not been rehearsed. It is an adventure, and a discovery, and it is the final goal that matters.

Emmett Fox

The crucial task of old age is balance: keeping just well enough, just brave enough, just gay and interested and starkly honest enough to remain a sentient human being.

Florida Scott-Maxwell

Growing Older

As I grow older, I am more and more aware of that spiritual principle the psychologist Carl Jung often spoke of and which he called "synchronicity": those "unexpected coincidences" that prove, as Scripture would say, "God works all things for good for those who love him and are called according to his purpose ..." Or, as my mother would say, "by the time we know a problem exists, God has already been working on it and his solution is on the way-- in fact, already here! I just have to be on the lookout for its manifestation." At least that's my version of her philosophy, augmented a bit by Jung's psychology.

I had evidence of that this morning. As I near the end of these reflections, I have found myself reflecting on my motives for writing and detailing the events of my life and those who have lived it with me. Are these just narcissistic ramblings to convince myself that I have been "sinned against more than sinning?" Are they perhaps the consequence of a hidden yearning to leave just a bit of myself behind so that my own descendants will know that once I lived and loved, hopefully to some purpose? Or is it written so that I will have a record of what I have been and done and seen and believed, an account that I can read and remember as I drift into an unknown future? Or is it to share the experiences and conclusions of a poem I once wrote and called:

"The Swimmer."

My life was always thrummed with fingers too inept
and cautious, never plumbed to inner, unknown depths.
I skimmed across the surface of its mirrored pool
as though I were a stone, thrown by some clumsy fool.

I thought I walked on water, I was God on a rug,
a water-walking skipjack, an ambitious little bug.
A skipjack skitters forward, sideways, tentative.
It never knows which way it's going, yet still lives,
anticipating endlessly that good will come
of ever constant moving, for to rest is to be done.

But yet one day I stopped, and like a rock I fell
into that unplumbed deep that I had thought was hell.
And when the water shattered like a pane of glass,
I learned to swim the lake of life to save my ass.

Irreverent, of course, but very true. Or, as I've often heard someone in Alcoholics Anonymous say, "I came to AA to save my ass, and found out my soul was attached."

I went to bed last night with my little egocentric question to God on my mind and woke this morning to find the answer to my dilemma (synchronistically!) in one of my meditation books and summarized:

1. "Know everything you can know about you! Know what makes you tick, what makes you laugh, what makes you

cry, what opens your heart, what happens when your heart is open. Share what you discover with as many people as possible.

2. *"Know what life is all about! What is important in life. Know what is sacred and holy in life. Know what life is and what life is not. Know where life comes from and why. Know what makes you want to be alive. Share what you discover with as many people as possible.*

3. *"Know why you are alive! Know that you are essential. Know that you are valuable. Know that every experience is an important step toward helping you figure out your purpose. Share what you discover with as many people as possible.*

"The more you learn about life, the more you learn about yourself. The more you learn about yourself, the greater is the purpose you serve in life. Some people live their entire lives never sharing what they discover about themselves or about life. Others never explore these questions and never experience what the answers can uncover. Don't be one of them!

"Until today, you may have been wondering how to go about developing a greater perspective of yourself and your life. Just for today, spend some time pondering and reflecting on these three simple points and sharing your discoveries with others."

So that's my answer, my "full speed ahead." God knows I've been sharing the deepest secrets of my heart with my fellow members of Alcoholics Anonymous for the last 46+ years.

About this Writing Business: I sometimes think about all the books I've written that were never published, never even sent to a publisher for consideration. I remember them all and have first drafts and sometimes finished books still in a box at the back of the guest room closet. They lie there in their hiding places--half dead, half alive--and I have not for a long time taken them out in the middle of the night and read them awake, then put them back in their secret places, as I once dreamed my mother took her dead baby from the closet shelf to rock it back to sleep.

Writing has been, at one and the same time, my retreat from life, my secret life, my way of talking to myself and explaining life, the stories I told myself when there was no one else to talk to. And I think I know why. As my long ago mentor told me: "I know everything I need to know, I just don't know I know it." Today, I still don't know everything I think I need to know, but I find it difficult sometimes to remember what I do know. That's also, I'm sure, why I keep so many books. Once I find an answer, I hold it close lest I forget. My head is too full of answers to hold them all, and they become even more crowded when more questions come to join them.

As I read over the events of my life, I am aware that I have consciously and deliberately not included many details about the personal lives of my children, or my grandchildren, just dates of births and weddings, mentions of especially significant events. No crowing over their successes or recriminations for what I might have perceived as their (and/or my) mistakes. For just as I realize that the choices I have made in my life were influenced by those who came into my life from birth onward (and perhaps even before, as genetics imposed its own strengths and weaknesses), I also realize that I could see and know that only in retrospect, and then only with a great deal of self-examination. So, too, I cannot know who or what has or will influence my children, my grandchildren, and all who come after, for good or for ill. That is for them to discover. I can never know the whys and wherefores of their lives, the impacts of even passing strangers. I am still coming to know and understand my own.

I do know I have loved each of them with all the love I was capable of, which might not have been the kind of love they wanted or the manner of expression they would have wished. I was not taught to speak my love but rather to show it in practical ways. I never saw my parents or my grandparents kiss or embrace. I do not remember any of them ever saying, "I love you," except my mother, once, as she lay dying. And I wish now that I had said, "I love you," to more people, more often. And yes, I may be inadvertently quoting or paraphrasing Maya Angelou. Imitation is the sincerest form of flattery, I've heard. But as I once wrote and have already repeated once in this story:

"There was a time when I thought many things to say,

Finding myself speechless then, they went away."

I realize that my children's, and *their* children's and grandchildren's, tomorrows will look very different than my yesterdays and even my todays. I was born into, and grew up in, the very beginning of an era that has been described as the "New Age." In the last 150 years, from my grandmother's birth in 1881 up to these moments in the waning months of 2023, there have been incredible changes in life as we live it. In those years, a rural society has been replaced by an industrial one, and technological advances that were once the stuff of dreams have become reality: airplanes, moon landings, electricity, radio, television, internet, antibiotics, indoor plumbing, and now "artificial intelligence." Although I must admit that today that as a worldwide drought threatens to become nearly as disastrous as the one in 1934, the year I was born, I have a deep concern that, with two bathtubs and two commodes: Will I someday, before I die, find myself without water to flush my toilet?

If it is true (as science, especially quantum physics, proposes) that we live in an evolving world and (as others suggest) that Spirit expresses itself in our "collective unconscious," then I must believe that there are profound changes to come, that we are indeed at the beginning of a "new *eon*," when "more will be disclosed." I quote Jung here (dated just over 100 years ago), from a book I picked up to read just this morning in one of those synchronistic moments I have come to trust, because his words mirror my own thoughts those two years as I waited out a pandemic that changed our world so profoundly. And he says it much better than I ever could.

> *". . . the contents of the collective unconscious accumulate so much energy that they start influencing the conscious mind...when the life of a large social group or of a nation undergoes a profound change of a political, social or religious nature. Such a change always involves an alteration of the psychological attitude. Incisive changes in history are generally attributed exclusively to external causes. It seems to me, however, that external circumstances often serve merely as occasions for a new attitude to life and the world, long prepared in the unconscious to become manifest. Social, political, and religious conditions affect the collective unconscious in the sense that all those factors which are suppressed by the prevailing views or attitudes in the life of a society gradually accumulate in the collective unconscious and activate its contents. Certain individuals gifted with particularly strong intuition then become aware of the*

changes going on in it and translate these changes into communicable ideas."

Carl Gustav Jung (London, 1919)

If I have regrets as I anticipate my slippery slide into eternity, it is that I will not live, at least not in *this* lifetime, to see those changes. (I do consider reincarnation a distinct and hopeful possibility!) Perhaps my children, and certainly my grandchildren and great-grandchildren, will be a part of that future. Just for now, I am still reflecting upon the past. And I always seem to be able to express my feelings best in poetry, and usually by poking a bit of fun at myself and my own pride, vanity, regrets, mistakes, and mere missteps, even my fears and my griefs. There are some I have saved to the (hopefully not bitter) end.

We learn many lessons about love and intimacy through the years, and some even late in life, as evidenced by another poem:

Last Dance

If there be diminution of desire
As age collects its toll from passion's hands;
If siren's song is stilled by vesper's choir,
And feebled heart resists ardor's commands –

As lust retreats, or in defeat lies low,
Will love be still in chill tranquility
Or clasp its fading comrade close in slow
Adagio, at last in harmony?

Tinder may kindle, but it keeps no flame,

And fuel piled up careless chokes the fire.
Soft-blown breaths brighten darkest coals, the same
That blust'ry winds would scatter and expire.

Lust spends itself too soon when youth's at play.
Come, then, old friend, and let us love all day.

And about that "Great Conversation" I mentioned at one point in my story:

Socrates, and Before

A million years ago, it was,
In the corner of a darkening cave, alone,
A man chipped away with his clumsy tool
And carved his story in stone:
"I lived, I breathed, I slept, I woke
And I laughed, sometimes I cried.
I ate when hungry, I fought for life"
(and the unwritten coda)
"I suppose, I died."
Others followed the one-without-name.
Instead of a picture, they used a word.
But the plot, the plea, remained the same:
"Listen, I must be heard."
Why toil away through those lonely hours
With paint, or chisel, or pen?

> *The ancient knew, his answer was there:*
> *"I leave to the future this message: 'I am.'*

Reflecting on my past and allowing myself to imagine the possibilities of what lies ahead tomorrow, and tomorrow, *ad infinitum*, I realize that I am not at all afraid of dying--though I certainly hope I do so as comfortably as possible--because I believe that I will live again, in some form which only the "God of my understanding" could conceive. I've even been gifted on occasion with a glimpse of that. (See "Things of the Spirit" in the Epilogue.) I am fond of some words on page 164 of AA's Big Book: "We realize we know only a little. God will constantly disclose more to you and to us."

As for what I might wish for, I am also very fond of a Navajo prayer which I read every year when I reach January 31 in one of my meditation books:

> "Happily may I walk,
>
> May it be beautiful before me.
>
> May it be beautiful behind me.
>
> May it be beautiful below me.
>
> May it be beautiful above me.
>
> May it be beautiful all around me.
>
> In beauty it is finished."

I am quite certain that the last line of that prayer is actually a sacred promise.

"There is no light without shadow and no psychic wholeness without imperfection."

- Carl Jung

"As we turn to face our shadow side, we can learn to embrace our imperfections....Making peace with our shadow side teaches us about the gift of grace. Grace frees us to love ourselves for both our shadows and our light and connects us with the shared humanity of one another.

-from Seasons of the Spirit

To live in a reverential manner is . . . to create an autobiography in which we tell the stories of the unique epiphanies that have informed our lives. - Sam Keen

Epilogue
Things of the Spirit

Coming to terms with God has been a lifelong struggle for me, although a recent book by the theologian Albert Nolan contains a paragraph that seems to offer some wiggle room for an escape from the tentacles that have tried to clasp and hold me to the ideas about God I was taught:

> *"Everyone has a god—in the sense that everyone puts something first in his life: money, power, prestige, self, career, love and so forth. There must be something in your life that operates as your source of meaning and strength, something which you regard, at least implicitly, as the supreme power in your life. If you think of your priority in life as a transcendent person you will have a God with a capital letter. If you think of your highest value as a cause, an ideal or an ideology, you*

will have a god with a small letter. Either way you will have something that is divine for you."

I believe I have a "small-letter god," but I also bow to the convention of capitalizing it. That might be called "going along to get along," but it works for me, although I'm sure it confuses a great many people—some of them good friends and even close kin of mine.

There's a quote from Shakespeare that comes to me when I think about spirituality. In Act 1 Scene 5 of *Hamlet*, his friend Horatio finds him talking to his father's ghost, and says, "O day and night but this is wondrous strange!" And Hamlet responds, "And therefore as a stranger give it welcome. There are more things in heaven and earth, Horatio, than are dreamt of in your philosophy." Horatio, it seems, was a model of rationality, studying a philosophy at university that was a compound of ethics, logic, and natural science. That emphasis pretty much excluded talking to ghosts. Yet my grandmother spoke of having conversations with the wraith-like appearance of her dead mother on a fairly frequent basis, and my mother was comforted by a feeling that amounted to assurance of my father's presence in the months after his death.

I am sometimes just as awed by the presence, evidenced by the actions, of God in my life as poor Horatio was when confronted by a man talking to a ghost. And that presence can be as simple, and as profound, as a mockingbird, which I wrote about just this week:

About This Mockingbird:

I think my Mother's come again to visit me.
She's built a nest that I simply can't fail to see:
tucked it up high, between gutter and post,

knowing, I'm sure I won't mind being host.
She's lining it with slender twigs, shaping it 'round,
just like last year's—the one that I took down.
How could I not have seen her quilter's hand in it?
The piecing and the padding and the forming it to fit?

Each year, since she went far away and seemed forever gone,
she has come back in spring to sing her sweet and tender song.
And though I move my home, she seems to follow me,
this guardian in feathered guise, now flying wild and free.
Mockingbirds will often do that; did you even know?
They are, the Indians and mystics say, protectors of the soul.
I have been told, of course, that this is all just fantasy,
an old wives' tale perhaps, and only half-believed.

Yet it seems far beyond strange that this little bird,
would nest itself so close, to sing its trilling words
that tell me every morning, and 'til the encroaching night,
that I can and must believe our world will be all right.
Before my Mother died, she spoke in metaphors—
dementia had taught her to speak that elegant discourse.
I wonder if she's since learned the Great Spirit's poetry,
And this new language has become the one God speaks to me.

    The psychologist Carl Jung called these actions of God "meaningful coincidences without logical explanation" and labeled them "synchronicity." And I'm sure there are many people—including members of my own family--who believe that I have followed Hamlet's advice far too diligently in bidding "strange things" welcome. Most recently there's been my intense curiosity regarding quantum physics and its correlations with spiritual matters, sparked 20 years ago by my introduction to another book, *The Dancing Wu Li Masters*.

There are, I've been told, some children who seem to have been born "old souls." But for most of us it seems to take a while to even become a human grownup. And even longer to become, as the childhood story of *The Velveteen Rabbit* tells us, "real," and then to discover (or rediscover) and come to believe in our "true self." For we wear several layers of body and ego protected by stubborn self-centered fear, and a softer and more permeable layer that is a simple and entirely human longing to be loved, to be "connected," to be "part of." What we long for, I think, is what some call at-one-ment: NOT atone-ment, but at-*one*-ment. Just adding a hyphen results in a completely different theology.

The mystics tell us that the goal of meditation and prayer is to experience that at-*one*-ment: unity with an ultimate reality. Mahatma Gandhi, a Hindu, has said, "I believe in the essential unity of all people or, for that matter, of all that lives. Therefore, I believe that if one person gains spiritually, the whole world gains, and if one person falls, the whole world falls to that extent." That's what the Buddhist Thich Nhat Hanh calls "interbeing."

The Belgian pioneer in cell biology (and winner of a 1976 Nobel Prize) Christian de Duve confesses his own lifelong struggle with the God/god conflict, that while "my whole life as a scientist has been permeated with the conviction that I was participating in a meaningful and revealing approach to reality," still, at the same time, "On exceptional occasions, I have felt close to something ineffable, utterly mysterious but real, at least to me, an entity that, for want of a better term, I call Ultimate Reality." (And he capitalizes those two words!)

An astrophysicist I met years ago and became very fond of (Alfred Schild, for the curious) told me he believed in "One." As a protegee of Albert Einstein, I figured Al knew a thing or two about the cosmos. And almost all major religions would agree with all of the above.

I recently discovered a little book, *The Common Heart*, which actually describes those agreements, and I was not at all surprised to realize that they conform almost precisely with what I, too, have come to believe during the last half of my life.

It takes time and patience, and more than a few temptations and tribulations, to abrade and tear away our many layers of fear and pride to discover, acknowledge, and begin to actually experience the freedom to speak and finally live our own truth. For it is the truth that sets us free. But until then there is trial and error, doubt and despair, in our search for anything and everything to fill that God-shaped hole in the center of our being until we are finally, either literally or figuratively, brought to our knees–as my mother once prayed I would be–and ready to humbly and willingly ask the God of our own understanding for help. If there is salvation in that, and of course there is, it is that moment when we are—yes, let's *call* it "saved"--pulled up from a seemingly bottomless pit where we have been dragged and dropped by the Four Horsemen: Terror, Bewilderment, Frustration, and Despair–the pit we have dug for ourselves.

Some mystics—*Christian* mystics, by the way--have called that time of doubt and despair *The Dark Night of the Soul* and our escape as an entry into, or out of, *The Cloud of Unknowing* (and have written books so-named). Matthew Fox (Catholic turned Episcopal priest) would describe that "Dark Night" as the *Via Negativa*. But on the other side is light, divine light, an aspect of divine presence. In Genesis, God says, "Let there be light, and there was light." In Zoroastrian belief, the Supreme God, Ahura Mazda, is the source of that light. It is also incorporated into the teachings of the Sufi branch of Islam. Buddhists call such entry "awakening." In the Hebrew religion that light is called the Shekinah (and that light is feminine!). But whatever the name for the experience, and whatever the name for the Higher Power of *our* understanding, it brings with it a change of thinking, a *metanoia* – the Greek word that was always translated in the Bible as "repentance" but is actually (and I quote my friend Paul Meier in his book *Dry Bones)*:

"*a) change of mind that brings reformation,*

b) change in the way you think,

c) turn around in your thinking and

d) think differently."

With that in mind, I have come to believe that, as Paul continues, "The teaching ministry of Jesus was focused on changing people's minds about many things: [including] the image of God, the will of God, justice, equality, wealth, and more."

Carl Jung, as he is quoted in AA's Big Book, *Alcoholics Anonymous* (p. 27), described such "vital spiritual experiences [as] emotional displacements and rearrangements. Ideas, emotions, and attitudes which were once [lives'] guiding forces are suddenly cast to one side and a completely new set of conceptions and motives begin to dominate them." Or, in AA shorthand, we make a "180-degree turn." Sure sounds like *metanoia* to me.

That moment can happen at any time, anywhere. Many people have had such experiences without seeking them. The Apostle Paul was brought to his knees on the Road to Damascus. The Buddha had his moment sitting in meditation under a tree. Bill Wilson found himself talking to what he would later call the Spirit of the Universe while lying in a hospital where he was being treated for chronic alcoholism. It is, I believe, an experience of God's grace. Sometimes it is as gentle and fleeting as the wings of a butterfly, one of God's little creatures that has become a symbol of transformation. And once we are brushed by the wings of grace we are never quite the same.

I was first conscious of its possibility when I pledged my life to God's service when I was 14 or so, promising to take God's message to the "heathen." Well, promises to God can take strange twists and turns on their way to fulfillment. I promptly forgot that pledge as I went away to college and discovered another spirit and the change it wrought in my life. And I hope anyone hearing (or reading) this won't be insulted when I tell you that today, in this place, at this time, you are the recipients of the only message I have come to understand, though still incompletely: *you* may be one of the heathen I was destined to meet.

I wrote in an earlier section of this book that I first experienced that grace in a near-death experience, as my first child was born in a hospital in Rosiclare, Illinois. It was a journey toward a great light and, on the other side, such peace and joy that I did not want to "come back." Until, as I remember, a voice said, "Lona, wake up. You're killing your baby." I woke up. Or, perhaps, "came back?"

And I surely experienced it again after the birth of my third child when, in the grip of postpartum depression, I was so frightened that I couldn't bear to be alone. Until one night, lying in bed, I spoke to

God in despair and pleaded with him to take away my fear. And again there was that glimpse of light, and fear left me, and peace (which felt more like courage than serenity) came in its place.

Years later, when I was 41, divorced and alone, I wanted desperately to escape the life that I had created for myself. I was contemplating a "permanent escape from a temporary problem" and even said, right out loud, "God, if you don't want me to do this, you're going to have to stop me." My challenge was accepted. My recently installed phone rang and a little old lady on the other end of the line said, "Has anyone talked to you about God lately?" I believe now that she was one of those people I call "God with skin on." Nearly blind, she came with her deaf friend to talk to me. Or perhaps they just listened. I'm a sucker for listeners.

But it was another two years before I found myself on my knees on a witch's black carpet in a moment of complete surrender to a power I did not understand, could not possibly understand, and still do not understand, but have found it possible, nonetheless, to trust. For I have accepted that faith is, indeed, "The substance of things hoped for, the evidence of things not seen."

What do I believe today? *(There's a list at the end of this Section. I'm an almost compulsive list-maker.)* Bear in mind that it may change tomorrow, because I may outgrow those beliefs too. The main thing that always changes is the nature of the god of my understanding: always growing bigger and more powerful until he/she/it seems to pervade everyone and everything.

An acquaintance of mine whose higher power was something or someone named "Vol" used to say that he had learned from "Vol and other spiritual sources." Although I think a god named Vol was featured in an old Star Wars movie and seems to bear rather suspicious spiritual credentials, I know about those "other spiritual sources," and I have gathered from them bits and pieces, here and there, occasionally in hunks and chunks.

I have come to believe that there is no vengeful God, no manlike creature or Daddy in the clouds that watches us and punishes our "sins." There is instead a scientific principle based on the concept that we are all powerful, with equal access to the same source of power, and that we are all born with all the tools we need to create a life that is joyous, productive, and loving. That "our thoughts become things and what we dwell on we create." I cannot think of a better description of what scientists now believe is evidenced and will, perhaps, ultimately be proven by the principles of quantum physics. And I believe it's a good idea to, as Mahatma Gandhi once said: "*Live* as if you were to die tomorrow. *Learn* as if you were to live forever."

I am not a "Christian," at least not in the commonly accepted sense of that term. Nor do I believe that Jesus was. (How could he have been?) He is reputed to have said, "I am in God and God is in me." My ggggg-grandfather Stokes was a Quaker, and I suspect there is more than a drop of that inclination in my DNA. If he'd been born a bit farther East, he'd probably have been a Taoist. I may be a bit of both. (Not formally, of course.) Fair warning: the last time I said, out loud, "I call myself a Christian," the lights went out in the whole building. The lesson: Say what you mean, and mean what you say. I often read Emmet Fox, who says:

> "**There is no difficulty that enough love will not conquer;*
>
> **No disease that enough love will not heal;*
>
> **No door that enough love will not open;*
>
> **No gulf that enough love will not bridge;*
>
> **No wall that enough love will not throw down*

*No sin that enough love will not redeem."

From my off and on association with other spiritual paths, I strongly suspect that this also spells out the message of the Course in Miracles, amplified in a thick tome purportedly dictated by Jesus (though I don't think anyone is *really, **really**,* sure he did). Fox just says it in far fewer words. I read Thich Nhat Hanh, the Tibetan Buddhist, whose writings on meditation, mindfulness, and what he calls "interbeing" seem to mirror the beliefs of two Catholics, Thomas Keating and Thomas Merton. And a little book called "Just This," which is a distillation of Richard Rohr's thoughts.

My spiritual practice for the last 46 years has been the 12 steps and the principles of Alcoholics Anonymous, and I just recently realized that the 12th Step is possibly my personal way of engaging with the Hindu pathway of service, Hatha Yoga. I like the Hindu religion; they believe everybody is on *some* spiritual path and that they all lead to the same goal, although some paths get us there faster than others, and that we should allow everyone their very own. An Episcopal priest once told me the same thing, in almost exactly the same words.

Mahatma Gandhi also once wrote, "Religions are different roads converging to the same point. What does it matter that we take different roads, so long as we reach the same goal?" [and] "There will be no lasting peace on earth unless we learn not merely to tolerate but even to respect the other faiths *as our own*." And wasn't it Jesus who said we must "love our neighbor as ourselves"?

I sponsor newcomers to AA and as I listen to 5th Steps (AA's version of confession), I remind myself that I have never heard anyone tell me of something they have done and are now admitting with guilt and shame that I cannot imagine having done myself, given the same set of circumstances (and often actually have done at some time in the past).

Is that forgiveness? No, I think you'd call it empathy, which is akin to love and is perhaps the first step toward both compassion *and* forgiveness. I believe that I don't need a priest or any minister to forgive me anything (though I may need to make amends to anyone I've harmed), because the God of my understanding forgives *everything*, even before I ask, even as it is happening. He may have implanted my instructions for right living when I was born, and my only complaint is that those "seeds for good deeds" seem to have been incredibly slow to sprout.

My views on prayer have changed as well. I once asked a Catholic monk if one could be in prayer at all times, and he assured me that it was entirely possible. And Meister Eckhardt, the German mystic, once said, "The only prayer we ever need to pray is: "Thank you." Personally I think that is more than just a prayer; it is an attitude. In early Christianity, "prayer" didn't refer to some kind of problem-solving transaction between humans and God, nor was it about saying words to God, but was quite literally "putting on a different thinking cap." Jesus talked of "going to your inner room," which many now consider a simple description of contemplative prayer, or meditation. Those early Christians understood prayer as a transformation of the consciousness of the one who was doing the praying, the awakening of an inner dialogue that, from God's "listening" side, had never stopped. Quite simply then, prayer is not changing God's mind about us or *anything* else but allowing God to change our mind about the reality right in front of us—which we are usually avoiding or distorting.

Song is a part of my interior spiritual practice, part meditation and part prayer. I often find it difficult to listen when the views of the religion of my childhood are expressed or re-expressed in some Christian music. But there is also what I call "inspirational music" that expresses my own experience. Some of it wouldn't be described as "spiritual" at all --- but it sends a very strong message to my stubborn heart, and there are verses that hum through my mind like mantras.

When I was first in recovery, I'd walk the streets of Chicago with an old song running through my mind that goes: "Accentuate the positive, eliminate the negative, latch on to the affirmative, and don't mess with Mr. Inbetween." I have, sometimes, a nearly overwhelming desire to "mess with Mr. Inbetween in all his/its many guises. And my conscience forces me to admit that I have always wanted to give a talk where I actually sing part of that song.

The old hymn that begins, "Have Thine own Way, Lord, have Thine own way; Thou art the potter I am the clay. Mold me and make me, after Thy will, while I am waiting, yielding and still," is a 6th and 7th Step song for me. (The shorthand of that might be "Reinvent me.")

There is a song called *The Prodigal's Prayer* that I often think of when I do my 10th step at night: "If I have wounded any soul today, if I have caused one foot to go astray, if I have walked in my own willful way, dear Lord, forgive."

And "Open my eyes that I may see, visions of truth thou hast for me, place in my hands that wonderful key, that shall unclasp and set me free." – Now that's a beautiful 11th step prayer.

Diana Butler Bass, in her book *Christianity After Religion*, talks about people who leave old places and adopt new identities, trying to "find themselves." And "they [discover] themselves in a different sort of community, with different people, different religions, different practices and different languages. They [find] themselves in a new location, *in, with, among,* and *through things and people* they once would never have imagined. . . They find a new place of belonging, new communities of faith. And there, they [find] themselves and God." That resonates with me in a special way. I found my place, and myself, 46 years ago.

And then she quotes parts of a poem the theologian Dietrich Bonhoeffer wrote while he was imprisoned by the Nazis, torn from family and friends and all he loved. An exile, really. And there, in a *where* so different from all he had ever known, he found that he had not really known himself:

> "Who am I? They often tell me
>
> I stepped from my cell's confinement
>
> Calmly, cheerfully, firmly,
>
> Like a squire from his country house.
>
> Who am I? . . .
>
> Am I then really all that which other men tell of?"
>
> Or am I only what I myself know of myself? . . .
>
> Who am I? This or the other? . . .
>
> Whoever I am, Thou knowest, O God, I am thine!

Only a short time after that poem was written, he did indeed step from his prison and walk out to face a Nazi firing squad, and died. It was, I believe, the end of his hero's journey.

And so, as I still stumble toward God, escaping from the prison I made for myself, I hope to fall into the unexpected, into the arms of Grace, which is perhaps also simply God with a capital "G."

My Beliefs (which I hereby claim the right to change)

I believe in light, that light which signifies a divine manifestation of a supreme presence, which I may call by any name I choose, and which today I choose to call God--a light of love and mercy that lights the world and casts out all darkness. I believe that the spiritual experiences I have had are an affirmation that ***God is,*** that I am in God, and God is in me.

I believe that the five Cs of the Oxford Group, a Christian movement of the early 1930s, on which AA's steps are based: conviction, conversion, confession, contrition, and continuance, are a spiritual program that can lead me from despair to a life filled with hope and love.

I believe in God's grace, a free and unmerited gift with which God is always ready and willing to bless us abundantly if we simply ask.

I believe that time is a river and that God can see around the next bend and also around corners. (I just don't have any idea how God does it, but I suspect that quantum physics may have some clues.)

I believe that "Faith is the substance of things hoped for, the evidence of things not seen." (Or, as my first spiritual mentor, a kind of shade-tree guru, said, "You know everything you need to know, you just don't know you know it." My life seems devoted to rediscovering the things I already "know."

I believe in synchronicity -- those "coincidences" which prove that "God works all things for good for those who love him and are called according to his purpose ..." (Or, by the time we know a problem exists, God has already been working on it, and his solution is on the way-- in fact, already here! I just have to be on the lookout for its manifestation.)

I believe in Karma -- not the idea that I must pay today for the sins of past lives with punishment in this one, but that "all actions take place in time by the interweaving of the forces of nature" and that God created and *is* the loom. (I also believe in reincarnation, simply because it makes sense.)

I believe that following the golden rule, taught by Jesus and Buddha and the Koran and the books of many other faiths, is a spiritual path that leads to compassion and love, and that to "love one another--to love my neighbor as I love myself," is the goal of my journey. But I also believe in the silver rule, taught by experience, that "You should not help those who could and should help themselves."

I believe that all my thoughts are prayers, and while I do not believe that prayer changes the Mind of God, I believe it changes me.

And, most of all, I believe in ONE.

Lona Rae is the pen name of Lona Rae Babbington, born July 21, 1934, in Williamson County, Illinois, the daughter of Raymond Korte and Evelyn Jennings Korte. She grew up in Massac County, Illinois, attending New Columbia High School (1946-1949) and graduating from Metropolis Community High School in 1950. She attended Southern Illinois University from 1950-52 on a Normal School Scholarship and received a Bachelor of Independent Studies degree from Murray State University (Kentucky) in 2002. She has three children: John David Crabb, Rebecca Crabb Brooks, and Mary Elizabeth Crabb Culp; four grandchildren and nine great-grandchildren; one great-great-grandchild.

As assistant to the editor of Metropolis News (1960-64), she wrote a weekly column, At Our House; she was later the managing editor of both the Downers Grove (Illinois) Graphic (1964-65) and the DuPage County (Illinois) Times (1965-70); was an associate editor for Office Appliances and Office Design magazines (1971-1972), and Director of Public Relations for the American Institute of Steel Construction (1980-1990), writing and editing a number of industry publications as well as coordinating industry conferences, conventions, and trade shows.

She is also the author of a historical novel, Down River, published by Tower Books in 1981.

Lona currently lives in Murray, Kentucky.